UNDEFEATED

UNDEFEATED

How Father and Son Triumphed over Unbelievable Odds
Both on and off the Field

BOB AND BRIAN GRIESE

with

JIM DENNEY

A
JANET
THOMA
BOOK

THOMAS NELSON PUBLISHERS
Nashville

Published in Nashville, Tennessee, by Thomas Nelson, Inc.

Library of Congress Cataloging-in-Publication Data

Griese, Bob.
    Undefeated : how father and son triumphed over unbelievable odds both on and off
the field / by Bob and Brian Griese with Jim Denney.
        p. cm.
    ISBN 0-7852-7021-3 (hc.)
    1. Griese, Bob. 2. Griese, Brian, 1975– 3. Football players—United States—Biography.
4. Fathers and sons—United States—Biography. I. Griese, Brian, 1975– II. Denney, James
D. III. Title.

GV939.G76 A3 2000
796.332'092'273—dc21
[B]
                                                                    00-037214
                                                                    CIP

Printed in the United States of America

1 2 3 4 5 6 7 BVG 06 05 04 03 02 01 00

To Judi
Wife, Mother, Inspiration

CONTENTS

ACKNOWLEDGMENTS

It would be impossible to properly acknowledge all the special people who had an impact on our lives and on this story. You know who you are, and we appreciate you. So on this page we will simply acknowledge those friends and family members who had a hand in sharing their memories, shaping these words, and bringing the idea for this book into reality.

Thanks to Ida Griese, Scott Griese, Jeff Griese, Shay Whitney Griese, Jean McNamee, Ron and Becky Cordes, and Julie Twilley for sharing thoughts and recollections that filled in the gaps and rounded out the story. And thanks also go to Jim Denney for his creative work; to Matt Merola, Charles Morgan, and Bruce Barbour for advice and representation; and to Lane Convey, who handled endless details.

Clearly this book was a team effort—and we make a great team!

FOREWORD

When my father and I were approached about writing a book, not long after the 1998 Rose Bowl game, I didn't think it was a good idea. Throughout our lives, our family has been in the spotlight because of what my father accomplished with the Dolphins and his fame as a sportscaster. I was not eager to further open our private lives to the public.

But we discussed it as a family and I gave it a lot of thought. I realized that this was an opportunity to use what we had gone through in our family to help people in similar situations. The terrible disease called cancer had invaded our lives and taken away my mother, who was truly the heart and foundation of our family. But though she had physically left us, my mother's love and unconquerable spirit were still with us, holding us together.

This story is for those who have experienced losses or setbacks in life (and who hasn't?). It's the story of how a family of boys grew into men under the love and protection of a man who most people know as a Hall of Fame athlete—but who I know as a Hall of Fame father. I wanted to write this book as a tribute to my father for the courage and patience he demonstrated in accepting what God laid out for him as a widowed parent, raising three sons to become men of character.

I also wanted to write this book as a remembrance of my mother, and as an example to others of how life goes on, even after tragedy and loss. If there's one thing my dad, my brothers, and I have learned, it's that you can use the hurt and setbacks of the past as motivation for the future.

The title *Undefeated* refers to my father's perfect season with the '72 Dolphins, and my '97 season with the Michigan Wolverines. But more importantly, it refers to our lives and our family. Setbacks are a part of life, but setbacks are never the end of the story. As my father's example continues to teach me, whether in sports or in life, character and courage always bring you out on top.

That is why we have been undefeated.

—Brian Griese

1

TOUCHDOWN ON MOUNT EVEREST

Two seasons ago, Bob Griese was barred from covering Michigan games because of the perceived conflict of interest. But new management at ABC Sports changed that policy. "I had every confidence that Bob would handle this in the appropriate way," says executive producer Steve Anderson. The Michigan-Washington State matchup on New Year's Day will mark the sixth time this year that Griese and partner Keith Jackson will have done a Wolverines game. Initially Bob referred to his son, the Michigan QB, as "Griese." Now he usually just calls him Brian.

—TV GUIDE, MONDAY, DECEMBER 22, 1997

Brian

A few days before the Rose Bowl, my father and I were out in California, having dinner together. Dad said, "Brian, you can't lose. No matter how this game comes out, you win. There's no pressure on you. This is a fun game for you. You've gotten to where you want to be. Now just go out there and have fun!"

I laughed. "I'm gonna have fun, Pops—but I'm also gonna win the Rose Bowl!"

Bob

I just wanted Brian to stay loose. I didn't want him taking any extra pressure onto himself just because this was the Rose Bowl. I figured if he would approach this game like every other game during the season, he'd be okay. I told him, "You know, the Rose Bowl is just a football field like any other football field. It's a hundred yards long and fifty yards wide. You don't have to throw the ball any better than you have all year. Just play your game the way you've always played it, and you'll do fine."

When I watch Brian play, I see a quarterback who reminds me a lot of my younger days—after I got a little seasoning with the Dolphins. Brian's not a scrambler like I was in the early days, before Don Shula got hold of me. He's more like the seasoned, disciplined Bob Griese—which is amazing, because he never saw me play, except for a few of my old film clips from NFL films. So he was too young to have learned much football technique from me. It seems almost instinctive.

I like to think he's soaked up a little of his old man's approach to life— and maybe that's why Brian's approach to the game reminds me of my own. Brian is cool and patient in the pocket. His strengths are his intelligence, his decision making, and his leadership on the field. He's not the fastest quarterback in the game, and he doesn't have the strongest throwing arm, but he doesn't get rattled and he doesn't make many mistakes. And that's why he wins games.

Shortly before the Rose Bowl, the veterans of the undefeated 1972 Miami Dolphins got together for a twenty-fifth anniversary reunion, so my own perfect season was on my mind while Brian and the Wolverines were winning game after game in 1997. As the '97 season progressed, I started thinking, *Man, if this goes on, Brian's going to have himself an undefeated season—just like his old man!* I remembered what that season was like, so half joking, just trying to take the pressure off, I said, "Hey, Brian, don't go thinking you're going to win every game this season! That's something we did in '72! Don't you start infringing on my undefeated season with the Dolphins!"

And he came right back at me. "Hey, Dad, time to step aside! It's a new day, and you old-timers are going down! Time to make room for the next generation!"

ABC, the network for the Rose Bowl, wants its broadcasters to remain impartial, but any built-in biases should cancel each other out. Analyst Bob Griese is the father of

University of Michigan quarterback Brian Griese. But play-by-play man Keith Jackson graduated from Washington State in 1952 . . .

Griese said he's glad he won't be the only one dealing with questions about how his loyalties could influence the telecast. "It's interesting to see my partner having to answer these types of questions," Griese said, laughing. "I'm sitting back and kind of enjoying this."

—*DETROIT NEWS*, MONDAY, DECEMBER 29, 1997

Bob

My broadcasting partner, Keith Jackson, is a Washington State alum, so I was kidding him before the Rose Bowl. Everyone in the media was hitting him with this same "conflict of interest" business that I had been fending off all season. I just laughed. "Keith," I said, "now you can deal with all those questions I've been fighting all year long!"

Of course, Keith is too professional to show any bias in either direction. Like me, he calls every game right down the middle.

Brian

My first couple of years at Michigan, ABC wouldn't let my father cover any of my games because of a "conflict of interest." Some conflict! He bends over backward to be fair to the other side! He's always told me, "You're not gonna get a fair shake when I'm in the booth. If you make a great play, I'm gonna say it was a good play. If you mess up down there, you'll get no mercy from me."

I understood that, and it was fine with me. All I cared about was that my dad could come to my games. When he covered my regular season games, he'd come to town and we'd have dinner on Thursday night. Then Saturday night, after the game, he'd come down from the broadcast booth and meet me in the locker room like any normal parent. The price we had to pay was that he had to be pretty brutal during the broadcast. And I'm okay with that.

Afterward, I'd come home to visit and we'd put a tape in the VCR and watch the game together, and he'd be high-fiving me and hooting and hollering like he was my biggest fan. I'd be throwing a pass on the TV screen, and there'd be ABC analyst Bob Griese saying, "Griese's pass is complete" in a totally flat voice. But at the same time, he's right next to me, jumping up and down, whooping and spilling pretzels all over the place, yelling, "Son of a gun, that was a beautiful throw!" And I'd say, "Why didn't you say that on the air?" And he'd go, "Man, I wish I could have!"

So I'd tell all my friends, "If you really want to enjoy a Michigan game on TV, go to a sports bar where there's so much noise you can't hear the announcers—but whatever you do, don't listen to my dad calling my game!"

Bob

Hey, Brian, don't say that! It's bad for ratings!

Brian

Okay, okay! Actually, Dad and Keith do a pretty good job. I like the stories those old-timers tell when they cover a game. Dad has a job to do, and he's been doing it a lot longer than I've been playing football. If he has to bend over backward to be fair, that's cool with me.

Bob

The Rose Bowl marked the sixth and final game of Brian's that I would be covering. Since it was the Rose Bowl, and since I had played in the Rose Bowl, it was a special game for me.

I went on the field the day before the game, when the media was out taking pictures of the players. I looked around at the field and the stands, and I thought back to the day I was on that same field for the '67 Rose Bowl, when Purdue beat USC 14-13. I gave myself a few minutes to think about the fact that, the following day, Brian would be playing on the field where I won the big game thirty-one years earlier.

On game day, Keith and I were so busy rehearsing, checking our charts, taking care of this and that, there was no time to wander down to the field.

But while I was up in the booth, getting ready for the pregame show, I allowed myself a few minutes to get caught up in the emotions, to think, *Here I am at the Rose Bowl again, and there's Brian, warming up on the same field for the game of his life.* I don't do that very often, but this was different, this was special.

I just sat there and thought, *Isn't this something? Here he is, he's made it, he's got the whole family around him, the whole country watching him, his mother smiling down on him from Heaven—he can't lose. If he wins, hey, that's just icing on the cake!* As a father, I couldn't have been prouder.

Brian came into the eighty-fourth Rose Bowl with a record of 2,402 yards, twenty-four touchdown passes, and only five interceptions. As the quarterback in Michigan's eighteenth Rose Bowl appearance, he was about to become part of a great Rose Bowl tradition, going all the way back to the first Rose Bowl in 1902, when Michigan flattened Stanford so badly (49-0) that Stanford walked off the field in the third quarter.

When Brian played in the Rose Bowl on New Year's Day 1998, it had been five years since the Michigan Wolverines had been to the Rose Bowl (the Wolverines had lost to the University of Washington in 1992, then came back and beat them in 1993). During Brian's first four years at Michigan, the Wolverines suffered four straight four-loss seasons.

But Brian's fifth year at Michigan was another story altogether. The Wolverines arrived in Pasadena with an 11-0 record, and a perfect season on the line. The Wolverines were also aiming at their first national championship in half a century. Most of the media attention was focused on Washington State (a 10-1 record and an average of 42 points and 500 yards a game). But the Wolverines came to Pasadena with the number one defense in the nation, led by Heisman Trophy-winning cornerback Charles Woodson, along with All-American defensive end Glen Steele, outstanding strong safety Marcus Ray, and cornerback Andre Weathers.

Brian

While the press was hyping the Leaf-Woodson matchup, I was heading into that game under the media radar. I wasn't even on the scope—and that was fine with me. I grew up around the media, and some of my earliest memories are of sitting in the broadcast booth with my dad. So I've never been very impressed with the media. I wasn't going to Pasadena to grab the limelight. I didn't care about that stuff. I was going there to win a football game. If we kept doing what we had done all season, I figured it would serve us well.

Before the beginning of the season, Coach Lloyd Carr had challenged the team, using Mount Everest as a metaphor for the season ahead. He had just read *Into Thin Air*, Jon Krakauer's account of the ill-fated Everest expedition in 1996, which left eight people dead by the time the survivors reached the summit. He wanted us to know that we were facing a punishing challenge, and that it was our choice whether we beat the mountain or the mountain beat us. It was our choice whether to go all the way to the summit.

"There is such a thing as destiny," Coach told us, "but destiny is not something that happens to you. It's something you choose."

On game day, as we went through the tunnel and took the field, I thought about Mount Everest and the road we had traveled to reach that elevation in our game. We had made it most of the way up that mountain Coach Carr had told us about. We hadn't reached the summit yet, but it was in sight and within reach. We had just a little bit farther to go. In a few minutes, it would be time to get out there and make some touchdowns on Mount Everest. It was time to claim the summit.

In the moments before the game, I also thought about my mother. It had been just a month short of ten years since she passed away. As the game was about to begin, I knew she was there with me. I talked to her, and I could feel that she was happy for me.

I was ready.

Everything went as well as could be expected for the visitors from Ann Arbor. The weather back home was 20 degrees at kickoff; in Pasadena, it was a satisfying 70. The sky was powder blue and the champions wore maize and blue.

—*LOS ANGELES TIMES*, FRIDAY, JANUARY 2, 1998

(**Brian**)

There's nothing like the feeling at the beginning of a big game—
stretching out your body during final warm-ups; knocking helmets and
slapping pads with the guys you go to war with; hearing the stadium
announcer's voice echoing your name across the stands as you take the
field; feeling that swell of pride and the rush of anticipation as you stand
in your nice, clean uniform and your eyeblack, listening to the national
anthem; riding that adrenaline flow as you wait for the kickoff.

There's nothing like game day. Anything can happen. You could get
hurt, you could get beat, you could lose big-time—but you never think
about any of that. You're there to win, and winning is all you think about.
You have no fear on the football field, only fierceness. There's an intensity
of emotion, a surge of adrenaline at the beginning of a big game that nothing else matches. A thrill ride at Disneyland doesn't even come close.

After the kickoff, when the special teams guys have returned the ball as
far as they can, I'm on. There's an edge of tension as the offense takes the
field for the opening series—but there's also a kind of serenity. I know I'm
in control. I know my part, and everybody lining up around me knows his.

The reason I love playing quarterback is that the quarterback controls
the start of the play. Nobody's going anywhere until I say so. I always take
advantage of that. I know I can look at everybody on both sides of the ball
for as long as I want, up until the last tick of the play clock. The guys on
the other side of the ball don't have that luxury; they're all in suspense,
and there's a moment of indecision on their side. They're all thinking
about their responsibilities, about where they have to go and how they're
going to get there. The linemen are watching one another, the defensive
backs are watching the quarterback and the receivers, and the only one
who really knows when the ball will be snapped is me.

Before the play starts, the defense is in disguise—but each of those guys
has to get to the right position for that defensive play, and in the last
instant before the ball is snapped, they give themselves away. A good quarterback can recognize those telltale signs. When I step up behind the center, the defensive formation looks like pieces on a chessboard. In that

half-second before the snap, I get more information about what the defense is trying to do than at any other time.

The ball is snapped, I go back—and when things start to move, it just reconfirms what I already suspected before the snap. When I'm going back to pass, I think, *Okay, now I know for sure what's going on.* When everything works the way it's supposed to, I look over the scene and think, *Here comes the pass rush, and there's my receiver, and everything looks clear, just like in practice.*

There are times when everything is right where it's supposed to be—my receiver is out in the open, I throw the ball and he catches it, and that's all there is to it—a perfect play. Other times, I take my three- or five- or seven-step drop, I set up to throw—and all of a sudden this big lineman's paw comes out of nowhere and rips across my helmet. *Okay,* I think, *I'm still on my feet, but now the play is in doubt.* At that point, the pressure is very intense and I have to make some very important decisions in a fraction of a second. The guy who was supposed to be over there is about four yards closer than he's supposed to be, and the pocket is collapsing, and the defense is charging at me—but that's what makes it fun.

When you take the snap and drop back to throw or hand off the ball, you never know what's going to happen back there. If somebody comes charging at you, you have to move out of the way and avoid the sack. If somebody hits you from your blind side, you have to be careful not to fumble the ball.

A lot of variables go into being a quarterback. Sitting in the pocket is like sitting inside a pinball machine while someone pulls back the plunger and sends the little silver ball flying. Once the ball is snapped, all sorts of unpredictable things start to happen all around you. You hear the thunder of hoof beats, the clash of pads and helmets on each side of you, the wheezing and grunting of guys getting the wind and the stuffing knocked out of 'em. Your job as a quarterback is to get the ball away before it all happens on top of you.

As the Rose Bowl got under way, I was eager to get in there and do my job. My first order of business was to keep possession of the ball. Second order of business was to get the ball into the end zone. In the entire regular season, I had been intercepted only five times—and three of those picks were in the first half of the Iowa game that we came back and won. Now here I was in the opening series of the Rose Bowl—and I got intercepted.

Bob

He sure did.

Brian went back to pass, and he just kind of chucked the ball down-field—sort of a lazy-armed throw. I don't know who the intended receiver was, but the guy who caught the ball was Lamont Thompson—and he was wearing Cougar crimson and gray instead of Wolverine maize and blue. Sitting in the booth and watching Brian throw that interception was really tough on his old man! I had to bite my tongue to keep from saying what was really on my mind! I've always told Brian that the first rule for quarterbacks is: *Only throw to the guys wearing the same color jersey as yours.* If you do that, you'll never go wrong.

Brian

I said to myself, *There's nothing I can do about it now. I just have to do better on the next series.* I wasn't going to let it throw me off my game.

Washington State took over the ball, and our defense hit them with a blitz-heavy pass rush. The Cougars' quarterback, Ryan Leaf, was dodging linebackers, corners, and safeties coming at him from every direction, play after play. By the end of the game, he'd been sacked four times.

On his second series, Leaf completed a 15-yard touchdown pass to Kevin McKenzie, putting the Cougars up 7-0 with 3:17 left in the first quarter. But a short time later, the Cougars' 1,000-yard rusher, Michael Black, got knocked out of the game with a bruised right calf. With Black out of the game, our blitzing scheme kept them from establishing the run, so they were forced to keep the game in the air. That's when the Cougars discovered they couldn't establish the passing game, either.

Leaf really struggled in the first half. Those five Cougar receivers—the ones the media called the Fab Five—kept dropping passes. In the first half, Leaf completed only 8 of 20 passes for 106 yards.

Bob

In the second quarter, the Cougars rolled upfield and were getting ready to score again. Ryan Leaf completed a pair of passes, getting his team to the Michigan 12-yard line. On third down, the Michigan pass rush flushed him to his left. He lofted a wobbly floater into the left corner of the end zone, intended for Kevin McKenzie. But Michigan cornerback Charles Woodson, seeing that McKenzie had only enough room to run a shallow route, shadowed the Washington State receiver perfectly. Woodson leaped high in front of McKenzie and picked the ball out of the air, turning Leaf's TD into an interception. That key defensive play kept the Wolverines from falling behind by two touchdowns. A couple of series later, Woodson set up Michigan's first scoring drive with a 15-yard punt return to the Michigan 34.

Three snaps later, Brian hit Tai Streets on the sideline for a game-tying touchdown. Now that I'm not in the broadcast booth, I can say what I really think: Brian's 53-yarder to Streets was a *great* pass!

The first half was [what] . . . the fight mob calls an "agony fight." . . . The final half was a slugfest, playground football.

— *LOS ANGELES TIMES*, FRIDAY, JANUARY 2, 1998

The second half was textbook Michigan football. The Wolverines turned the Cougars' defense numb with short, powerful runs. When Griese caught Washington State cheating too much toward the run, he burned the Cougars with touchdown passes.

— *THE COLUMBIAN*, FRIDAY, JANUARY 2, 1998

Bob

The second half was a whole different ballgame from the first. Both teams came out slugging. Midway through the third quarter, Washington State took the lead again with a 14-yard reverse by Shawn Tims. Michigan's James Hall blocked the point-after attempt by Rian Lindell, holding Washington State to a 13-7 lead.

On the next series, Brian hit Tai Streets again—this time with a 58-yard pass, his longest completion of the season. Streets hauled down the pass at the 7, burning Washington State defender Dee Moronkola. Moronkola could do nothing but pound the turf with frustration as Streets ambled across the goal line. The extra point, kicked by Kraig Baker, gave the Wolverines a 14-13 lead.

I thought Brian had thrown a sensational pass—but of course, I kept my enthusiasm in check as I recapped the play. Our producer, Jay Rothman, thought our sideline reporter, Lynn Swann, had a good view of the play, so he cut to the sidelines. Lynn analyzed the replay of Brian throwing the ball and Streets beating the defensive back on the play. Then he capped his commentary with a nod to me—and to Brian: "Bob, my hat's off to your son."

The second-half turnaround in Michigan's game was really something. While Brian and the Wolverines had failed to convert a single third down out of five attempts in the first half, they converted *ten straight* third downs in the second half. The capper came early in the fourth quarter, at the end of a 14-play, 77-yard drive.

Brian

With 11:21 left in the game, we were on the Washington State 24-yard line. I took the snap, faked an inside handoff, and bootlegged to the right. I looked downfield and saw my primary receiver, Jerame Tuman, running wide open. It was one of those moments I described earlier, when everything is working according to plan—my front line was blocking exactly as they were supposed to; my receiver was right where I wanted him; the passing lane was as clear as glass; all the X's and O's were in place—everything was textbook.

I released the ball, a high floater, leading Jerame just enough so that he could easily catch it. The ball settled into his arms, and he loped into the end zone for an easy touchdown. Though we still had plenty of work ahead of us in that final quarter, that play-action pass was the game winner for us.

But my favorite part of the game was still to come.

Bob

Brian's TD pass to Jerame Tuman put Michigan up 21-13 early in the fourth quarter. All Washington State could muster in response was a 48-yard field goal kicked by Rian Lindell with 7:25 left in the game. Washington State still trailed Michigan by five points, but they had cut into Michigan's lead. Brian and the Wolverines took over the ball with plenty of time on the clock in which to lose the Rose Bowl. More than anything, Brian had to keep the ball out of the hands of Ryan Leaf.

Brian

We started our final drive on our own 19. The first couple of downs didn't go too well, and we soon found ourselves facing a third and 11 on our own 18. I took the snap, looked for my receiver—and discovered I had a problem. The pocket was collapsing, and I had a tackler coming after me in the backfield. This play was not textbook at all.

I fought off the tackler, found a hole in the line, and took off running. I needed 11 yards for a first down—and by the skin of my teeth, I gained *exactly* 11 yards before I was brought down.

A few snaps later, I again found myself in a third-and-5 situation on our own 32. In the huddle, I told Charles Woodson we were going to a trick play. I would throw the ball backward to Charles, and then he would throw downfield to Chris Howard. "And Charles," I said, "this is a big play, so if the receiver's not there, just run it yourself."

So we lined up and I took the snap. I flipped a lateral pass to Charles behind the line of scrimmage. He looked deep for Chris Howard, but the Cougars had Chris well covered. So Charles did exactly what he was supposed to. He fought off a couple of guys and streaked up the sideline. He gained 6 yards and converted the down. A few snaps later, he caught another first-down pass at the Washington State 40.

In all, we converted four straight third downs on that series, consuming 6 minutes and 56 seconds in 15 plays, moving the ball a total of 51 yards. By every measure, that was the biggest drive I led all season. When I left the field, I knew our offense had done everything possible to win the game. Jay Feely came out to kick what everyone thought would be a 47-yard field goal—but the field goal setup was a fake. Instead, Jay booted a nice little 23-yard punt, and our guys downed the ball on the Cougars' 7-yard line. Ryan Leaf got the ball with only 29 seconds left in the game—and 93 yards of prime Pasadena real estate to cover.

Later, the media would ask me about my three touchdown passes in that Rose Bowl game. But when I look back on that game, it's not the touchdown passes I remember best. The thing I'm most proud of in that entire game was that seven-minute drive in the fourth quarter. It was a team effort, conducted by an offense that had spent most of the season in the shadows.

That drive was personally satisfying for me because I got to use all the skills I hold important as a quarterback. I didn't just throw the ball. We used a mix of runs, downfield passes, and short passes on third downs. I made sure that the clock wound all the way down to two seconds on each play before I snapped the ball. I reminded our guys to stay in bounds to keep the clock running. I ran the ball myself for 11 yards. We picked up the blitz, we adjusted, we got first downs. I did all the things I love to do as a quarterback—and that's why I love that drive.

Bob

That's the kind of ball control that leads many sportswriters to compare Brian's style with mine. A lot of facets of the quarterback position don't get a lot of notice but go a long way toward winning a ballgame—things like ball control, clock management, and attention to the fundamentals of the game.

That's what Brian did on that final drive in the Rose Bowl. He chewed up almost half of the fourth quarter on a single drive that went only 51 yards. For almost seven minutes, Ryan Leaf was standing helpless on the sidelines, just eating his insides out, wishing he could get back in the game. It must have been the longest seven minutes of his life. By the time the Cougars finally got the football, they had only 29 seconds left—and no timeouts.

Brian

Some of the media guys reported that I was "nervously" or "anxiously" watching Ryan Leaf's final drive in the last half-minute of the game. Not true. The fact is, when Washington State was driving down, my mind wasn't even on the game anymore. I knew it was over, and we had won.

At that moment, I was thinking of my mother. She was the only thought on my mind. She was definitely there with me, and I knew she was celebrating with me.

When I walked off that field for the last time and turned the game over to our defense, I knew I had done everything I could do throughout the season, that it was completed, it was perfect, and we were undefeated. I had an incredible peace and a strong sense of finality within me. I thought, *I'm done, the pressure's off, we accomplished everything we set out to do. Now I just want to celebrate with my family, with my mother.* During Washington State's final drive, and long after the game was over, I was thinking of her.

Bob

Leaf began his final drive by throwing two incompletions. Then, on third and 10, he hit Nian Taylor with a big 46-yard pass. Though Taylor pushed off on Charles Woodson to beat him on the play, there was no flag for offensive pass interference. The play gave Washington State half the yardage they needed, plus a first down. But they were still on the Michigan 47, with only nine seconds of game time left.

On first and 15 after a delay-of-game call, the Cougars hatched an old-fashioned, sandlot-style hook-and-ladder play. Leaf tossed a short pass to tight end Love Jefferson; Jefferson lateraled to Jason Clayton. Clayton had a chance to run out of bounds and stop the clock around the 30, but he went for broke instead. He was tackled inbounds at the Michigan 26 for a 21-yard gain and a first down. Technically, the clock was still running, but it was stopped with two seconds remaining so the officials could move the chains.

The Cougar offense got into position while the first-down marker was reset. Meanwhile, the crowd revved up like the engine of a DC-10—man, it was noisy in Pasadena! The referee signaled for the clock to resume. Instantly, the ball was snapped to Leaf, and he spiked it, hoping to burn a down and stop the clock.

Too late. The clock had run out.

> The ending? As good as it gets.
>
> "We had to fight to the last second," said Michigan's senior quarterback, Brian Griese, who was voted the game's outstanding player.
>
> Make that the last two seconds. Washington State was a mere 26 yards from the Michigan end zone when the referee came waving his arms, indicating that time had expired. Cougar players stood by, helplessly. Their fans did the same, in disbelief, as the final 0:02 ticked off the clock. Michigan's fans stormed the field, to hail the victors.
>
> —*LOS ANGELES TIMES,* FRIDAY, JANUARY 2, 1998

Brian

At that point, things got a little crazy.

There are a lot of Washington State fans who think one more tick was left on the clock. But before the ball hit the grass, the officials ruled that time ran out. And me? Well, I've got to side with the officials. We had won, 21-16.

The moment referee Dick Burleson ruled the game over, the entire Michigan bench—me included—ran out into the middle of the field and began celebrating a Rose Bowl victory. Charles Woodson took a victory lap around the stadium, high-fiving the Wolverine fans along the way. We had just put the capper on an undefeated season—Michigan's first since the last title season, 1948.

We gathered on the 20-yard line for the presentation of the Rose Bowl trophy, and for a few moments it was like being in the middle of a riot. People were all around me, screaming themselves hoarse, slapping my pads and rubbing my head, just going crazy. That's when the emotions really welled up inside me—the most incredible, exhilarating moment I've ever felt. It was hard for me to believe that, just a year earlier, I had almost walked away from football altogether.

I never would have forgiven myself if I hadn't come back.

Bob

The game was over—and that's when I lost my composure. I mean, how could any father keep his cool at a moment like that? I saw Brian and his teammates high-fiving one other, celebrating their victory and their perfect season, and I was just overcome. Of course, the big question at that moment was the selection of Most Valuable Player—but my broadcast partner, Keith Jackson, already had that question answered. "If you want to know who the Rose Bowl MVP is," he said, "I'm standing alongside his proud daddy." Then he turned to me, saw how choked up I was, and said, "You want to cry, you go ahead. I'll hold you up. Hey, you're going to make me cry!"

Brian had earned the MVP honor. Though he wasn't known for his scrambling ability, he rushed for 28 yards. Underrated as a passer by the media, he had completed 18 of 30 passes for 251 yards, with one interception and three touchdown passes. Though the media predicted that Brian would put all his reliance on Heisman-winning receiver Charles Woodson, Brian had shown great ingenuity and adaptability, spreading his 18 completions around to eight different receivers. He'd played a great game.

A platform was set up in the middle of the field, and they brought Brian and Lloyd Carr up to the stage. I stayed up in the booth, though I didn't say much on the air at that moment—I was too choked up. When Coach Carr presented the MVP trophy to Brian, he couldn't resist giving me a little dig. "Did his old man ever win this trophy?" he asked.

Up in the broadcast booth, I just threw my hands up in surrender. "I knew that was coming," I said. "Michigan's had a great year—a magical year for Brian. I'm really proud of him."

Just then, Shay came into the booth and we hugged each other while the ABC cameras captured the moment and beamed it across the country. Then the cameras cut back to the field, and I looked at the monitors, dabbing my eyes, while my son talked to everyone in the stadium, and to TV viewers from coast to coast:

"I will cherish this game and this university for the rest of my life," said Brian. "I wanted to be part of this team because I knew it would be something special. All of us have opportunities in life, but those who stand out are the ones who take advantage of those opportunities. It's just sweet for us to capitalize on an opportunity to make history.

"This is the greatest moment of my career, because we gave all of our effort—everything we had—and we came out victorious. To win this game was my ultimate goal, but to be named MVP is something I never expected. I never wanted to be in the limelight. I just wanted to be part of the team."

What can I say? Spoken like a true Griese.

Brian never set out to be a star or win a trophy or impress the NFL scouts with spectacular plays. He set out to win a football game, end of story. He did that by playing within the offense, by remaining cool and confident after one early mistake, and by maintaining his poise when his team twice fell behind—7-0 and 13-7. In my book, those are the marks of a good quarterback.

Keith and I stayed up in the booth for maybe half an hour, while the celebration on the field and in the stands went on and on. Finally, the team went into the locker room, and Keith left the booth with his wife and daughter and son-in-law. I took off my headset and just sat there with my thoughts, waiting for the stands to clear a bit so I could make my way down to the locker room.

Finally, I left the booth and made my way down the stands. People saw me and applauded, which was nice, but the applause was really for Brian and what he had accomplished that day. When I got down to the locker room, I looked around for Brian and finally found him. He was a sight with that big, broad grin, and his eyeblack dripping down his face from tears of joy. We reached each other and wrapped our arms around each other. It's moments like those when you really know what being a dad is all about.

Some of Brian's eyeblack got smudged onto my face, and he reached over and rubbed it off. We didn't say much. There wasn't much that needed to be said. Brian knew how I felt about him. And me? Well, I had won a Rose Bowl with the Purdue Boilermakers, and I'd had a perfect season with the Dolphins, so I had a pretty good idea what Brian was feeling.

He said, "I love you, Dad," and I said, "I love you, too." What else needed to be said?

I couldn't have scripted a more perfect ending for this story. When I think of the frustration Brian felt a year earlier, and how close he came to missing the entire season and the Rose Bowl, it's just unbelievable. A year earlier, Brian had almost decided to quit football and join the "real world" of 9:00 to 5:00. If he had done that, I hate to think what would have been going through his head if he had sat home New Year's Day, watching the game on TV instead of playing in it.

Shortly before Brian's mother, Judi, died of cancer in 1988, she told me her only regret was that she would miss her three sons' great moments— their big games, their graduations, their weddings, and the grandchildren. Well, Judi was wrong about that. She didn't miss a thing. All these years since she left this world and went to a better one, she has continued to have a big influence on Brian and his two brothers. Brian thinks about her and talks to her. She helps him to remain calm and confident in tough situations, and she's one of the reasons Brian plays so well.

Officially, they say that 101,219 people attended the Rose Bowl that day, but I know the attendance was undercounted by one. Judi had the best seat in the house.

> I've said all along that he's been underrated. I wouldn't trade Brian Griese for any quarterback in this country. If I were an NFL coach, I would take Brian Griese in a heartbeat.
>
> —MICHIGAN FOOTBALL COACH LLOYD CARR,
>
> IMMEDIATELY AFTER THE ROSE BOWL

Brian

Though my father had won the Rose Bowl with Purdue in 1967, the MVP trophy went to a Purdue defensive back. So I told him after the game, "I finally did something you haven't done—you were never Rose Bowl MVP."

He grinned and said, "You just let me know when you win a *world* championship, hotshot, and go undefeated in the process."

"Sure, Dad. You're on."

In the locker room after the game, Coach Carr told us, "This game was the stuff of legends. You guys have left a powerful legacy for every Michigan team that comes after you. This team has just won the national championship."

Actually, we wouldn't know for sure if we had won our first national title in half a century until the balloting was completed in the Associated Press poll. The results would be released two days after the Rose Bowl, and one day after Nebraska played Tennessee in the Orange Bowl. But there was no doubt in my mind who the national champions were. As I told the press, we had played the toughest schedule in the country by far, and we finished undefeated. Then we went to the Rose Bowl and beat a very tough Washington State team.

I mean, what else did they want us to do?

We had done it all. We had *earned* that title. And when the votes were tallied, the title was ours.

I don't believe in fate, except the fate we make. I don't believe in destiny, except the destiny we choose. I believe in not giving up.

We had risen to Coach Carr's beginning-of-the-season challenge. We had climbed Mount Everest. We had reached the summit.

2

COMPETITIVE FROM THE GET-GO

Having lost his own father to a heart attack when he was only 10, Bob understood his importance to his family.

"My father was never a quarterback to me," Brian says. "He was always first and foremost a father."

—*USA Today,* TUESDAY, APRIL 21, 1998

Brian

When my mother died, I had to grow up faster and face the real world sooner than I wanted. But my father was there for me in every way. He set aside his own life and made sure I had everything I needed for a normal, healthy life. He knew exactly what I was going through.

Bob

After Judi died, I just wanted Brian to have a normal life—well, as normal as possible under the circumstances. I remembered how it felt when I was ten years old and my dad died. Losing a parent is devastating to a kid, and I was no different from any other kid with that kind of loss. My father died of a heart attack in his sleep, early one morning. It was sudden—he was gone just like that. He was a smoker, and there was no second chance for him.

So I went from being a normal kid, going to school and playing Little League baseball, to being a kid without a dad. After that, I always had a big hole in my life—a sense of *Gee, my father died*. It was a kind of dull ache that never went away.

After Judi died, I never went to my mother and asked, "How did you do it, Mom? How did you carry on as a single parent?" But I did remember the things she did for me. She made sure my life would go on as normally as possible. She made my breakfast, sent me to school, and always made sure that my baseball uniform was clean, my socks and cap were laid out, and I had my glove. Dad was usually the one who had gotten me to the ballpark for games and practice, so after he died, Mom assumed that role. She did whatever she had to do.

When Judi died in February 1988, I knew what Brian was going through and I remembered what my mother did for me. I just tried to do the same for Brian. Losing Judi was hard on all my three boys, of course, but Scott was away at college and Jeff, who was a senior in high school at the time, would be leaving for college in August. So after Jeff took off, it was just Brian and me. I just tried to keep Brian's life going the way it was before his mother died. I did that for Brian's sake, of course, but I also did it for Judi, because I knew that's what she wanted.

I didn't want anything to change for Brian. I didn't want him to have to change his routine. I wanted his life to continue as normally as possible, because that's the way I wanted it when I was growing up without a dad. I had already lost a parent—I didn't want to lose my friends, my routine, my athletics and sports. I didn't want to have to change. When you're young, you want to keep doing what you do. If you've lost something over here, you don't want to lose all this other stuff.

Bob's dad died when Bob was only ten years old. The doctor said he had a massive heart attack in his sleep. I said, "Well, okay," and I just accepted it. Then I went to break the news to my three kids. I just told them that their daddy had died. I don't really remember what transpired then, because I was in so much shock myself.

You know, when something like that happens, it has a terrible impact on a ten-year-old boy. The day my husband died, all the neighbors and relatives gathered at the house. All of a sudden, I realized I couldn't find Bob. I looked all through the house, and I got very worried. Nobody knew where Bob was.

So we had people running up and down the block, looking for him, calling his name, but nobody could find Bobby. I was at my wit's end—I had just lost a husband and now my son was missing. Just then, we all heard a thumping coming from somewhere in the house.

I went looking and found the thumping came from one of the bedrooms. I opened the door, and found Bob sitting on a big cedar chest, all alone. He was banging his heels up against the cedar chest—thump, thump, thump. I guess that was his way of showing his grief because he had lost his daddy, and maybe his frustration because everybody was so busy and nobody was paying attention to him.

Bob has always been a quiet person. He's always been kind of to himself, you know—he likes to be left alone. And I think it probably goes back to the day he lost his father.

—MRS. IDA GRIESE, BOB'S MOTHER

Bob

I grew up in Evansville, Indiana, with a brother, Bill, two years older than I, and a sister, Joyce, three years younger. Dad was a plumbing contractor, and he had to work every day. He'd often get called out on a job at night or on the weekend, so he was busy a lot, but he was never too busy to play pitch and catch with Bill and me. We were a very close family. Dad loved us and he was good to us. He was proud of all three of his kids, and he came to all my games.

I remember one time—I think it might have been my first Little League game—I hit a double. I took off running the bases, and my dad stood up in the bleachers, yelling, "That's my son! That's my boy!" Trouble was, I hit a two-bagger, but I didn't stop at second. I kept going and got thrown out at third. But my dad was so busy yelling that he didn't see me get thrown out. So my mother tugged on his shirt and said, "Sit down, Slick, he just got thrown out at third."

That was what they called him—Slick. With a name like Sylverius H. Griese, it was a natural nickname for him.

Everyone always thought my brother Bill would be the athlete in the family—I think I surprised a lot of people when I ended up in the NFL. Bill was the big, athletic type, while I was small and scrappy as a kid. But somehow my dad knew I was a tough competitor. One time my mom and dad were sitting in the bleachers at one of my Little League games, and he leaned over to her, pointed at me, and said, "That boy is gonna be a great athlete one day." And she looked back at him and said, "You're crazy! That little bitty kid out there is going to be a great athlete?" She couldn't believe it.

But my father must have known something. I don't know what he saw in me, but he saw something that nobody else saw, not even my mother.

I loved every kind of sport—football, baseball, basketball, anything where there was athletic competition. I always had a ball in my hand. I played a lot of football with my brother, Bill. He was about twice my size, and so were his friends, but I loved to get in there and scrimmage with the big guys.

We would always play with a neighbor kid, Ted Temple—though we have to call him *Father* Temple now. He became a Catholic priest and is still a close friend of our family. He married Judi and me, as well as my brother and my sister, and he baptized all three of my boys.

Bill, Ted, and some other kids would play football on the big lawn outside the public library in Evansville, and I would tag along. I couldn't block too well, but I could snap the ball, run routes, and catch passes. After every game, I'd walk home between Ted and Bill, with my nose bleeding and a big grin on my face. Another game, another bloody nose. Mom was alarmed the first time or two, but after a while it got to be routine. She'd just send me into the house to wash up and pack my nose. Getting scuffed up and bloody was part of the game.

Like all kids, I had my share of fights with my brother. But we were close, and he was a good big brother. He included me in his games, and I looked up a lot to Bill and his friend Ted—probably even more so after I lost my dad. Joyce, the baby of the family, was very pretty, with wavy blonde hair. Bill and I used to tease her without mercy, because that's what brothers do. Teasing was our way to show how much we cared about her—though she didn't see it that way. She'd run to Mom, wailing, "I hate them! I hate them!" Today Bill, Joyce, and I are very close, even though we live in different parts of the country.

I went to Assumption Elementary School in Evansville, where I was taught by nuns. My third-grade teacher, Sister Annette, had a big impact on me when I was in her class but even more so a couple of years later when my dad died. She often came to the house to visit and help my mother. She was a very good friend to me, Bill, and Joyce, and she remains close to my mother to this very day.

After Dad died, I turned to sports. My male role models were my coaches—my Little League baseball coach, my grade school basketball coach, my high school coaches. I was a good student, I was very coachable, and I listened. I still tell kids today: "Keep your eyes and ears open. Learn from those who have more game experience and life experience than you have. Listen to your coaches. If they're in that position, it's because they know more about the game and about the real world than you do. So listen to them and do what they say." I doubt that I would have gotten anywhere in football or in life if I hadn't been coachable when I was young.

I was competitive from the get-go. I wanted to play. I wanted to learn. I was always eager to pick up some little nuance, to gain some little edge that would enable me to play better, to make the team, to be the starter. I never considered myself a master of the game—I was always a learner, an eager student, even when I got into the NFL.

My Little League coach at the time my dad died was a guy named John Wainman. He has since passed away, but he had a huge influence on me because he was there, investing in me and spending time with me, helping me to get past the grief and get on with my life after Dad died.

My brother and I went to different Catholic high schools. My school, Rex Mundi, was a brand-new school, and when it opened, the boundary lines of the district were changed. Since my brother, Bill, was already attending Memorial Catholic High School, he was allowed to finish there, even though we lived in the Rex Mundi district. So he went to Memorial while I went to Rex Mundi.

We had a lot of fun with the rivalry between Memorial and Rex Mundi—and the rivalry between Bill and Bob Griese. Memorial was the longtime, established power in football in the area, especially among Catholic all-boys' schools. Bill was a big, bruising senior playing nose tackle—he must have weighed 275 pounds at the time. By contrast, Rex Mundi was the new school, and I was the school's young upstart quarterback. I did a little bit of everything—I threw passes, ran the ball, punted, and kicked extra points.

Once, when Rex Mundi played Memorial, Bill was playing right over the center, away from me, and on one play I got the ball and started to run with it. He saw me coming and I guess he figured it would make him look pretty bad if his little brother got past him. So Bill tackled me just short of the end zone, and a few plays later, we got the touchdown. Now, I have to tell you that Bill remembers that play a little differently from the way I do. The way I tell the story, it was a 7-yard quarterback sneak. When he tells it, it was a 7-yard sack! But Rex Mundi won the ballgame.

My family thought it was great—two brothers competing against each other. On the field, it was sibling rivalry to the bitter end, but off the field we were great friends. Blood is thicker than water—but hey, football is football!

From 1964-66, Bob Griese quarterbacked Purdue to a 22-7-1 record, including a 1967 Rose Bowl victory over Southern California. While he lacked the arm strength of contemporary standouts John Elway, Dan Marino and Troy Aikman, he was the master of making the right throw at the right time.

—GANNETT NEWS SERVICE, SATURDAY,
NOVEMBER 11, 1995

Bob

After my dad died, my mother tried to keep his plumbing business going. She had helped when Dad was alive by answering the phone and keeping the books and doing the billing, but she wasn't really able to manage the business after he passed away. So eventually she folded the business and took a job as a secretary for an Evansville businessman named Ferris Traylor. Ferris was a big Purdue alumnus, and he had seen some of my games . . .

Brian

Dad doesn't like to blow his own horn—so I'll blow it for him. He made All-State in high school football and basketball. And he was a pretty good pitcher in high school baseball as well—so good, in fact, that the Baltimore Orioles offered to sign him the summer of his senior year at Rex Mundi. That spring and summer, he was 7-and-0 in high school baseball and 11-and-0 in American Legion baseball. By the time he got to the American Legion World Series, he was 18-and-0 . . .

Bob

Yeah, but I got absolutely waffled in the opening game of the series. Anyway, the Orioles had a scout at the Series, and they wanted to sign me, but I said, "Thanks, but no thanks. I'm going to college."

My mom's boss, Ferris Traylor, had been following my high school career, and he knew I was a pretty good athlete. The brand of football we played at Rex Mundi was pretty simple. We were a brand-new high school with new, young players. Our coach, Ken Coudret, built us into a disciplined team, but he was careful not to overcomplicate things for us. We had the basic running plays and five passing plays—a short out and a deep out on the left, the same on the right, and a crossing route. And that was it. We didn't do anything flashy. We just snapped the ball and battled our way downfield—and it worked pretty well. But, of course, when I graduated from high school, I was not schooled in any kind of well-oiled offense or a precision passing game.

Ferris Traylor was a Purdue alum, and he believed in me. He knew I didn't have the money to go to college. The only way I could go to school was on a scholarship. So he went to the people he knew at Purdue and said, "This kid, Bob Griese, is an athlete. You oughta give him a scholarship and suit him up." Indiana showed some interest, too, but other schools weren't exactly standing in line to give me a scholarship—just Indiana and Purdue. I chose Purdue.

The athletic director at Purdue was Red Mackey, and the head football coach was Jack Mollenkopf, who was a good friend of Ferris Traylor. Freshmen were ineligible for NCAA sports in 1963, so I played junior varsity basketball during my freshman year, and varsity basketball and football my sophomore year. It was tough going back and forth from basketball to football, because as soon as I finished basketball season, it was time for spring football practice to begin. I was either having to get rid of my basketball muscles to get into football shape or the other way around. So in my junior and senior years, I gave up basketball and concentrated on football.

The crazy thing was, the sport I really loved was baseball! I asked Coach Mollenkopf about it in the spring of my sophomore year, and he said, "Well, yeah, you can play baseball if you want—but you know, our starting quarterback just graduated, and there's a battle here in the spring for the starting QB job next fall. And if you're playing baseball, you won't be in line for that job." So I passed up baseball that year and concentrated on football.

My junior year, I was really thinking hard once again about baseball. So I went to Coach again and said, "What about baseball?" And he said, "Well, yeah, you can play baseball if you want—but you know, you've already been the starting quarterback for a season, and in the spring you have to work with your receivers in spring practice . . ."

So I never played baseball again.

Looking back, I think I did all right sticking with football. My junior year, we beat Notre Dame. They were ranked number one, and we were ranked number six. It was a tough game—we battled back and forth. We were up, then down, and we came back by the end of the game and beat them—a very memorable game.

Brian

How did you play?

Bob

I don't know. Something like 19 of 22 for I don't know how many yards. I just remember it was a great game for Purdue. We beat the number one team, and after that, we were number one.

(**Brian**)

And you were All-American that year?

(**Bob**)

Yeah. I made All-American my junior and senior years. People kept saying to me, "You're going to play in the pros after college, aren't you?" Well, I enjoyed football, but I had no grand designs to play in the pros. My plan was to graduate in four years with a degree in industrial management. Then I would interview and get a job someplace like Procter & Gamble or Johnson & Johnson. I was planning to go into business and get into the real world.

Purdue went to the Rose Bowl for the first and only time in 1967, my senior year. It's funny, but I really don't remember a lot about that game. As Rose Bowls go, it wasn't all that exciting a game—even though it was decided by one point. I'm not the kind to remember all the good plays I made. I'm the kind who remembers all the interceptions, not the touchdowns. I remember the bad things, not the good. The good is what you're supposed to do; the bad is what you build on and learn from.

What I do remember clearly is that it was a beautiful, sunny day in Pasadena, and my family came out from Indiana for the game. It was a big event for the family—just like when Brian played in the Rose Bowl thirty-one years later.

Purdue's offensive coach, Bob DeMoss, called the plays in that game (more than thirty years later, Bob is still a good friend of mine). As I recall it, we were leading the USC Trojans 14-7 by the fourth quarter, and I remember that I kicked both extra points. Then, with about two and a half minutes to play, the Trojans scored a touchdown, but failed to make a 2-point conversion that would have won the game. So we got the ball, ran out the clock, and won, 14-13. The Rose Bowl MVP award, by the way, didn't go to the quarterback, but to a Purdue defensive back, John Charles.

A Rose Bowl win was a nice way to cap off my senior year, and I look back on my Purdue career with a lot of pride and satisfaction. Jack Mollenkopf was a great coach, and he deserves the credit for what the

Boilermakers accomplished that year. His name is still legendary among Purdue fans and alums.

After I made All-American again my senior year, people kept telling me, "You've gotta play pro ball! You're crazy if you don't!" But I kept saying, "I'm just going to graduate and go into business."

But when I was drafted by the Miami Dolphins in the first round, I said to myself, *Well, okay, I guess I'll go do that for a year or two and see how it works out*. I never imagined I'd end up playing pro ball for fourteen years, with two Super Bowl rings, a Hall of Fame ring, and a lot of great memories.

(**Brian**)

How did you find out you'd been drafted?

(**Bob**)

I don't really remember.

(**Brian**)

You don't remember?!

(**Bob**)

Well, being drafted in pro football wasn't as big a deal back then as it is now. I mean, today they show the entire NFL draft live on ESPN, and there's a lot of drama and hype. But it wasn't like that in '67. I think maybe one of the coaches came to me and said, "Hey, you know you got drafted by the Dolphins?" or something like that. It was in the off-season, a couple of months after the Rose Bowl—in March or April, I think. I was the fourth player selected in the first round.

I had only one contact with the Dolphins before the draft, and that was on the day of the Rose Bowl—January 2, 1967. Joe Thomas, vice president of the Dolphins at the time, came into the locker room right after the big game and introduced himself. He later told me why he came down to meet me. "Anybody I draft in the first round," he said, "I like to talk to him first-hand." I guess he wanted to talk to me as close to the game situation as he could. I didn't give it much thought at the time—I wasn't planning a career in the pros. I was going to get my degree and get on with life in the real world.

And, by the way, I was going to get married.

> Bob Griese . . . was an All-American football star at Purdue before joining the Dolphins in 1967 and quarterbacking them to two consecutive Super Bowl wins in 1972 and 1973. Yet despite the demands of his dazzling 14-year career, Griese always found time for Judi, whom he'd met at Purdue.
>
> —*PEOPLE* MAGAZINE, MONDAY, DECEMBER 11, 1997

I met Judi at a party in Bloomington after an Indiana-Purdue game, the last game of the year. It was a Purdue party with a bunch of Purdue people, and she was there. We were introduced and never really said more than hello to each other. It's funny how your whole life can take a big turn on such a small event. There were no fireworks, no violin music, no cherub with a bow and arrow kicking me in the backside and yelling, "Hey, stupid! This is the girl of your dreams!" We just said hello and enjoyed the party, and that was that.

Back at Purdue a couple of days later, I was sitting in the frat house (I was a Sigma Chi), and I looked up on the wall. There were posters of girls who were running for Army Ball Queen or Homecoming Queen or some kind of queen. I looked at the picture of one of the girls and I thought, *I know her from somewhere! Where did I meet her? Oh, yeah! That's Judi, the girl from the party!* I found out she was a Pi Phi, so I called her, asked her out, and we began dating.

Judi was in the nursing program. She was a year older than I, and she came from Fort Wayne. We dated during my junior and senior years. Because she was a year ahead of me, she graduated and started work as a nurse in Evanston, Illinois, while I completed my senior year. We commuted back and forth to see each other—some weekends I'd go up to Evanston; other weekends she'd come down to the Purdue campus in West Lafayette.

Judith Ann Lassus was a rare combination—beautiful and talented, yet modest and unassuming; confident and secure in her own abilities, yet far more interested in others than in herself; very ladylike, yet very athletic and competitive. Everyone who knew Judi loved her. She was that kind of person. I graduated on Saturday, June 3, 1967, and Judi and I were married the following Saturday, on June 10.

Judi's family had a lot of friends in Fort Wayne. Her friends gave several wedding showers for Judi, and we got a lot of nice gifts. Judi wanted me to come up for some of the showers so that I could meet her family's friends. Well, I wasn't wild about the idea—to me, showers were a girl thing; guys didn't go to showers—but I agreed to go to some of them. And they weren't so bad. Her family's friends were all nice people.

The wedding was huge and elaborate, with flowers everywhere. I had never seen so many flowers in one place in my life! It was also a very hot day in Fort Wayne, and the church where Judi grew up, St. Joe's, was not air-conditioned, so I was very uncomfortable in my tux. It was a beautiful ceremony, and afterward we had a big, lavish reception at the Fort Wayne Country Club, and again there were flowers all around.

When we were making our honeymoon plans, I went to a travel agent and got a lot of brochures, and we decided on Grand Bahama Island. That shows you what a couple of kids fresh out of college know about travel! We went to the Bahamas for our honeymoon, and it was hot and humid. If I had it to do over again, I wouldn't pick the Bahamas in the summertime for a honeymoon—but it really didn't matter. Judi and I were together, we were starting off on a new adventure, and we had a great time.

After our honeymoon, I came back and played in the All-Star Game in Chicago. Then Judi and I loaded our wedding gifts and belongings into a rented truck and moved to Miami. Because of the All-Star Game, I missed some practices, and I think I even missed one or two of the preseason games. But the Dolphins organization was easygoing about it—things were a lot looser in the NFL in those days.

Finally we got settled in. I was a Miami Dolphin—and Judi was a Dolphin wife.

Bob Griese and my husband, Howard, were close friends on the team, and they're close to this day. Howard thinks the world of Bob. In fact, our second son is named for Bob. That tells you that we think pretty highly of Bob Griese.

It was a much different NFL in those days from today. I think Howard and Bob were both making about $25,000 a year. It was long before the big money came in.

Howard and I used to keep a house in Tulsa and a house in Miami. We decided to sell the place in Miami and just rent during the season. One year we rented a house from Bob's backup, Jim Del Gaizo, and another year we rented Jim Kiick's house. Judi was always my real estate agent. She was great at finding the perfect house. We had a special bond, and our families spent a lot of vacation times together.

Bob and Howard took Judi and me to Marco Island one time for vacation. This was in the early Dolphin days, before Howard and I had children. I was a schoolteacher, and I remember that just before we were to leave for Marco, I had given my class a standardized test. Bob, Judi, and Howard came to pick me up at school in our car, and I had this huge stack of standardized tests to grade before I left town.

So I said, "Okay, you guys can help me." I gave everybody a stack and I read off the answers. It was a funny sight—two big pro football players hunched over these little classroom desks, checking the tests so we could get away on vacation.

When Bob and Judi had their first son, Scott, I baby-sat for them. Then when Jeffrey came along, I helped with him, too. Then I started having kids, and we just had a great, great time during those early years as Dolphin wives together, with marriage and motherhood.

Years later, when Brian was born, Howard and I were living in Tulsa, and Bob and Judi were in Miami. Brian was born in March, and my son Blaine was born in May. So those were the only two babies that she was not around for me and I was not around for her.

But even when we were apart, we had a wonderful friendship and kept in touch. She was very giving, very thoughtful, and utterly loyal. I don't remember her ever saying anything bad about another person. She had such a sweet spirit. She adored Bob and her boys, more than you can imagine, and she was just a great mom and a great wife. Losing her was a tragedy for her family, and for me, and for anyone who knew her.

I miss her so much.

—DOLPHIN WIFE JULIE TWILLEY

Bob

Football is a job. It's not like most jobs, but it's still a job.

A lot of guys get caught up in the whole celebrity thing. A lot of players go Hollywood and live the fast-lane, celebrity lifestyle. I was never into that. I was married, and after practice, I wanted to go home and be with my wife and kids. I figured you do your job, you work hard, and then you go home and spend time with your family. That's what life is really all about—family.

I didn't go out for drinks with the guys very often. I'm not critical of the guys who do, but that's not for me. Judi and I would get together with two or three other couples and have a dinner party or play bridge. We were close friends with Howard and Julie Twilley, and some other couples.

That's where my values are to this day—family is number one. When it gets to be 5:00 or 6:00 P.M., I say, "Gee, I'd better get home—dinner's about ready." That's the way I was brought up, and that's the way I brought up my three boys.

When I drive down the highway around dinnertime, I pass a lot of bars with full parking lots. The places are packed. I think, *Who are those people? Don't they have families?* I don't think you should be in a bar drinking when you have a wife and kids waiting at home for you.

During the season, Judi and I always had a date every Tuesday and Friday night. Even after we had kids, we'd get a sitter and go out together, just like when we were dating. I think it's important for a husband and wife to spend time together, just the two of them. More than that, I enjoyed being with Judi. I was always crazy about her.

Our oldest son, Scott, was born September 17, 1968. That was during my second season with the Dolphins. I remember that we had a practice that day, but Coach Wilson said I could skip the morning meeting to take Judi to the hospital. So I did, and after a difficult labor, Judi had the baby. The baby was perfect and Judi was okay, so I said to her, "Okay, I've got to go to practice."

As I was driving up U.S. 1, I was so happy and relieved that everything went okay that I just started laughing in the car. I just laughed and laughed, all by myself, because I was so happy to be a father, happy that life was so good. When I got to practice, I took some cigars and passed them around to everybody on the team.

I was so proud when all three of my boys were born.

Brian

Were you in the delivery room when we were born?

Bob

The delivery room? No, no, no! I didn't do that! When all three of you guys were born, I was in the waiting room, not the delivery room. That was a more civilized era when fathers weren't expected to actually be a part of the childbirth experience. I mean, the sight of blood—hey, that's not for me!

Brian

You've seen plenty of blood on the football field.

Bob

That's different. That's football blood. Football blood is a whole different thing from *that* kind of blood.

I've had a lot of fun playing football, and there's a lot of satisfaction in being a part of what the Dolphins accomplished while I was a part of the team. But none of that compares with the fun of roughhousing and playing with your kids or the satisfaction of watching your boys grow to be solid, responsible, straight-up young men.

With all three boys—Scott, Jeff, and Brian—I coached their Khoury League (like Little League) baseball teams. I coached their teams from the time they were playing T-ball (though that's more like baby-sitting than coaching) right through their school years. I suffered through a lot of Little League-type games, where the action is excruciatingly slow because the kids are young and just learning to play the game, and they can never get anybody out.

As my boys grew up, there were always balls around our house—golf balls, tennis balls, footballs, basketballs, baseballs. Whatever season it was, we'd pick up a ball, and the boys and I would play. I'd come home after practice and we'd play games in the yard.

I raised my three boys pretty much the same way I was raised. They had the same routine I had growing up: You go to school, and after you've studied all day, you're rewarded by getting to play sports from 3:00 to 6:00 P.M. Then you come home, have dinner, do your homework, and go to bed.

That's a good, healthy way to raise a kid—a good mix of education, exercise, and family time. You work your mind a while, then get out for some exercise and fresh air. That keeps you out of trouble and helps you to stay away from drugs and all that other stuff. You get to hang out with athletes—and most athletes are good people with good values and good habits—and you get your mind, body, and values in shape.

As my kids grew up, I never pushed one sport over the other. I never said, "You ought to go out for this sport" or "You shouldn't do that sport." Though all my sons played football in college, I never pushed them toward the sport I excelled in. I encouraged them to try everything, and whatever they chose to do, to give it everything they've got.

Judi and I raised our kids in the church because God is the ultimate reality. Life is short but eternity is forever, and we wanted our boys to be prepared for life and for the life to come.

As in any American household, holidays were special times in the Griese household—though we sometimes had to be flexible in how we celebrated holidays because of my job. Football players sometimes have to work on Thanksgiving and Christmas. So we didn't get too stuck on celebrating holidays on the actual day. We would just celebrate whenever I could be home. The important thing is family and the meaning of the holiday—not a specific date on a calendar.

We had three boys, and Judi always wanted a girl. She had a girl's name picked out for Brian—he was supposed to be named Christine or Christina. Somehow, though, I don't think someone named Christina Griese would have ended up as a Rose Bowl MVP.

We stopped at three kids. I have friends who have had four or five kids, and they were all boys! But Judi and I felt that three was all we could handle. We didn't necessarily want to have quantity—we wanted to have quality. We weren't sure we could live our lives the way we wanted to while raising more than three children, so we said three is enough. Though we never had a daughter, we figured there'd be a granddaughter or two in the picture one day (and sure enough, Scott and his wife, Jennifer, came through—their first child was a girl, Reneé Judith).

So we began our family in 1968, while I was getting started playing pro football in Miami. In those early years of my career, I got a lot more satisfaction out of my family life than I did out of football. During my first three years in Miami, the Dolphins were strictly a losing proposition.

3

A Punch in the Face

In 1967, the Miami Dolphins snapped up Purdue quarterback Bob Griese in the first round of the AFL draft. He and the young franchise struggled until 1970 when Don Shula became the team's head coach.

—Roland Lazenby, *The 100 Greatest Quarterbacks*[1]

Bob Griese was a Rose Bowl-winning quarterback out of Purdue who . . . [signed] with the (then) not-so-hot Miami Dolphins in 1967. While Griese couldn't turn the Dolphins into winners [before Don Shula arrived as head coach], he did manage to complete over 55 percent of his passes in every season he played. This meant Griese was of championship caliber, just waiting for the chance to prove it.

—Nigel Cawthorne, *World of Pro Football*[2]

Brian

You don't have a great team without great coaching. Without Lloyd Carr's coaching, Brian Griese doesn't have an undefeated season and go to the Rose Bowl. And without Don Shula's coaching, Bob Griese wouldn't have had an undefeated season and gone to three Super Bowls.

A great coach is a spiritual leader—he knows how to motivate you and inspire you. He's a mentor and a teacher—he knows how to elevate your character, endurance, and skill level. He's an example and a tough-love friend—he knows when to put his arm around you and when to kick you in the tail. A great coach cares about winning, and he knows how to get you to care about it as much as he does.

Without a great coach, all the talent in the world won't get you to the big game. Men like Lloyd Carr and Don Shula know how to get a chaotic collection of talented, competitive egos to fly in formation. There are no great teams, no great seasons, without great coaches.

Bob

My first three seasons with the Dolphins were miserable, losing seasons. There were a lot of reasons for that, but the number one reason was that it was a young expansion team. The Dolphin organization was born in expansion in 1966, and I came aboard in 1967, the second year of the team's existence. Dolphins owner Joe Robbie had hired George Wilson as head coach of his brand-new Miami franchise. Wilson had been a great player with the Chicago Bears, and had gone on to coach the Detroit Lions. He was a likable guy, a real player's coach, the kind who would go out after practice with the players. I liked George, but his style of coaching was not going to get us to the Super Bowl. We didn't need a buddy for a coach. We needed someone who would get on our butts.

I was getting paid pretty well—for the 1960s, that is. I wasn't making anything like the money players get today. But no amount of money can make you feel good about losing week after week. I had always been a fierce competitor, and no true competitor can stand losing as many games as we were losing.

In those days, I was scrambling around a lot. We were behind a lot. I had to throw a lot. I was getting hurt a lot. I didn't know what I was doing out there. I vividly remember the pain of those years—the pain of losing, the pain of being the worst team in the league, and the physical pain of getting sacked and stomped all the time. We didn't have much of an offensive line. I got a separated shoulder, injured my knee, and got punished in game after game because there wasn't much pass protection.

We weren't losing because of lack of talent. We had good players. We were getting killed because we hadn't been whipped into shape as a team. We finished the 1969 season with a pathetic 3-10-1 record—the absolute worst in the league.

Despite the 'Phins' poor won-lost record, I got favorable attention from the media and the fans. I guess some people might take solace in favorable press clippings, but I didn't. I read those articles and thought, *They think I'm playing well? I think I'm playing awful! Wait 'til they see my game when I get rid of all the mistakes!* Each year, I focused on getting better and better. But I was frustrated because I didn't have a system to play within, I didn't have effective coaching, and I didn't have pass protection. I knew we weren't going to start winning until some changes were made.

We didn't need a pat on the back. We needed a punch in the face.

At Miami, I was asked to take over a group of players who never had a winning season and had only a 3-10-1 record the year before. The first thing was to learn as much as I could about the players . . .

Bob Griese, Larry Csonka, Jim Kiick, Mercury Morris, Nick Buoniconti, and Dick Anderson were quite impressive. Norm Evans looked as if he was a player who was capable of excelling. We also could see the potential of Larry Little, although he didn't play much the year before because of a knee injury. Larry Seiple looked like a fine punter. The player that I felt had the most ability was Griese. He first made a tremendous impression on me when I was at Baltimore and played the Dolphins in a preseason game in 1968. Griese was exceptional that night and we had trouble winning 22-13 because of the way he threw the ball.

–DON SHULA, *THE WINNING EDGE*[3]

In 1970—the same year the National Football League and the American Football League merged—Joe Robbie lured Don Shula, head coach of the Baltimore Colts, to Miami. As coach of the Colts from 1963 to 1969, Shula had amassed the best win-loss record in the league—73-26-4. One thing was sure: Don Shula was no player's coach. Asked to describe his coaching style, Don Shula once said, "I'm as subtle as a punch in the face."

Just what we needed!

So Don Shula took the job—but there was a big bump in the road on his way to Miami: Colts owner Carroll Rosenbloom complained to the league that Joe Robbie had "stolen" Shula from the Baltimore franchise. It was a specious claim. Don Shula had been completely open and aboveboard with Colts ownership and management. While Rosenbloom was out of the country, Shula conducted negotiations with Rosenbloom's son, Steve, who was president of the Colts organization. Steve Rosenbloom understood that the Miami offer was a big advancement opportunity for Shula, and he promised that the Baltimore organization would not stand in his way.

But soon after Shula's hiring was announced by the Dolphins, the Colts accused Joe Robbie of "tampering"—a very serious charge that carries stiff league penalties. It looked like an out-and-out stickup—Carroll Rosenbloom was making the charge in order to get the Dolphins to come up with extra cash for the Colts. No one seriously thought the charge would stick. Sure, there are formalities that must be observed when one team hires a coach from another team, but those formalities had been observed in this case.

Surprisingly, NFL commissioner Pete Rozelle sided with the Colts in an April 1970 decision—and he penalized the Dolphins, taking away our number one college draft pick and giving it to Baltimore. It was completely unfair. There had been no double-dealing, secrecy, or underhandedness in the deal, and Don Shula had kept Steve Rosenbloom apprised every step of the way. But you can't fight City Hall, and you couldn't argue with Pete Rozelle.

In the end, it didn't matter. Having Don Shula in Miami would have been worth a dozen number one draft picks. Just a couple of weeks after Rozelle slapped us with the penalty for the "tampering" that never was, the Dolphins got to meet the new head coach. He laid out for us his vision for the team, and told us what we could expect in the months ahead: an all-new system, a heavy emphasis on execution and technique, and an intense regimen of long, punishing workouts. Best of all, he promised that we would start winning games.

That was all I needed to hear.

Though Don Shula and I are great friends now, at that time he was just Coach to me. When I met him at that first meeting, "Shoes" was a young guy in his mid-thirties, and he had the bearing of a marine colonel. I knew at first glance that he was exactly what the team needed. I was instantly impressed by his work ethic, his toughness, his take-no-prisoners approach to the game. I was ready to follow this guy into battle—all he had to do was say the word.

Shoes spent a lot of time working directly with me, getting me ready for training camp in July, while assessing the talent pool he had to work with. We had a solid nucleus of veterans—guys like Larry Little, Larry Csonka, Jim Kiick, Norm Evans, Mercury Morris, Nick Buoniconti, Dick Anderson, and my roommate on the road, wide receiver Paul Warfield. We also had a great crop of rookies—Mike Kolen, Jake Scott, Tim Foley, Doug Swift, and Curtis Johnson. To top it off, Shoes signed a couple of talented free agents—tight end Marv Fleming from the Packers and field-goal kicker Garo Yepremian. Shula also released a number of players he thought would not make the team.

At his first press conference as Miami head coach, Shula announced that he didn't have a timetable for turning the team around. "I don't have a one-year, three-year, five-year, or ten-year plan," he said. "I'm just going to work as hard as I can to put the best team on the field."

Well, Shula may not have had a timetable, but the Dolphins owner sure did! A reporter asked Joe Robbie if he was going to give Don Shula time to turn Miami into a winning ball club. Robbie's terse reply: "Sure—he's got all summer." As it turned out, Shoes didn't even have that long. Just as we were about to launch into training camp, Coach Shula's game plan got sacked by a players' strike—the first such strike in the history of the NFL.

Even before the strike, Shoes had been working against the clock, trying to turn this losing team into a winning machine. But he's such a shrewd team-builder that he was even able to use the strike to his advantage. Though he couldn't work out his veteran players during the stoppage, he got his rookies together in a mini-camp and used the time to work them, observe them, and jell them into a strong, young platoon. Then, when the strike ended, he brought all the veterans in—and suddenly we had a team!

Brian

Didn't they call you The Scrambler before Shula took over?

Bob

They called me that—and worse. But when Shoes started working with me in training camp, he told me the first thing he wanted to do with this team was to get the quarterback to quit scrambling around, to stay in the pocket. I said, "Hey, I'd love to stay in the pocket—but there's no pocket! You get me a pocket and I'll stay put!" So Shoes worked with the offensive line, working on techniques, and that season, we had a pretty darn good offensive line. It was great!

Once Shoes got hold of me, they stopped calling me The Scrambler. They started calling me The Thinking Man's Quarterback, and even The Chess Master—but none of it would have happened without Don Shula's coaching. Shula built the pocket, and more often than not, that's where I did my job.

Because the players' strike had robbed us of so much of our summer, we really had to hustle to make up the time in an abbreviated training camp. Shula had us doing *four* grueling workouts a day. We started with a workout at 7:00 A.M., then a break for breakfast, followed by a team meeting, then a morning workout in pads. Then we had lunch, another team meeting, an afternoon workout under the hot Florida sun, a break for dinner, and a final workout until dark. We capped the day with a final meeting at 9:30. It was a football boot camp, and we worked harder than we'd ever worked before, pitting offense against defense in intensive "Oklahoma drills," "seven-on-sevens," and scrimmages; sprinting endless "gassers" from sideline to sideline to build up our endurance; and watching hours of film of our own practices that had been shot and rush-developed by the team cameraman.

It was a punishing, even murderous, schedule, but there were few complaints, because Shoes had pared the team down to a hard-core bunch of guys who wanted to win. We knew that to win, we needed to be tougher and more dedicated than the guys on the other side of the ball. We understood that pro football is not the kind of job where you put in your eight hours and pick up your paycheck. If you're not ready to do whatever it takes to win, you shouldn't be there.

We had already had our fill of losing. We were hungry to win.

After the victories, you can look back at all the hard work and laugh . . . We were convinced that we could be a good team, a winning one. It was amazing how intelligent Griese was, how quickly he picked up our system. Fleming's blocking ability enabled us to run the ball better. A trimmed-down Csonka and Little made it obvious how much their contribution was going to be to this team. And it happened early, before training camp actually started, when these players went out on their own and worked out. They accomplished a great amount of work by their intensity in a time-shortened training camp.

—DON SHULA, *THE WINNING EDGE*[4]

Joe Robbie would surely have given a man with Shula's proven track record a number of years to turn around the Dolphins' fortunes. Well, if Rome wasn't built in a day, Miami sure was. With Shula in control, the Dolphins went from the 1969 doormat of the AFL to a 10-4 record and a wild card berth in the playoffs in 1970 . . . The Dolphins, who drew a paltry 34,000 attendance per game in 1969, rocketed to 78,000 (capacity) in 1970. The people of Miami had obviously been waiting for a winner to whom they could give their undying allegiance.

—NIGEL CAWTHORNE, *WORLD OF PRO FOOTBALL*[5]

Bob

We got off to a good start in the preseason, winning our first four exhibition games. Even though we dropped the fifth and sixth preseason games, those first four wins emboldened us and helped us believe that this team could have a good season. For the first time since I began suiting up as a Dolphin, I believed I was on a winning team. We *all* believed!

Our season opener was against the Patriots in Boston. The game started out well, but turned disastrous: we went from a 14-3 lead to a 27-14 loss. After that game, Don Shula gave us the verbal reaming we deserved. The Patriots weren't that good a team, and for us to lose that game, especially after leading by a TD and a half—well, there was just no excuse for it. We had made a lot of mistakes, and the Patriots had turned our mistakes into a rally. We were capable of more, and we all knew it.

So we took our medicine and we went to Houston the following Sunday and sacked the Oilers, 20-10. It was a good game, and we didn't make the same mistakes we had made in Boston. We went on to beat Oakland 20-13 in the Orange Bowl (first time we ever beat the Raiders), then we beat Joe Namath and the Jets in New York, 20-6 (another first), followed by the Bills in Buffalo, 33-14. With a 4-1 record, we were as good as any other team in the NFL. Suddenly, we didn't just *believe* we were a winning team— we were *proving* it.

We had played four of our first five games on the road, and we had proved we could win on the road. Miami fans were going wild, now that they finally had a team they could cheer about. We couldn't wait to get back home and show the hometown crowd what we could do. Our next home game, against the Cleveland Browns, drew our first capacity crowd—seventy-five thousand fans. So we came out on the field of the Orange Bowl. . .

And the Browns cleaned our clocks. I mean, it was nasty—a 28-0 humiliation in front of a packed house. We couldn't have played a worse game if we had tried! The Monday morning postmortem on the game was that it looked like the return of the 1969 Dolphins.

From there, it was back on the road to—of all places—Baltimore. The Colts and their fans were ready for the return of their former head coach. It was another embarrassment for Shula and the Dolphins—a 35-0 shutout. This was followed by a third consecutive loss, this time to the Eagles, 24-17. That game was especially hard for me. Shoes pulled me out when the Eagles were up 24-0, and I had to watch from the sidelines while my backup, John Stofa, put 17 points on the board, trying in vain to overcome the deficit. Now, instead of 4-1, we were 4-4. We weren't a winning team anymore—we were a mediocre .500 team.

I took a lot of flak in the press after Philly, and there were some who said Shula should bench me and go with Stofa. But I believed I could turn things around, and Shoes told me he believed in me, too. He promised to stick with me as the starter, and his confidence in me elevated my own confidence.

The following week, we broke our losing streak, beating New Orleans 21-10. Then we beat the Colts in a rematch at home, 34-17. That was followed by a 20-6 Monday-night win over the Atlanta Falcons. After a three-game slump, we were now on a three-game roll—and we were making a statement. Shula put it this way in *The Winning Edge:*

> The victory [over Atlanta] established our identity as a tough, hard-nosed football team. All week long we had talked about how tough and physical the Falcons were. But we were the ones who were physical that night. We knocked the Falcons off the ball—our defense upended the Falcon blockers, swarming, gang-tackling—the kind of defense you like to see. We became a physical team that had the personnel who could run with the ball and a quarterback who had the intelligence of knowing how important a running game is, directing it, mixing his passes well, and coming up with the big play. This game was one of the early milestones in the development of the Miami Dolphins as a successful team.[6]

And we just kept on winning. We beat the Patriots 37-20, the Jets 16-10, and the Bills 45-7. We closed the season with a 10-4 record and made the playoffs. In a single season, we moved from the bottom of the barrel to the cream of the crop—perhaps the most remarkable one-year turnaround in the history of pro football.

Our first-round play-off game was against Daryle Lamonica and the battle-hardened Raiders in Oakland. We flew out of Miami on Christmas Day, and that night, Joe Robbie and Don Shula treated the team to a party in San Francisco, to sort of make up for the fact that we were away from our families on the holiday. The game was played on a rain-sodden field, and Oakland put the first touchdown on the board. Just before halftime, I hit Warfield with a TD pass that tied the score at 7. Oakland pulled away from us in the second half, thanks in part to a pass I threw that was picked off by Raiders defensive back Willie Brown. He ran it 50 yards for a touchdown. Lamonica outsmarted a fourth-quarter safety blitz, launching an 82-yard TD pass to Rod Sherman, giving the Raiders a two-touchdown advantage. I answered with a touchdown pass to Willie Richardson late in the quarter, and the game ended 21-14, Raiders.

It was tough losing that game and being knocked out of the play-offs, after we had gotten a good taste of winning. In the locker room after the game, nobody said a word. Every man on the team had his own thoughts and emotions to deal with. But I believe we were all thinking and feeling pretty much the same thing: after putting together a 10-4 record, after tasting what winning is really like, we hated losing more than ever. Even though this was the end of our season, this wasn't the end of the road for the Dolphins.

We knew we were going to be back. And we were right.

In Shula's second Miami season, the Dolphins made it all the way to the Super Bowl with a 1971 record of 10-3-1 . . .

Don Shula is the type of coach who wants to have control of all aspects of his team's play on the field. In Baltimore he used to have difficulties with the legendary Johnny Unitas, who definitely had his own thoughts on how best to move the ball. But upon moving to Miami and meeting the Dolphins quarterback, Shula changed his tune.

"Bob Griese understands perfectly what we are trying to do," Shula said. "He likes to work within the system and gets a kick out of calling the right play at the right time."

—NIGEL CAWTHORNE, *WORLD OF PRO FOOTBALL*[7]

Brian

This is all ancient history to me, Pops. I wasn't even born until five years after Shula came to Miami. But I know that you and Paul Warfield made a pretty strong passing combination.

Bob

Well, we had a number of good receivers—Warfield, Howard Twilley, Jim Mandich, Marv Fleming, Marlin Briscoe, Jim Kiick, Otto Stowe—so I spread the ball around a lot. But the two real go-to guys I had out there were my wideouts, Warfield and Twilley. I roomed with Warfield on the road and with Twilley in training camp. When you spend a lot of time with your receivers—not just training but really living with them—I think you build a kind of rapport and trust that shows up in the game.

Though we were predominantly a running team, we could throw. Paul Warfield and Howard Twilley gave me good opportunities for big-yardage plays. Warfield had speed, intelligence, and precise routes. And if you only put single coverage or double coverage on Warfield, you'd better believe I would throw to him—and we'd make you pay. On the other side, Howard had intelligence, excellent routes, and I swear he had a clock in his head— he knew exactly when to get open.

As we geared up for the 1971 season, Shula saw the Griese-Warfield connection as one of the keys to the Dolphin offensive strategy. He later recalled:

> I wanted to utilize our training camp to minimize last year's mistakes and felt that Bob Griese was the key. I consider him a no-fault quarterback. He has a complete understanding of all offensive situations and makes very few errors himself. This would be his second year of working with Warfield, of getting their timing synchronized.[8]

So we took the lessons of our first winning season and built on what we had learned to become a more consistent, poised, and winning team for

1971. A winning record wasn't enough. We wanted a world championship. But as we worked our way through the preseason, it was clear we had a lot of fine-tuning to do. We finished our exhibition games with a lackluster 2-3-1 record, including an embarrassment at the hands of the Vikings, 24-0. Our season opener against the Denver Broncos ended in a frustrating 10-10 tie. Our field-goal kicker, Garo Yepremian, missed four field goals in that game—any one of which would have won it. But Garo redeemed himself the following Sunday, kicking five field goals in a 22-14 win over the Bills in Buffalo.

In our next game against the Jets, we blew a 10-0 lead and lost 14-10 at home. That loss was all the more bitter in that the Jets beat us with a backup quarterback—Broadway Joe was sidelined with a broken leg.

We took our lackluster 1-1-1 record into Cincinnati to play the Bengals, a very tough team at the time. Our morale was in the tank, so the night before the game, Shoes called a team meeting. He gave us a tough talk about what winning meant, and about what it takes to get the job done. Then he opened it up to the floor and let anyone talk who wanted to. I spoke, and so did Paul Warfield, Larry Csonka, and our tough middle linebacker Nick Buoniconti. We laid it on the line: It was make-or-break time. A loss to the Bengals would make us a losing team, and could well sink our chances for play-off contention. We *had* to win that game, and we had to *keep* winning, no letup, throughout the season.

That meeting had a lot to do with lifting us out of a slump and pulling us together as a team. We came out the next day and hammered the Bengals offensively and stuffed them defensively. As a team, we learned a lot about turning a setback into a comeback. The oddsmakers had Cincinnati as the tougher team and our backs were against the wall, but we pumped one another up in that meeting, then came out swinging and beat a very tough team—and we kept winning from there.

That win in Cincinnati kicked off a streak of wins. We beat New England 41-3, the New York Jets 30-14, the Los Angeles Rams 20-14, the Pittsburgh Steelers 24-21, the Baltimore Colts 17-14, and the Chicago Bears 34-3. In the New England game in Miami, I surprised a lot of people (including myself) by throwing three touchdown passes on three consecutive plays. I threw one TD pass, then we got the ball again on an interception, and I threw another on the very next play. Then we kicked off, the Patriots fumbled the return, and we recovered. So I threw a third TD pass on the very next play.

Three games later, we played the Steelers in Miami. The night before the game, I was in the hospital with food poisoning. I couldn't keep anything down, so they fed me with an IV. The doctors released me the next morning, and I went straight to the Orange Bowl and reported for duty. Shoes took one look at me, and it was like he'd seen a ghost. "How do you feel?" he asked.

"Not too bad."

"Well, why don't you get dressed, stand on the sideline, and maybe throw a few? We'll see how it goes."

The game got under way, and it was a disaster. Just a few minutes into the second quarter, we were down, 21-3. I kept looking over at Shula, and he'd sneak a glance at me, like he was thinking it over. I must have looked worse than I felt, because I was really ready to go, but Shoes kept holding off a decision. Maybe he was just waiting for me to say something, because finally, when I couldn't take it anymore, I got up off the bench, walked over to him, and said, "I'm ready."

He didn't think twice. "Okay," he said. "You're in."

So I took the field, called a play in the huddle, lined up, took the snap . . .

And promptly fumbled the ball on my very first play. The Steelers recovered. I walked back to the sidelines feeling down on myself. But Shula was 100 percent encouraging. "Come on," he said, "you'll be okay. Don't worry about that one."

So I shook it off, the Steelers went three and out, and we got the ball again. Before the quarter was over, we scored two touchdowns, bringing the score to 21-17 at the half. We were back in the game. The Steelers never scored again, and I hit Warfield with a 60-yard TD pass in the fourth quarter that sealed the game for us, 24-21. That was a big victory for the Dolphins, because we had proved to ourselves and to our fans that this was a team that could come from behind.

Another example of turning a setback into a comeback was the very next game against the Baltimore Colts in Miami. By the third quarter, the Colts were leading us, 7 to zip. Then we tilted the game in our favor with two third-quarter touchdowns—Jim Kiick ran one in from the Colts' 1-yard line, and I hit Marv Fleming with a go-ahead TD pass. The Colts scored again in the fourth quarter to tie it at 14, and Garo Yepremian kicked a 20-yarder to win it, 17-14. That was a big game for us in a couple of ways. First, we beat the defending Super Bowl champions and Coach Shula's former team, something we all really wanted to do for Shoes. Second, it was an inspiring game, because Larry Csonka was playing hurt. Zonk had pulled something in his leg, and we could all see that he was in a lot of pain. But he played with such courage and emotion that he gained 93 yards on 15 carries. When you see a guy playing that way through all that pain, it elevates your own performance.

Brian

After that winning streak, you also had a couple of losses.

Bob

We were upset by the Patriots in New England, 34-13, after we had given them a sound thrashing earlier in the season. We were never able to establish the run in that game, and they shut down our passing game with double coverage on my outside receivers.

Even so, we went into Baltimore the following week with a half-game lead over the world champion Colts. But we left Baltimore a half-game behind them, losing our second game in a row, 14-3.

We finished the 1971 season with a 27-6 win against the Green Bay Packers. That win, combined with a loss by the Colts the same day, gave us the first divisional championship in the short history of our franchise.

> The Dolphins and Griese capped off an astounding 1971 season by sneaking past the Kansas City Chiefs in a Christmas Day playoff battle, the longest game in NFL history.

Griese played despite a painfully injured left shoulder. The game was a kicking duel pitting Miami's Garo Yepremian against KC's Jan Stenerud. Griese was left with the duty of getting the ball close enough to let Yepremian use his toe. After six periods of play and two sudden-death overtimes, the game came down to a photo finish . . .

—Roland Lazenby, *The 100 Greatest Quarterbacks*[9]

Brian

At the end of the '71 season, you were voted Outstanding Player in the AFC.

Bob

That was a nice honor, but the main thing to me was the team accomplishment. And our biggest accomplishment of that year was when we went into the divisional play-offs against Hank Stram's Kansas City Chiefs, who had won Super Bowl IV two years earlier.

The game was on Christmas Day 1971. We went into Kansas City's old Municipal Stadium determined to play our game and continue doing everything we'd been doing all season long. The Chiefs were a big-time team—along with the Colts, one of the two powerhouse clubs in the AFC. Their roster was stacked with big-name talent—Len Dawson at QB, receiver Otis Taylor, running back Ed Podolak, cornerback Emmitt Thomas, defensive tackle Buck Buchanan, and linebacker Willie Lanier. And who were we? Just the brash, young, upstart Dolphins, newly emerged from the bottom of the league, coming to play in the Chiefs' backyard. The oddsmakers didn't give us much of a shot.

The Chiefs stacked their defense to stop our running game. Our plan was to come out and establish the run against their veteran defense, then mix in some quick slants to the wide receivers, Warfield and Twilley, taking advantage of the Chiefs' man-on-man coverage. We wanted to control the ball and keep their offense off the field. But it didn't go the way we planned.

We received the kickoff but struggled in our first series. The Chiefs' defensive line sealed up the middle and stuffed the run, and their secondary contained our aerial attack. While we struggled offensively, the Chiefs put points on the board—a field goal and a Dawson-to-Podolak TD pass in their first two possessions.

Well, we had been in worse spots. We just had to reach back and remember what we had learned against the Steelers and Colts. If we were patient, we could overcome a 10-point deficit. There was no panic on our side of the ball. We just went to work and stayed with our game plan in the second quarter. We gradually tilted the playing field back to level with a touchdown and a last-minute field goal. We left the field at halftime with the score tied at 10. We had kept our poise, and we felt we had nudged the momentum of the game slightly in our direction.

During the third quarter, the Chiefs and Dolphins each scored a touchdown, so we went into the fourth quarter knotted at 17. In the first three quarters, it seemed that the Chiefs always scored first, and we had to answer back to keep up. We weren't satisfied with answering back—I wasn't, Shula wasn't, none of us were. But we could never seem to gain the upper hand on the Chiefs—and the fourth quarter was no exception. Once again, KC quarterback Len Dawson struck paydirt with a 63-yard pass that led to a touchdown on the next play. The Chiefs were once again on top, 24-17, and we were once again playing catch-up ball.

On our answering drive, I threw a change-up at the Kansas City defense: five straight passes, concluding with a game-tying touchdown pass to Marv Fleming with about a minute left in the game.

Even though we had come from behind and tied the game at 24, we still had a lot of football left to play. And the kickoff after that touchdown brought us right back to the brink of disaster.

Garo Yepremian booted the ball deep, where it was caught by the Chiefs' Ed Podolak, who found a hole and dashed down the sideline for the end zone. Yepremian and Curtis Johnson combined to force Podolak out of bounds, but not until he had gotten all the way to our 22-yard line and within easy field-goal range. The Chiefs ran the ball three times, but our defense stopped them each time. With half a minute left in the game, Jan Stenerud (who is now a Hall of Famer, and perhaps the best kicker in NFL history) stepped up to kick the winning field goal for the Chiefs. He booted the ball . . .

And incredibly, it went wide left—no good! It was still a tie game.

We could feel the surge of energy and excitement on our side of the ball. We went into sudden-death overtime having to kick off to the Chiefs. All they needed was one score—any kind of score—to win. The Chiefs' Ed Podolak returned the kickoff to their 46-yard line for excellent field position. They worked the ball down to our 35, then called Stenerud out again to boot the winning field goal. He kicked . . .

But Nick Buoniconti was right there, leaping high and blocking the ball. Another busted field goal for the Chiefs, and another reprieve for the Dolphins. Our offense took over and worked the ball downfield, but the best we could do was set up a long 52-yard attempt by Garo Yepremian. He kicked it—no good.

So we went into a *second* sudden-death overtime. And we were thinking, *They can't beat us! They're tiring out, and we've still got plenty of steam left!* That's when we understood why Coach Shula had put us through all those grueling "gassers" in the hot Florida sun. We were the better conditioned team!

We took over the ball on our 30 and started moving it, pounding the ball for short but steady gains. Finally, I called a play we hadn't used yet— a misdirection play, 39 roll right, trap left. It was one of my favorite plays, but at the start of the game, we had known the Chiefs were looking for it, so we kept it in reserve. Now it was the sixth quarter, and I was pretty sure the Chiefs weren't looking for it. The play sent guard Larry Little and tackle Norm Evans to the left, drawing the KC defense with them. At the same time, the tailback and I went right, which opened the way for number 39, Larry Csonka, to cut left and up the middle. Zonk stunned the Chiefs' defense, rumbling downfield for 29 yards to the Kansas City 36-yard line. Just like that, we were in field-goal range. We used three more plays to move the ball an extra 6 yards, then called on Garo. He kicked—

And it was good! Merry Christmas, Miami!

That game was the key to everything we accomplished the following year. It set up the franchise, it made the Dolphins what they soon became, it taught us all that we could be a championship team. The experience of being a young team going into Kansas City against a tough, physical, veteran team really built our confidence and our toughness. We all grew up a lot during that one game.

Of all the games we played, that was the game that truly prepared us to go undefeated in 1972. We came back home and were mobbed by about twenty thousand delirious fans at the Miami airport. I had never seen a celebration like that in my life.

The following week, we beat Don Shula's old team, the Baltimore Colts, in the Orange Bowl. Our defense controlled Johnny Unitas all day long, and our offense was unstoppable. In the first quarter, I hit Paul Warfield with a 75-yard play-action pass. The Colts' cornerback, Rex Kern, had gone for the fake handoff, leaving Warfield wide open. Then, in the third quarter, Curtis Johnson deflected a Unitas pass into the hands of Dick Anderson, who ran the interception in for a touchdown.

In the fourth quarter, on a third-and-2 situation on our 45, I saw that the Colts were in man-to-man coverage, so I checked to a long pass. Just as I thought, Paul Warfield beat the secondary and went deep. I hit him with a pass that he carried 50 yards, to the Colts' 5-yard line. Then Zonk scored on the next play. When the game was over, we had shut out the Colts 21 to zip—Baltimore's first shutout in 96 games—and the Dolphins had won their first AFC championship.

(**Brian**)

Then came Super Bowl VI.

(**Bob**)

You had to bring *that* up!

In the heat of the moment, ex-scrambler Bob Griese had reverted to his old wild ways. Griese's 29-yard loss was a dramatic evidence of the trend of Cowboy domination.
–JOHN FACENDA, "SUPER BOWL VI–DALLAS COWBOYS, WORLD CHAMPIONS"[10]

———————————✗———————————

[Miami's] opponent in Super Bowl VI was a Dallas Cowboys team that had dominated their division every season since 1966 and contested the previous Super Bowl.

> Experience won out over youthful enthusiasm that day as Dallas defeated the Dolphins 24-3. Shula and the Dolphins gained valuable information on how to handle the tremendous pressure of being in a Super Bowl. They learned from their loss. The future was all Miami's.
>
> —NIGEL CAWTHORNE, *WORLD OF PRO FOOTBALL*[11]

Bob

Super Bowl VI in New Orleans, January 16, 1972—when we talk about Super Bowls, that's the one we *don't* talk about. Tom Landry's Cowboys just outplayed us in that game. They were dominant; they were the better team. They beat us 24-3, and the Dolphins became the first team not to score a touchdown in the Super Bowl.

Brian

You set a record in that Super Bowl, didn't you, Pops? You scrambled for the longest sack in Super Bowl history.

Bob

That's another thing we don't talk about!

But it's true. I was sacked for 29 yards on a single play. The NFL films recap of the game shows the play in slow-mo, from the snap to the sack, then they back up and show it all over again from every angle—I mean, the agony seems to last ten minutes! I remember taking a seven-step drop and before I could set to pass, I looked and my whole front line was gone. There was nothing in front of me but Dallas defensive linemen, with number 74, Bob Lilly, leading the charge. So I took off running, slipped one tackler, rolled to my right, and put my arm up to pass, but there was nowhere to throw. So I rolled to my left, and Lilly wrapped me up from behind and planted my face in the ground. I got up off the ground and looked back at the line of scrimmage, and it looked like it was about a mile away.

For me, that was the worst moment of a very bad day. When the game was over, we went quietly into the locker room. I remember thinking, *We had our shot and now it's gone. We worked all season long just to get to this game, and when we got here, we got our tails kicked. Now it's gonna take us a whole year just to get back to where we were just three hours ago, and there's no guarantee we'll ever get that close again. Now we erase the blackboard and start over.*

Shula came in and he gave us a very straight-from-the-shoulder talk—no shouting or berating, but no sugarcoating, either. It went something like this: "We embarrassed ourselves out there today. We lost a shot at a world championship, and that wipes out everything we accomplished this season. Nobody's going to remember that we won the AFC championship, that we beat the Colts in our last game, or that we beat the Chiefs the week before that. They're going to remember that we lost the Super Bowl. We lost our season today, and there's no way we'll ever get that back."

Don Shula wanted us to feel every last drop of pain and frustration we had earned that day, but he also wanted us to learn the lessons of that game. "Something good can come out of this," he went on, "if we can reach back to this game for the experience we gained today. Something good can come out of this if we can use this loss to fuel future Super Bowl wins. That's the only way we're ever going to erase the embarrassment of this loss."

We got the message. We took the lessons of that Super Bowl loss with us into the 1972 season. The bitterness of Super Bowl VI set us up for the sweetness of the Perfect Season. We told ourselves and one another, "Hey, don't let up; don't stop working and training; don't make mistakes. We've got another entire season to go through to get to Super Bowl VII, so if we've gotta go through this, let's make sure we do it right."

We lost Super Bowl VI because we had not absorbed all the lessons of the '71 season. We had learned how to elevate our play to a very high level against very tough teams, but we had not learned how to be *consistent* enough to *stay* at that level. The first time you reach the point where you can play against that level of competition—against a team like the '71 Chiefs or Colts or Cowboys—you find that sometimes you can play to that level one week, but the next week you can't. Once we found out what it was like to be at that level, we were able to come back in 1972 and stay at that level all season long.

We had a goal in front of us: to get back and win the Super Bowl and become the world champions. If it meant winning every game to ensure that goal, so be it. We'd do it. If Don Shula was the first "punch in the face" the Dolphins needed to become a winning team, losing Super Bowl VI was the second. We didn't need to take any more punches. We were ready to start punching back.

Our goal was nothing less than perfection.

4

PERFECTION!

Don't ask Bob Griese to compare his '72 Dolphins with any other team in football history. And whatever you do, don't bring up the Steelers or the 49ers or even the Cowboys. 'Cause if you do, all you'll get is a quick look and the company line: "Look, we did something that no other team, before or after, has done. You cannot compare teams of different eras." In other words, "Listen, squirt, we were great, and don't you forget it."

—CNN/SPORTS ILLUSTRATED, "SUPER BOWL COVERAGE"[1]

Brian

Question: How many NFL teams have ever reached perfection?
Answer: Just one—the Miami Dolphins. In 1972, they won every game—the regular season, the postseason, and the Super Bowl.

Bob

When we started the 1972 season, though, we weren't thinking about perfection. We still had Super Bowl VI stuck in our craws, and our only thought was that we had to get the burden of defeat off our backs. No one ever thinks at the beginning of a season, *We're gonna go undefeated this year.* You only look one game down the road. You only let yourself think about winning the next game. That's how you keep your focus.

Despite what we accomplished that year, the '72 Dolphins were an underrated team in their day, and I think in many ways we continue to be underrated today. Maybe that's because it was not so much a team of flashy superstars as it was a team of disciplined, motivated, intelligent overachievers.

Sure, we also had some talented stars. Paul Warfield made a name for himself with the Cleveland Browns before coming to Miami. Mercury Morris certainly had a lot of flash, and Larry Csonka had the raw power. It was always fun to watch Zonk go chugging upfield like a freight train, while tacklers bounced off him and got squashed under his wheels.

But the *real* talent of the 1972 Dolphins was the ability of each man on the team to play a disciplined game of football, working within Don Shula's system. Our offensive platoon was a bunch of very bright players. So were our defensive guys—the so-called No-Name defense: cornerbacks Tim Foley and Curtis Johnson; safeties Dick Anderson and Jake Scott; linemen Manny Fernandez, Bob Heinz, Bill Stanfill, and Vern Den Herder; linebackers Doug Swift, Mike "Captain Crunch" Kolen, and Bob Matheson; and defensive captain and linebacker Nick Buoniconti. The No-Names were all very bright guys. They weren't just dumb jocks—and the very fact that they were called No-Names is proof that these great, smart players never got the credit and respect they deserved.

Of course, the perfect season couldn't have happened without Don Shula. Shoes was relentless. He set one goal for the team: Get back to the Super Bowl and *win* it. He had already lost two Super Bowls—Super Bowl III when the Jets beat the Shula-coached Baltimore Colts, and then Super Bowl VI, Dolphins versus the Cowboys. He wasn't about to lose a third Super Bowl, so he drove us like a man possessed. And that was good. We all wanted it. We said, "Go ahead, Coach! Bring it on, we want it, we're willing to work for it!" Our attitude was, *We know we can play well. We also know we can play badly. We know what it takes, so let's get back to where we were and let's do it right this time. We've got some unfinished business here—so let's finish it.*

Shula made us understand that we were not going to get there as individuals, but as a team. He told us to expect injuries on the team, and when that happened, the backup had to be ready to step up on a moment's notice. And he was right. Many players suffered injuries—including me. But every time someone had to be carried off the field, the next guy in line would run on and take his place. A lot of guys stepped up and played that year. Again, it goes back to Coach Shula and what he drilled into us: Left tackle gets hurt? Okay, backup tackle steps up. That's what he's here for. He plays just like a starter. Defensive end pulls a hamstring? Next guy moves in; he plays. Quarterback breaks a leg? Backup quarterback, you're on; let's go.

We had good coaches, bright coaches. They didn't ask guys to do what they couldn't do. They built on the things they could do. We were not a great athletic team, but we were a smart team. And that's how we did what we did.

There was no question in my mind. I knew this was the year.

I didn't have any doubts about Griese getting the job done on offense. He is a remarkable individual. He grasped the system quicker than I ever imagined. It has been only two years since he was introduced to it, which tells you something about his intelligence. He has more talent than any quarterback I have ever coached.

—DON SHULA, *THE WINNING EDGE*[2]

The '71 Dolphins had flopped in their first title try—Super Bowl VI—losing 24-3 to the Dallas Cowboys. Seven months later Miami had something to prove, and it launched the '72 campaign with an offense that was heavy on the run and a defense that was young and unknown. These Dolphins ultimately won consecutive championships (Supes VII and VIII) and became the only team ever to play in three straight Super Bowls.

—PAUL ZIMMERMAN, "THE ROAD TO GLORY"[3]

Perfect season, game one, September 17, 1972—a steamy, 100-plus degree day. It was the Chiefs' first game in their brand-new stadium, Arrowhead. We had closed their old stadium for them by beating the Chiefs in a Christmas Day play-off game, winning in double overtime— the longest NFL game ever. After spoiling the Chiefs' previous season, we were back, and we ruined their season opener, 20-10. Larry Csonka rushed for 118 yards and a touchdown, and I threw for a TD. Beating Hank Stram's Chiefs twice in a row set us up for the season and made us believe we could do anything.

Perfect season, game two, September 24, 1972—a rainy home opener at the Orange Bowl against the Houston Oilers. For the new season, Don Shula had come up with an innovative approach to the running game: a three-man backfield rotation. Instead of having a pair of starters plus backups, Shoes had three starters—Csonka, Jim Kiick, and Mercury Morris. The sports reporters kept asking Shoes which two were his starters. He'd say, "I have three starters—Zonk, Kiick, and Morris." It had never been done before, but it gave our running game a lot more flexibility than we'd ever had before. Shoes would dial our running backs into various combinations that gave us added weapons—and gave our opponents a lot more to worry about.

The three-back system worked because those three guys didn't let ego and competition get in the way of team performance. Whoever was on the sidelines would be pulling for whoever was on the field. The three-back system paid off big-time against Houston: Zonk, Morris, and Kiick combined for 228 yards rushing and three touchdowns. Dolphins 23, Oilers 13.

Perfect season, game three, October 1, 1972—Miami at Minnesota—man, that was a game! The 1972 Vikings were a very good team. Their defense was brutal, physical, and punishing—which is why they were called the Purple People Eaters. But the No-Names gave it right back, sacking Minnesota quarterback Fran Tarkenton five times and intercepting three passes. Tarkenton burned us with a long bomb for an early lead in their opening series, and they maintained the lead through most of the game, but Garo Yepremian kept us in the game with field-goal kicks of 38 and 42 yards.

Late in the fourth quarter, we were down 14-6 and we found ourselves backed into our own territory on a fourth and short. That's a textbook punt situation—unless you are down by 8 points with time running out. Then, if you've got a gutsy, granite-jawed coach, you go for it. We went for it. I handed off to Mercury Morris, and he got us the first down. We worked the ball downfield, getting a couple more first downs. Then we stalled out. Now it was fourth and long, and none of our options—to run, pass, punt, or attempt a 51-yard field goal—looked very attractive. Garo Yepremian was not known for hitting long field goals, but Shoes gambled on him, and Garo hit it for three points.

With the score 14-9, we were down just 5 points—less than a touchdown—when we handed the game over to the defense. Nick Buoniconti and Company did what they had to do—stopped the Vikings in their tracks without yielding a first down. Our offense reclaimed the ball with good field position and two and a half minutes on the clock. "Don't hurry," Shula said as he sent me back on the field. "You've got plenty of time." Well, I wasn't worried about the clock; I knew we were going to get it done. I relied on the passing game to move us quickly downfield, completing two passes to Howard Twilley, a down-and-out and an over-the-middle. When the Purple People Eaters lined up with their backs to the goal line to stop the run, I knew we had them beat. I faked a handoff to Csonka, then dumped the ball over the middle of the drawn-up defense to Jim Mandich in the end zone—one of the most effortless passes of my career. As I left the field, there was still a minute and a half on the clock. Final score: Dolphins 16, Vikings 14.

That was a very satisfying win for all of us. Shula later observed that the win over the Vikings on the road "demonstrated how we didn't collapse even though we fell behind and had trouble scoring against them. We never panicked and we stayed with what we had, making the big plays when we had to . . . Maintaining poise and coming from behind are characteristics of a championship team."[4]

Perfect season, game four, October 8, 1972—against the New York Jets at Shea Stadium. The focus of that game was to frustrate Joe Namath, and to do that, our defensive coordinator, Bill Arnsparger, threw something at the Jets offense that he had devised for the '72 season: the "53 Defense." In that defensive scheme, linebacker Bob Matheson played a wild-card role, sometimes dropping back in pass protection, sometimes rushing like an end (the "53 Defense" got its name from Matheson's jersey number). The scheme worked beautifully, keeping the Jets' offensive line off balance and keeping Namath out of rhythm. It gave our defense a powerful element of surprise.

Namath played tough, and at one point he drove to a first and 10 on our 1-yard line—but our defense made a goal-line stand and the Jets had to settle for a field goal. On my side of the ball, I had great pass protection throughout the game, and when it was all over, it was Dolphins 27, Jets 17.

One week later, during a home game against the San Diego Chargers, my own "perfect season" took a sharp, painful turn.

Judi and I always sat together at the games throughout those Dolphin years. We wore out each other's knees at the games, because we were so tense and excited—we would grab each other's knees and squeeze to relieve the tension. I remember Judi would always have a huge knot in her stomach before every game. I don't think Bob was really aware of it, but she was very worried that he would get hurt out there.

We never talked before the games—no chitchat, nothing. We were so tense, we just sat and waited for the game to begin, then we dug our fingernails into each other to get through four quarters. It was very hard for Judi when Bob was injured in the game with San Diego. My husband, Howard, got banged up a lot over the years—he had five major surgeries, and Judi was always there for me through each one. But Bob had been relatively injury-free up to that point, and it hurt her deeply to see him in pain.

We were sitting next to each other in the Orange Bowl the day Bob broke his leg. I hugged her while Bob was down on the turf, holding his leg. Then, after they wheeled him off the field, I drove Judi to the hospital. By the time we got to the hospital, Judi and I were nervous wrecks! She was worried sick about him.

We went into the emergency room and found Bob sitting on a gurney with the TV on, just glued to the game. And Bob looked up at me with a big grin on his face and he said, "What are you doing here? Your husband just caught a touchdown pass!"

That was typical Bob Griese. He was more concerned about the game than anything else—even his own leg. Judi and I just looked at each other and shook our heads.

—DOLPHIN WIFE JULIE TWILLEY

When Bob was with the Dolphins, I watched every game of his that was on TV. And every year, I used to manage to get down to Florida to see at least one of them at the Orange Bowl. I worried about him some. I worried about him more when I was at the stadium watching him than when I was watching him on TV. I didn't want to see him get hurt. I saw that game on TV in 1972 when he got hurt and he was out for most of the season—that wasn't very nice.

—Bob's mother, Mrs. Ida Griese

On the game's 14th play, quarterback Bob Griese was sandwiched between Chargers defensive linemen Deacon Jones and Ron East. As Griese went down, he let out a blood-curdling scream . . .

—Bob Glauber, "Unbeaten, Untied, Unsung"[5]

Bob

Game five of our perfect season was made especially memorable for me, thanks to a pair of San Diego linemen, Deacon Jones and Ron East. We were in the Orange Bowl, October 15, 1972, and it was late in the first quarter. I called a pass to Jim Kiick over the middle. The ball was snapped and I dropped back to pass. I saw two Chargers come bull-rushing right through the line. I threw the ball, and on the follow-through, Ron East came in low and fell into my right leg. I felt something give right then. As I went down, the Deacon went flying over the top of me, pounding me into the Poly-Turf.

After East and Jones climbed off me, I sat up and looked at my leg to see if it was still there. It was, but it didn't look right. The lower part of my leg turned out at a funny angle. My initial reaction was, *Oh, man. There goes my season.* But there was no use crying over it. Once it's done, it's done. If you don't want to get hurt, don't play football.

The next few minutes were kind of eerie. The Orange Bowl is normally a loud, raucous, rowdy stadium, but suddenly it was very quiet. I was sitting up in the middle of the field, looking at my skewed right leg. My teammates were all standing around looking worried, and Bob Lundy, the trainer, was out on the field checking me over. On the sidelines, Don Shula was ashen-faced. It was all very solemn. The trainers strapped me to a gurney, wheeled me off the field, and rushed me to the hospital.

Meanwhile, Don Shula sent in backup Earl Morrall, a thirty-eight-year-old veteran QB we had claimed off waivers from the Colts just six months earlier. Morrall had played for half a dozen NFL teams, and that kind of experience turned out to be just what the Dolphins needed after watching their starting quarterback leave the game on a stretcher. Morrall went on to complete 8 of 10, with two touchdowns. The Dolphins rallied around a quarterback they called "the last of the crew cuts," and won a very emotional game, 24-10. The 5-0 Dolphins were still perfect.

At the hospital, the doctors told me I had a broken leg, and an even more serious dislocated ankle. My reaction was, *Maybe I'll get to play again and maybe I won't. If my career is over, well, it was fun while it lasted.* Whether or not I would play again, all I wanted was to get well enough to run around the yard with my kids and go out on the course and hit golf balls. Football had been good to me; it had been fun—but if it was over, I could live with it. I knew there was life after football.

If at all possible, however, I wanted to play again. So after the cast came off, I was very conscientious about my therapy. I did everything the doctors told me to do so that I could get my leg and ankle back in shape. Most of it was just simple little exercises, going up on my toes, running around a bunch of orange cones on the field, stepping back and forth on each side of a line. My ankle had tightened up while spending six weeks in a cast, so I had to stretch it all out again.

I kept up with the team—went to the workouts, went to all the team meetings, watched film, and took notes. For two months, I was limited in my workouts and couldn't do all the things the team was doing. While the other guys were doing their stuff, I was doing my therapy. But as soon as I was able, I started throwing the ball, running laps with the team, and doing all the preparation I did when I was a starter. I kept up mentally and physically, because when Shula needed me, I was going to be ready and up to speed. Soon I was on the roster again as a backup quarterback.

Twenty-some years later, my son Brian would be going through the same experience at Michigan—a backup quarterback, standing on the sidelines, chomping at the bit, going through game after game as a spectator-in-uniform. So when he called me and complained about how hard it was to be prepared every week and never get to play, I told him, "I know, I know, I know." And I really *did* know. I had been there.

I told Brian what I had learned while I was pacing the sidelines throughout most of the '72 season: "Be ready. Don't let up. I know it's hard, I know you hate it, but just make sure you're ready to play. The worst thing in the world is when the coach finally turns to you and says, 'Okay, you're in the game,' and you go in and drop the ball because you don't know what you're doing. The coach will yank you out and say, 'I thought you said you could do this! You're no better than the other guy!'"

I wasn't a backup very long, but it seemed like an eternity. You never know when your chance to play is going to come, but you have to prepare yourself as if you're going to start every game. It's tough to go through it week after week, saying, "I'm ready for this game," but nothing happens. After five or six weeks of this, the temptation to just let down sets in. But you can't let down—not if you want to be a champion.

I don't know if Brian was listening to me or not—

Brian

Sure, I listened—even though I didn't want to. I didn't want to hear my dad telling me, "Be patient; your time is gonna come." I spent a lot of time walking the sidelines at Michigan, standing in the shadows. I would complain about it, and he'd say, "I know. I know. I know." That's what he'd always say, whatever your complaint—"I know."

Bob

Well, I *did* know.

Scott: I remember watching your road games on TV at home with Mom. It drove her crazy. She worried so much about you. She was always afraid you were going to get hurt.

Bob: She was? She never told me she worried.

Scott: Well, of course not. She would never say anything.

Jeff: She used to chew on ice all the time, because she was so nervous. She had this whole big thing of ice, and she used to chew on it to relieve the tension.

Scott: If she saw you getting in trouble out on the field, she'd stand up and yell, "Throw the ball! Get rid of it!" She'd see the pocket collapsing, and she knew that if you dumped the ball off, they'd go chase the guy with the ball.

Bob: You mean she was yelling at the TV?

Scott: Oh, screaming!

Jeff: Yeah, screaming. I couldn't be in the same room with her.

Bob: I never knew that.

Jeff: She was just as tense at the home games, but she wouldn't get up and yell in the stands. She just sat there and quietly endured it. We went to the games with her, and she would sit on the 30-yard line with the other Dolphin wives.

Scott: She worried about you all the time.

Bob: I never knew that. But my mother was like that, too. She worried about me. If she was watching one of my games on TV, and things weren't going well, she would have to leave the room. She told me about that, and I said, "Why don't you just change the channel for a few minutes? You don't have to get up and leave the room." She'd say, "Oh, no! I don't want to miss anything!" So she'd go out and listen from the other room. But she couldn't stay and watch.

—CONVERSATION BETWEEN BOB GRIESE AND SONS SCOTT AND JEFF

What I tried to do in the '72 season was really try to make them concentrate on the next ballgame and not be looking back over their shoulders. If we had won a game the week before and didn't play as well as I thought we should've played, I treated it like a loss. I was really tough on them. Csonka described me as a man possessed because at times, even after a win, I just talked about all the mistakes that we had made and that if we continued to play that way, there wouldn't be a win the next week.

—DON SHULA, ON THE PERFECT SEASON

Bob

There were a couple of games during our perfect season when perfection hung by a thread. Game six, when the Buffalo Bills came to Miami on October 22, 1972, was one of them. That game was largely decided by the No-Names. In the first half, the defense held O. J. Simpson to 13 yards rushing; in the second half, defensive tackle Manny Fernandez stole the ball right out of quarterback Dennis Shaw's hands as Shaw was about to make a handoff. That turnover set up the go-ahead touchdown. Another key play in that game: Garo Yepremian's 54-yard field goal—his longest ever. If Garo had missed that field-goal attempt or if Manny hadn't gotten to that ball, there wouldn't have been a 17-0 season. As it turned out, we won it by a single point, 24-23, while I stood on my crutches and watched the game from the sidelines.

For game seven, October 29, we went to Baltimore and shut out the Colts, 23-0; the Colts never got closer than the Miami 28. Then, on November 5, we went to Buffalo for game eight, a rematch with the Bills. Mercury Morris rushed for 106 yards and two TDs, while Garo tacked on three field goals. The No-Names held O. J. to 45 yards rushing, and we won that one, 30-16.

Game nine on November 12 was our second shutout of the season— Dolphins 52, New England Patriots 0. That game was special because it made Don Shula the first coach in pro football to win 100 games in his first ten seasons.

On November 19, the Dolphins clinched the AFC East title with a 28-24 home win over the Jets in game ten. Afterward, Jets coach Weeb Ewbank predicted that the Dolphins would go undefeated and called us "the best team in the league." Game eleven, November 27, was a Monday night home win over the St. Louis Cardinals, 31-10. Howard Cosell was covering the game for ABC Sports, and in his pregame interviews, he raised the question of an undefeated season. Everyone on the team refused to talk about it—we were afraid of jinxing it. It was like telling a pitcher in the seventh inning, "Hey, do you know you've got a no-hitter going?"

In game twelve against the Patriots in New England, December 3, the Dolphins rolled up 501 yards, winning 37-21. In game thirteen, December

10, Miami went to Yankee Stadium and beat the Giants, 23-13. It was an incredible experience, standing on the same field where one of my heroes, Mickey Mantle, had played. My cast had just come off a short time before, and I tested out my leg by jogging around the field before the game. It was rainy and my ankle was still stiff and tight, and with all the mud puddles and chuckholes around the field, I thought, *Nope, no way, not today.*

The last game of the season was on December 16 (in those days, we played fourteen regular season games in the NFL, versus sixteen today). We clinched the season with a 16-0 shutout of the Colts at home. I went in and took some snaps in the fourth quarter of that game—maybe eight or ten plays. Zonk and Mercury Morris became the first backs in the NFL to gain 1,000 yards in the same season on the same team. We had been perfect all season long. Now, in order to reach the goal Shoes had set for us—getting back to the Super Bowl and winning it—we had to be perfect three more times.

The day before Christmas, we hosted the Cleveland Browns for the AFC divisional play-off game—game fifteen of our perfect season. In the course of that game, our perfect season once again hung by a thread. The Browns were a wild-card entry and not expected to be much of a problem in that game, but they roared out of the tunnel determined to put a hurt on us. It turned out to be one of the toughest games of our 17-0 season. By the fourth quarter, we were trailing, 14-13. Earl Morrall rallied the Dolphins for an 80-yard, six-play drive that ended in the final five minutes with an 8-yard TD run by Jim Kiick. We preserved perfection by a margin of 20-14.

I had watched the better part of the perfect season from the sidelines. But before the year was out, I would get my hands on the ball again.

> The worst season of all was the '72 season, the 17-and-0 season. Judi and I both felt the pressure and tension of that winning streak. They'd win a game, and we'd think, They just won another—and that's just a bit more pressure on our husbands. Judi and I both felt a lot of the stress and strain our husbands carried for maintaining that perfect record.
>
> —DOLPHIN WIFE JULIE TWILLEY

> "The Dolphins didn't scare us," says Pittsburgh quarterback Terry Bradshaw. "They didn't have those mean, intimidating-type people. I mean Earl Morrall . . . and that defense of theirs . . . basically nice guys. They didn't have a Mean Joe Greene or a Mad Dog White like we had."
>
> "We didn't scare him, huh?" says Buoniconti. "Please remind Mr. Bradshaw that our defense gave up the fewest points in the NFL that year."
>
> And knocked Bradshaw out of the game. On a first-quarter scramble, he was hit, he fumbled, the ball was recovered for a Steeler TD, and Bradshaw nursed a bruised shoulder. Miami, which hadn't done a thing, got back in the game on a 30-yard run off a fake punt by Seiple.
>
> "But what really turned the game," Seiple says, "was Shula coming in with Griese for Morrall in the second half." On his first possession, Griese threw a 52-yard pass to Warfield to set up the go-ahead touchdown.
>
> —PAUL ZIMMERMAN, "THE ROAD TO GLORY"[6]

Bob

On the last day of 1972, we went to Pittsburgh for game sixteen, the AFC championship game—the final step before Super Bowl VII. To place that game in a historical context, we went to Pittsburgh one week after Steelers rookie running back Franco Harris made his celebrated last-second "Immaculate Reception." If he hadn't caught that deflected pass, we would have played the Raiders instead of the Steelers for the AFC championship.

In those days, quarterbacks called their own plays in the huddle. Earl Morrall had his favorite plays and I had mine. I had kept my head in the game all season. I knew that if I was needed in Pittsburgh, I was ready. Best of all, Don Shula knew I was ready, too. There's one good thing about being hurt in the fifth game of the season: at the end of the year, you've got fresh legs and a fresh arm. Shoes knew I was fresh—I was throwing the ball well, I had my legs back, I had five years' experience in the league, and I knew what was going on. But he also knew that I wasn't quite ready to go for a full four quarters, so he started Earl Morrall in the first half.

The Steelers jumped to a 7-0 lead very quickly, using only four plays to score the first touchdown. Our offense struggled during the first half, unable to move the ball past midfield—but we got some unexpected help from a brilliant move by our punter, Larry Seiple. On a fourth-down play, he received the snap to punt—but Seiple is a very bright, alert guy (he's now quarterbacks coach for the Dolphins). He saw that the Steelers were trying to set up a big punt return down the right sideline, and were sending only one man to rush the punter. So instead of kicking, Seiple slipped the rusher and took off with the ball. He got all the way to the Steelers' 12-yard line before they brought him down. It only took two more plays to get Zonk into the end zone for a game-tying touchdown.

We left the field at halftime with the score tied at 7. In the locker room, Shula came up to me and said, "Are you ready to play?"

"I'm ready," I said.

He nodded. "You start the second half," he said.

"Okay."

It must have been tough for Shoes to tell Earl that he was putting me in—and it must have been hard for Earl to hear it. But Earl accepted it, and told Shoes that he would be ready if needed. That was one of the things that was so special about the '72 Dolphins—every single player on that team thought in terms of team first, self second. Winning mattered, not egos. That was one of the key elements that made the Dolphins work so well together. Earl Morrall was no exception. Earl kept the team moving toward a championship while I was sidelined, and he made an incalculable contribution to the team. Earl and I are good friends to this day.

We went out for the second half. Early on, the Steelers pulled ahead, 10-7, with a field goal. The Dolphin offense fought back, producing two touchdowns, while the No-Names held the Steelers to only one more touchdown. We had won a hard-fought championship game on the road. Final score: Dolphins 21, Steelers 17. For the second year in a row, the Dolphins were AFC champions.

But the job wasn't finished. We were 16 and 0, and we had won the right to play in the Super Bowl. But everything we had accomplished, all sixteen of those hard-fought victories, would be washed away if we didn't win the world championship.

It was 17 and 0 or bust.

I remember being at the hotel the night before, thinking about how proud I was of the fact that we were 16-0, but also realizing that if [we lost] again, it would destroy everything. There were a lot of negative things being said about me when I left Baltimore, and one of the things that was being spread around was that I couldn't win the big one. That's something you don't want to be associated with. If we had lost, it would have been devastating. For me, that would have been almost like death.

—DON SHULA, RECALLING HIS THOUGHTS
BEFORE SUPER BOWL VII

The '72 Dolphins were very close to perfection as an offensive unit. They. . . had perfect balance in the backfield: Larry Csonka and Jim Kiick for muscle, Mercury Morris for flash, Kiick for third-down receptions out of the backfield. Their middle three on the offensive line—guards Larry Little and Bob Kuechenberg and center Jim Langer—were the best I've ever seen. Their wideouts were the classic matching pair, Paul Warfield deep and Howard Twilley as the possession receiver. They had the old Packer, Marv Fleming, as the blocking tight end and Jim Mandich as the catcher. And in Griese they had a mechanically precise quarterback who wouldn't let ego get in the way of the offense.

—PAUL ZIMMERMAN, "MIAMI DOLPHINS VS. WASHINGTON REDSKINS,
SUPER BOWL VII"[7]

Bob

Game seventeen of our perfect season was the only game that really mattered: the Super Bowl. The previous year, after we had lost Super Bowl VI to the Dallas Cowboys, Don Shula had told us that losing the Super Bowl had wiped out everything we had accomplished in the 1971 season.

We weren't about to let that happen to our '72 season. We had worked too hard, gone too far, and achieved too much to let it slip through our fingers on a single Sunday afternoon.

Losing Super Bowl VII was not an option.

The Super Bowl is different from any other game. Even when you clear away all the hype and nonsense that surround a Super Bowl, it's still a very different game from all the other games you play during a season and a post-season. You have to prepare yourself physically and mentally for a Super Bowl more than you do for any other game. After playing week after week for sixteen weeks, there is a lengthy break in your routine. It can be a luxury to have a couple of weeks to prepare for one game—but that extra time can also be a negative. You don't play during that time, and it breaks your rhythm and interrupts your momentum. It's easy to let down and lose your focus.

The first time you get to the Super Bowl, there is an excitement and an exhilaration that can be dangerous. It's a trap to think, *Hey! We're going to the Super Bowl!* You have to be careful, or that's going to be your last celebration of the season.

We celebrated a lot after we won the AFC championship in 1971. When we won it again in '72, our celebration was a lot more subdued. There was an unspoken agreement throughout our team that we were not going to celebrate until we had put a Super Bowl win in the history books.

There are a lot of distractions around Super Bowl week. Ticket prices go sky-high, and people—close friends and relatives, distant friends and relatives, and friends and relatives you never heard of—start calling you about tickets and accommodations for the big game. You go to the Super Bowl city a week ahead of time, and your routine is changed. Your practice routine is not like your practice routine at home, where you can drive back and forth from home, relax and watch football films in your own living room, and get the food and rest you're accustomed to. Instead, you watch films in your hotel room, you have to figure out where to get your meals, you can't go anywhere without being mobbed, and it's not as easy to get a good night's sleep.

Having been to the Super Bowl the year before, we had a good idea of the upsides and downsides. Not only did Don Shula have us better prepared for the game ahead, but we were all more seasoned, more experienced, and more determined than the year before. I don't think any of us were as impressed with our 16-0 record as some fans and sportswriters were. We knew that our perfect record had hung by a thread at several crucial moments during the year. Though we were confident, there was no swagger, no arrogance, no sense that we were unbeatable. Fact is, I don't think we realized what we had accomplished in going undefeated until it was all over.

Today, of course, all of us veterans of the '72 Dolphins look back in amazement and pride at what we accomplished back then. More than a quarter of a century has passed, and no other team has duplicated the feat. To this day, we remain the only undefeated team in NFL history. Many have tried, but none have done it—they can't do it. So what we achieved in 1972 means more and more to us with each passing year. But at the time, we didn't really grasp the enormity of what that perfect season meant.

Going into the Los Angeles Memorial Coliseum on Super Bowl Sunday, we still had something to prove to the world. Despite our unbeaten record, there was a lack of respect shown to us that got under our skin. Here we were, going to the Super Bowl for a second consecutive year with a flawless 16-0 record, the unbeaten Dolphins versus a defense they called the "Over the Hill Gang"—yet the oddsmakers still had us down as 2-point underdogs to George Allen's Washington Redskins! It made us mad, and Don Shula used it to motivate us.

On game day, under a pale-blue southern California sky, we boarded the team bus for the stadium, a few hours before kickoff. You could feel the emotional intensity on the bus. Every man was thinking his own thoughts and getting mentally prepared to play. Shula stared straight ahead—probably going over the game plan in his mind. A few seats back, one of our safeties, Jake Scott, called out, "Hey, Coach! What's the matter? You worried you might go down as the losingest coach in Super Bowl history?" A few guys chuckled—then, seeing Shula's hard-nosed scowl, they turned those chuckles into a throat-clearing cough. "Just be ready to play," was all Shoes said in response.

With the very first snap, we took control of the game. We controlled it on offense; we controlled it on defense. Our offense scored two touchdowns in the first half, while our defense only let the Redskins cross the

50-yard line *once* in the entire half. We caught Washington off balance with surprise moves like a quick-strike pass on first down to Paul Warfield and a 28-yard TD pass to Howard Twilley.

Our defense kept Redskins QB Bill Kilmer off balance with the 53 Defense, while completely controlling and manhandling Redskin running back Larry Brown. On a third-down play in the second quarter, Kilmer fired a pass into heavy coverage, intending to hit his receiver, Charlie Taylor. But Dolphin safety Jake Scott stretched out one arm, plucking the ball out of the air with one hand as he landed on the turf with an interception. That was just one way the precision-drilled Dolphin defense smothered the Redskin offense (and much of the credit, of course, goes to the Dolphins' brilliant defensive coordinator, Bill Arnsparger).

Another example of No-Name dominance came just after the first two-minute warning. The 'Skins had just moved the ball to our 48—their longest penetration of the first half. Kilmer took the snap and dropped back to throw over the middle when he saw Dolphin linebacker Doug Swift coming at him on a blitz. Kilmer tried to force the ball in—and was intercepted by Nick Buoniconti, who returned it to the Washington 27. So ended the Redskins' best drive of the half.

Our offense took over and I fed the ball to Kiick and to Zonk, then completed to Mandich for 19 yards, then handed off to Kiick again for the TD run. Kiick's touchdown left only eighteen seconds until intermission. When we left the field for halftime, we had completed 6 of 6, and the score stood at 14-0. We had simply played Dolphin football, and the Redskins were just not able to get into the game.

The Redskins came out with a little more fire in the second half. Kilmer launched a passing attack along the seams, with his receivers running short outs underneath the No-Name zone. Finally, the Redskins had a drive going, and they took it right up to the brink of a touchdown—but the drive was flattened when Manny Fernandez sacked Kilmer at the Miami 25 on a third-down play. Forced to settle for a field-goal attempt, the Redskins sent Curt Knight in to put 3 points on the board—

And Knight's kick sailed wide. It was the Redskins' best drive of the day—and they had still come up empty!

Our offense took the field and we began moving the ball, using our basic up-the-middle ground attack. Larry Csonka went after the Over the Hill Gang like a battering ram, punching Zonk-shaped holes wherever he went. One play in particular demonstrated Csonka's total domination of the ground game—a thundering 49-yard rumble that brought us within striking range of our third touchdown. I threw a pass to Marv Fleming in the end zone—but Redskins left safety Brig Owens jumped up in front of Fleming for the interception.

At that point, Washington had eight minutes to overcome a two touchdown deficit. Again, Kilmer took the field and began working the ball toward the Miami end zone. At the end of the drive, it looked like the Redskins were going to score. Kilmer fired a pass to Jerry Smith, who was wide open in the end zone. But before the ball could reach Smith's waiting hands, it was deflected—by the goalposts.

And then, for Kilmer, it got even worse. Again he passed to the end zone—but it fell into the hands of Jake Scott, who collected his second interception (and clinched MVP honors for the game). At that point, we all thought we had achieved the first shutout in Super Bowl history.

We thought wrong.

Our offense moved the ball to the Washington 34 before stalling out with just over two minutes left to play. Garo Yepremian came in for the field goal—and that's when the game took one of its strangest and most memorable turns. If Garo had simply kicked the ball between the uprights, the game would have ended on a score of 17-0—a fitting score with which to finish out our perfect 17-0 season. But Garo's kick was low and blocked. The ball came right back to him. He scooped up the ball and ran to his right, putting his arm back to throw a pass, quarterback-style. But when Garo tried to throw, the ball slipped out of his hands. Desperately trying to reclaim the ball, Garo only succeeded in knocking it up in the air, where it was picked off by the Redskins' Mike Bass. Bass took off down the sidelines and ran it all the way for a Redskins touchdown.

Today, Garo Yepremian is an author and a motivational speaker, and he has gotten a lot of mileage out of retelling the story of that one humiliating play. He says in his Cypriot accent, "I wanted to pahss de futbol!"

Today we can laugh about it, but watching from the sidelines I couldn't believe what I was seeing. There were about forty guys on our sidelines who wanted to wring Garo's neck. As he came back to the sidelines, only two people said anything to him. Absolutely beside himself, Shula growled, "Why didn't you just fall on the @#&! ball?" But tackle Norm Evans—who is a Christian minister today—said, "Don't worry about it. God loves you even if you mess up."

Suddenly the score was 14-7, and Washington was back in the game with two minutes remaining—plenty of time to win if they could stop our next drive and then manage the clock well on offense. What had been a laugher was suddenly a tight game. My thought as I went back on the field was, *All right, we've just gotta go out, keep the ball, make some first downs, and burn up the clock.*

In the huddle, I told our guys to stay in bounds—don't stop the clock whatever you do. On first down, I handed off to Mercury Morris on a sweep right. He gained 4 yards and tried to stay in bounds, but Redskins cornerback Pat Fischer did a good job of dragging him to the sidelines before dropping him to the ground, stopping the clock at 1:51.

On the next play, I completed to Paul Warfield for a first down with 1:45 remaining. We gained three on the next down and the 'Skins took a time out. On third and 7 at our own 33, I gave the ball to Morris on another sweep right. Just as he was about to break free, he slipped and went down, forcing us to punt. The 'Skins used their last timeout. When the ball was snapped, the Redskins swarmed at punter Larry Seiple with a ten-man rush, and he barely got the ball away in time.

The Redskins got the ball with 1:09 to play. Kilmer had time for a couple of desperation passes, but in the end he was completely smothered by the Dolphin defense. On Kilmer's last snap of the day—a fourth-down, last-ditch passing play—he found himself pursued out of the pocket and sacked by a pair of No-Name defensive ends, Bill Stanfill and Vern Den Herder. Though we had possession deep in Washington territory, there was no need to run another play. We allowed the clock to mercifully expire.

And so the Dolphin season ended—a perfect 17-0.

Finally, it had ended. Emotion spent, the Redskins realized—as had Miami the year before—that reaching this game meant nothing without final victory. Washington's powder blue Sunday was now backlit with failure while Miami's year of doubt had ended in the sun. Don Shula had wiped clean a clouded past. His team had established an incredible precedent for the future. Don Shula and the Miami Dolphins—undefeated champions of the world.

—JOHN FACENDA, "WORLD CHAMPION DOLPHINS 17-0"[8]

The Miami Dolphins finally demonstrated rather conclusively that they are the biggest fish in the pro football pond. In the seventh Super Bowl they defeated the Washington Redskins 14-7 before 81,706 sweltering and smog-beset fans in the Los Angeles Memorial Coliseum. This meant that the Dolphins went an entire season without a loss, 17 straight. No other NFL team has ever gone undefeated for a season, and no other club is likely to do it again soon, either. On the record, then, Miami is the best club in pro football history.

The Dolphins won the game with a nearly impeccable first half; with an extraordinarily accurate passer in quarterback Bob Griese; with a rhino of a runner, Larry Csonka; and, above all, with a defense that may have been No-Names, but was plenty of adjectives. Try tough, tight, dashing and daring for starters.

—TEX MAULE, "UNBEATEN SEASON"[9]

Bob

I remember that when it was all over, the scoreboard flashed the words "Best Ever." Those two words vindicated everything we had gone through, everything we had dedicated ourselves to during the 17-0 season. Those two words proved that Don Shula and the Miami Dolphins could not only win the big one, but could win the whole enchilada, something no other team had ever done.

Once the Super Bowl was over, my first emotion was not so much one of exhilaration—"Hey, we won!"—but one of relief: "Hey, I don't have to win a game next week! The pressure's off!" It had been a long season, and now it was over—a perfect season, the first in NFL history. We had played the last and biggest game, we had won it, and now we could say, "We're the best."

Someday, another team may be good enough to go undefeated. I doubt it, but anything's possible. If it happens, more power to 'em. But we did it first, and no one can ever take that away from us.

Brian

You look back over the story of that 17-and-0 season, and what you see, again and again, is a bunch of guys who faced adversity and overcame it, both as a team and individually. One quarterback goes out on a stretcher, and another comes in—and the team pulls together to keep the championship dream alive. When adversity comes, you stand up to it. You accept some hits and some losses, but you keep battling back. In the end, you finish the game on your own terms. You're undefeated.

That's not just football. That's *life*.

5

ATTACK OF THE PURPLE PEOPLE

Bob Kuechenberg, the Dolphins' left guard, once told me that the players felt the '73 team was better than the unbeaten '72 squad, mainly because the defense was better and Griese was healthy for the whole [season]. . . .

I remember reading something in the paper after the Dolphins beat Detroit 34-7 (and it wasn't a bad Detroit team, either—at least not like now) in the last regular-season game. Griese said he had thrown a lot in that game because it was necessary to get the passing attack tuned up for the playoffs. That was the expression he used, "tuned up." . . . I remember thinking, that's one heck of a tune-up.

—PAUL ZIMMERMAN, "MIAMI DOLPHINS VS. MINNESOTA
VIKINGS–SUPER BOWL VIII"[1]

Brian

A few weeks after I played in the Rose Bowl, I was watching ESPN and they showed the NFL Films recap of Super Bowl VIII, where my dad quarterbacked the Dolphins to a win over the Minnesota Vikings. It was surreal watching that game. He played so much the way I'd like to play. At the end, Steve Sabol said that Bob Griese had only completed 6 of 7 passes in that game—but every one of those completions was a key play. "Now, that's ball control," he said. That's exactly the way I like to play—control the ball, control the line of scrimmage, manage the clock, make every throw count, and win the game.

Bob

The 1973 Dolphins really were a better team than 1972 Dolphins, even though we didn't win all our games. Because of what we had already accomplished, we were more poised and confident—not cocky, but definitely confident. Everybody had us on their radar screen; everybody had us highlighted on their schedule. The '73 Dolphins were the team to knock off. They knew we were coming, they knew we were good, and they were gunning for us. Two of them beat us, but when we got into the play-offs, we just went right through three tough teams like a hot knife through butter, and we won another Super Bowl.

There was something very special about the '72 and '73 Dolphins. How many teams in NFL history can say they went two years and only lost two games? How many teams can claim a record of 32 and 2? In the entire history of the game, that team was unique.

There was Larry Csonka. Zonk was a guy who absolutely exuded toughness. He was not all that fast (but faster than you might think!), and he was not a great receiver. When he played with other teams—with the World Football League in 1975 and later with the New York Giants—he didn't do as well as he did with the Dolphins. We knew what he could do, and we didn't ask him to do the things he couldn't do. We shaped the offense around him.

Zonk was a one-of-a-kind character, and the central pillar of his character was *toughness*. He would play bruised and bloody, with pulled muscles and torn ligaments. He'd take hits that you'd think would finish any other player's season, if not his career—and incredibly, he'd get right up and keep playing. If you like real down-and-dirty, smash-mouth football, then Larry Csonka is your guy.

Csonka remains the Dolphins' all-time leading rusher with 1,506 carries for 6,737 yards and 53 touchdowns. He had three consecutive thousand-yard seasons, and at the end of each of those seasons—1971 through 1973—we went to the Super Bowl. No surprise, Zonk was inducted by the Hall of Fame in his second year of eligibility. He was a special player not just because of the way he played, but also because of the emotion he brought to the game

and the way he elevated the play of all of us on the team. His toughness inspired us all to play tough.

We had a lot of tough, smash-mouth guys on that team—guys like center Jim Langer and guards Bob Kuechenberg and Larry Little. Langer was a guy we picked up on waivers from Cleveland, and he was good. A quarterback has to have a good relationship with his center, and Langer and I worked together well. He was one of the first guys I ever saw snap the ball, then pull around the end. He was tough and smart, and I could always ask him on the sidelines, "What's going on up there on the line?" and he would give it to me straight. He'd either tell me, "We can handle 'em," or, "We've got our hands full with these guys." I'd say, "What plays do you like?" And he'd say, "They can't stop this play or that play." I'd put it in the old mental filing box, and when I needed a play, I'd call it. So I always knew where we stood, because Langer gave it to me straight.

Bob Kuechenberg was a wild man—no fear, smart, tricky. We had a nonrhythmic count—a stutter cadence—and Kooch knew my cadence as well as I did. Occasionally, if the cadence was on "three," he knew I was going to hit the "two" real hard. He'd be lined up, and he'd have his right hand on the ground, and the defensive man would be down in front of him. And I'd go, "Two-seventy-eight! Two-seventy-eight! Hut-HUT!" And he'd move his left hand like he was coming off—and he'd stay put. The combination of his motion and my emphasis on the second "HUT!" would pull the defensive man offsides. Kooch was pretty cagey, and he'd move in such a way that the defender would see but the umpire couldn't— and he grabbed us a lot of yardage from those 5-yard offsides penalties.

Like Zonk, Kooch was a tough guy. He would play with broken bones or with a steel rod in his arm. He'd always want you to run the ball over him. In the huddle he'd tell me, "Run it over here! Run it over here!" When I was a young quarterback, the veteran linemen would say stuff like that to me, and I would believe them. But once I got a little more experience, I began to figure out who to believe and who not to. Kuechenberg was one of the ones I learned to watch out for. Sometimes he would have a couple of defenders in front of him the size of Mack trucks, and there was just no way he was going to handle them—yet he was always saying, "Run it over me!"

Sometimes I'd come into the huddle and say, "All right, anybody got anything?" It would be third-and-short, and the guys in the huddle knew what I meant: *Anybody got a soft spot? Can anybody open a hole?* And I would look around the huddle, and some of the guys would have their heads down, looking at the grass. Others were looking down the field, watching the play clock and making sure we got out of the huddle on time. Still others were looking right at me. Kooch was one of the ones who always looked right at me. Whenever I said, "Anybody got anything?" Kooch would always say, "Yeah, run right over me!" I soon learned not to take his word for it every time. If he had Merlin Olsen over him, I knew not to run the ball over Kooch unless we also had Langer or someone there to help him out.

But that was Kooch. He thought he could do anything, he thought he could handle anybody, and he wasn't afraid of anything—and I admire that attitude. He was tough. He could run; he could get out and pull; he was competitive; he was tricky.

Larry Little was a tough, physical giant of a guard. One of the most underrated blockers in the game, he opened the holes and paved the way for Csonka and Kiick to rack up mileage on the ground. We called him "Chicken" Little because he loved fried chicken. He had a long career with the Dolphins, patrolling the trenches and anchoring the offensive line for twelve seasons, starting 152 of 158 regular season games. He was named AFC Offensive Lineman of the Year three straight seasons (1970–72) by the NFL Players Association.

Another underrated player on that team was halfback Jim Kiick. Jim was a solid, all-around player, and he could do almost anything—block, pound the ball, run pass patterns. He was a great receiver and a good, tough inside runner. We had a pattern we ran out of the backfield—the halfback short option—in which Kiick would release out of the backfield, then go one of two ways on the linebacker; he was great at running that pattern. He would do anything you asked of him—he kept drives going by catching short passes, he made tough yardage on the ground, he blocked for Csonka, and when you gave him the ball, he hardly ever fumbled.

Kiick, Csonka, Langer, Little, Kuechenberg—these guys were the key to our inside running game, and the running game was the strength of the Dolphins. Then we had Marv Fleming and Jim Mandich at tight end. Fleming was one of the best run-blocking tight ends the NFL has ever seen, while Mandich was a better route runner and receiver.

One time when we were playing in Buffalo, I threw a pass to Marv Fleming in the end zone. He caught the ball, then looked down at his feet, scooped something off the ground, and came running back yelling, "I hit pay dirt! I hit pay dirt!" Turned out he had found a twenty-dollar bill in the end zone. He was more excited about finding that twenty-dollar bill than he was about catching a touchdown pass.

Jim Mandich was a great receiver. While Marv Fleming was a great *blocking* tight end, Mandich was a great *receiving* tight end. In fact, Mandich was really a slow wide receiver playing tight end. He could block better than a wide receiver, but he couldn't block like Marv Fleming. So when Mandich was in the game, we liked to get him involved in the passing game. Or he'd come in on third-down plays. He was very bright; he knew how to get open; he knew who was covering him and how to break out of coverage.

Some receivers just run the route—they don't pay attention to who's covering them, they don't know if they are open, or even where the open spot on the field is. But a really bright receiver like Jim Mandich thinks, *I'm supposed to go down and break out here, but if I do that, I'll break right into coverage. Griese can see the coverage right here, so I'll just go down a few more yards, break to the outside, and hang in that open area.* He was creative, he could think on his feet, and he gained us a lot of completions and yardage that lesser receivers never would have gotten.

Most of our talent was focused on the running game, not so much on the passing game, so we did what we did best: we ran. Other teams knew that we were a running team, and they knew exactly what we were going to do from one week to the next: we were going to pound the ball. But even though they knew what we were going to do, they couldn't stop us. I'd look at these teams across the ball, and I'd say, "You know what I'm gonna do, and I know that you know, and I know what you're gonna do to try and stop us—but we're gonna run the ball anyway. Whatever you come up with, we're gonna adjust to it and we're gonna run the ball, same as last week and the week before that." And we did.

Yet even though we were a running team, we could go airborne anytime we needed to—and my favorite target for the aerial attack was Paul Warfield. Paul was the only player in Dolphin history to score four TDs in a single game, and he was inducted into the Hall of Fame in his first year of eligibility. During our undefeated season in 1972, Warfield was our leading receiver, even though he caught only 29 passes for the season. You might think that 29 receptions is not a lot of productivity for a star wide receiver. But get this: with those 29 receptions, Paul Warfield gained 606 yards—an average of almost 21 yards per catch. That's why the Dolphins were such a threat: Though we usually kept the ball on the ground, we could switch to the pass and continue to roll up yardage. Our passing game, sparingly used, became our element of surprise, our ace in the hole.

As a quarterback, you want to get reliable feedback from your receivers. If you ask them in the huddle, "Were you open on that play?" you want to hear, "Oh, yeah, wide open!" or "No, they had me covered." There were some guys I would ask, and they would say, "Yeah! Yeah! I'm wide open! Just throw me the ball!" And later, in the team meeting, I'd watch the game film and there would be that very play—and I'd say, right in the meeting, "Hey! You told me you were open on that play! Run that film back! Does that look like you're open?" I would put the guy on the spot—and at the same time, I sent a message to the other receivers: "Don't tell me you're open unless you're open! I need good information from you guys! I'm not saying you're no good if you can't get open—we all get covered. That's fine, I'll just go throw somewhere else. I just need to know, so be truthful." They learned pretty quickly—most of them, anyway.

But for some reason, I always had a hard time getting information out of Paul Warfield. All I could ever get from him was a noncommittal "Well . . ." I'd say in the huddle, "Paul, were you open on that play?" "Well . . ." That's all he had to say! I knew he was capable of beating double coverage, and I also knew he couldn't get open all the time. I just wanted to know if it was safe to throw to him or not. Fortunately, Paul Warfield was good enough and fast enough that I could usually take "Well . . ." as a yes.

Mercury Morris was a big addition to the Dolphins. I'd rate him as a fair receiver, because he was erratic, not consistent. When he was at his best, though, Merc made big plays. He was not a great blocker, but he worked well in sync with Zonk and Kiick in Don Shula's innovative three-back system.

One time, when we were playing the Baltimore Colts, we were having trouble with Colts defensive end Bubba Smith. On some plays, when the linebacker would blitz inside, we blocked so that the offensive tackle over Bubba would block down and pick up the blitzing linebacker. So our back in the backfield was expected to step up and block the defensive end, Bubba Smith. The Colts knew this meant that 5'9" 180-pound Mercury Morris would have to block 6'5" 280-pound Bubba Smith, so they blitzed a lot. During the first half, Bubba kept running right over Merc and sacking me, so Shula took Merc aside at halftime and told him, "Mercury, when they blitz, you've got to step up on Bubba and block him."

Mercury said, "Okay, Coach—how do I do it?"

"Hit him at the knees," said Shula. "Those big guys don't like to get blocked at the knees."

So we went out for the second half, and the first time a third-down situation came up, the linebacker started moving inside, showing blitz. I didn't want to check off because I knew Mercury was ready for Bubba. I left the play on, we snapped the ball, the linebacker blitzed inside, the tackle moved off Bubba and blocked inside, Mercury stepped up—

And here comes Bubba!

Well, Bubba thought he was going to blow right through Mercury Morris again, same as usual. Instead, Merc dropped and hit Bubba at the knees. Bubba went flying end over end and landed right on me. Fortunately, it was a quick pass with just a three-step drop, and I had already dumped the ball by the time Bubba squashed me.

Well, Bubba got up and he wasn't too happy. I peeled myself off the grass and just walked past him—I learned a long time ago that you don't talk to defensive linemen, because they think they can get in your head and get you off your game. So I just kept walking. But Bubba was mad and he had to unleash on somebody. So he looked down at Mercury, and he said, "Man, you do that again, and I'm gonna bite your head off!"

"Bubba," Mercury said back to him, "you do that and you'll have more brains in your stomach than you have in your head!"

Merc was a very talkative guy. He always had something to say. He was not a great receiver like Paul Warfield, he was not a great blocker, and he was not great at protecting the ball—he fumbled more than he should have. But when Mercury Morris did something, it was big. He made a lot of big plays.

Another great receiver on that team was my good friend Howard Twilley. Howard and I roomed together in training camp, and he was another very bright overachiever. He knew his limitations, I knew his limitations, and we didn't ask him to do things he couldn't do. Instead, we had him concentrate on the things he did best, and he excelled as a result. Howard was a good blocker and he ran good routes, precision routes. He didn't have a lot of speed like Warfield or Mercury Morris, but he was good inside the 20 or the 10 or the 5, because you don't need speed down there—you need moves, you need patience. Howard would go down and break to the outside and look back, and if the defensive back saw that, then he'd break out or in or up or down or around—whatever it took to get open.

Howard is a solid Christian with a strong sense of family, and his family and ours spent a lot of time together. Julie Twilley was always a good friend to Judi, and we spent holidays and vacations together. It was great having a guy like Twilley as a friend on the team, because training camp can be a rough time, especially for a couple of family men like us. We'd go through practice together, and between the end of practice at 5:00 P.M. and the team meeting at 7:30, we could either eat with the team or go out for a meal. Howard and I figured we'd been practicing, showering, and meeting with these other guys all day—let's get away for a little while. So sometimes we'd get in the car and go to a little bar and grill that served great steaks. I can't remember the name of the place, and it's probably not there anymore, but I can picture it in my mind and I remember how great it felt after a tough practice to go out with a good friend and get a good steak. You remember those simple things as long as you live.

Norm Evans was a great guy, very positive, a real encourager. As a player, he had a strong work ethic, and he blocked a lot of very good, strong defensive ends. Norm and I were good friends, and I still see him every now and then when I get up to Seattle, where he and his wife, Bobbe, have a Christian ministry of counseling pro athletes.

> In 1973 there was no letdown for the Miami Dolphins. They didn't go undefeated—that streak ended when the Oakland Raiders beat them in the second week of the season. But with the pressure of staying perfect put behind them, the Dolphins set out to add another chapter to the NFL record books. In 1973, they were trying to become the first team to appear in three straight Super Bowls. In some ways, they were better in '73 than they were in '72, particularly on defense with the now well-known No Namers yielding an NFL-low 150 points.
>
> —STEVE SABOL, "SUPER BOWL VIII: MIAMI DOLPHINS VS. MINNESOTA VIKINGS"[2]

I was closer to the guys on the offense because I worked with them all the time. But I had enormous respect for the No-Names—safeties Jake Scott and Dick Anderson; cornerbacks Tim Foley, Lloyd Mumphord, and Curtis Johnson; linebackers Mike Kolen, Bob Matheson, and Doug Swift; and linemen Bob Heinz, Manny Fernandez, Vern Den Herder, and Bill Stanfill. Of course, Nick Buoniconti was the glue that held that unit together. He was a bright lawyer with a quick mind, and he worked in the middle of the defense and moved his guys around like chess pieces. He studied film and understood the strengths and weaknesses of the opposing team's offense. He was a kind of defensive quarterback, directing the No-Name defense with every bit as much skill and tactical precision as a General Patton or a Norman Schwarzkopf.

It was fun practicing against the defensive squad. We didn't go all out against one another. If it was an offensive period, the defense was supposed to give. If it was a defensive period, the offense was supposed to let the defense get their work done. The real fun of the practices, where we pitted offense against defense, was the mental game that went on between me and Buoniconti.

I'd call a play in the huddle and we would go up to the line, and Buoniconti would call out to his guys, "It's gonna be a run left!" And I thought to myself, *Run left! How did he know that? Either the lineman's tipping it or the backs are giving it away.* So then I'd work on my fake check-offs.

So we would play these mind games in practice. I would come up and practice my fake checks. It's something you have to do in a game, so we would do it in practice. I'd come up and say, "Set!" And Buoniconti would yell, "Run left!" And I'd look right at him and grin, a look that says, *Okay, buddy, here you go!* Then I'd call, "Two! Forty-eight!" And Buoniconti would yell, "Watch forty-eight!" And it wasn't a check-off at all. It was always fun to burn Buoniconti, because it wasn't easy to do. There were games within games at practice, and those mind games kept both sides, the defense and the offense, on their toes.

I think it's a shame that none of the No-Names has ever been inducted into the Hall of Fame. To me, that's a crime. After all these years, after all those guys accomplished, they're *still* No-Names. Buoniconti certainly belongs in the Hall of Fame, and maybe he'll get there yet.

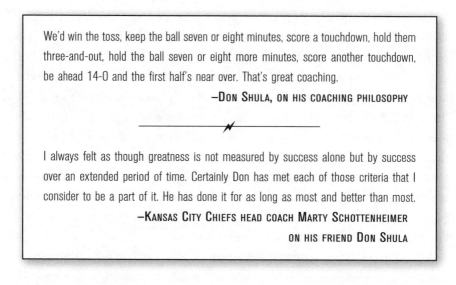

We'd win the toss, keep the ball seven or eight minutes, score a touchdown, hold them three-and-out, hold the ball seven or eight more minutes, score another touchdown, be ahead 14-0 and the first half's near over. That's great coaching.

—DON SHULA, ON HIS COACHING PHILOSOPHY

I always felt as though greatness is not measured by success alone but by success over an extended period of time. Certainly Don has met each of those criteria that I consider to be a part of it. He has done it for as long as most and better than most.

—KANSAS CITY CHIEFS HEAD COACH MARTY SCHOTTENHEIMER
ON HIS FRIEND DON SHULA

Bob

One piece of Dolphin lore from the early '70s is the story of Don Shula and the alligator. Shoes had a private shower in his office at Biscayne

College, and some of the guys caught a baby alligator and put it in the shower for a little "surprise." Shula found the alligator, all right—and within seconds, he was standing out in the parking lot wearing nothing but a towel around his middle. I think it was several years before Shoes found out who was responsible: Manny Fernandez, Bill Stanfill, and Larry Csonka. Certainly, those guys were in no hurry to 'fess up to it.

Without Don Shula, we wouldn't have made three trips to the Super Bowl, and we wouldn't have had a perfect season. Why is Don Shula such a great leader? No mystery: The man takes charge. Wherever he is, whatever situation he is in, he just takes charge. He takes charge in the meeting room. He takes charge on the practice field. He takes charge on the sidelines. He even takes charge on the golf course.

I remember one time I was playing golf with Don Shula, Eddie LeBaron, who was quarterback of the early expansion Dallas Cowboys, and Tex Schramm, the Cowboys' former general manager. Eddie's a good golfer—maybe a 3 or 4 handicap. Shoes is about an 18. Normally in a game, you throw the players' balls in the air, and the two that land closest together are partners, and the two remaining players are partners. But Shoes didn't do that. He just walked up to the first tee and took charge, "All right, Eddie," he said, "you and I will take on those two. We'll tee off first." Just like that, same old Coach—in complete charge wherever he goes. I kid him about that all the time.

I always liked that in Don Shula. Having a take-charge coach got our team places we couldn't have gone without him. Thanks to Shoes, I got to be a part of NFL history. He knew exactly what he wanted to do with that team, and he did it. There was never a question of, "Is this the right way to do it?" or, "Is this the wrong way to do it?" There was just Shula's way to do it, and that was fine with me. When something was wrong, Shoes set it right—pronto. He gave us a sense of direction, a sense of purpose, a sense of strong, forceful, forward motion toward a goal. When Shula came aboard, we were no longer just there to play a season. We were there to win a championship. Because Shula wouldn't settle for anything less, neither did we. I guess that's why he's the winningest coach in NFL history, with a record of 347-173-6 over a thirty-three-year career.

Come to the Miami area and you can drive the Shula Expressway, spend the night at the Shula Hotel, play golf at the Shula Golf Resort, and chow down at the Shula Steakhouse. The tough-as-nails coach also has a heart of gold: He established the Don Shula Foundation to fund cancer research (his wife, Dorothy, died of cancer in 1991) and the Don Shula Scholarship to help athletes at colleges in Florida. All in all, not a bad life's work for the fisherman's son from the little town of Painesville, Ohio.

Shoes earned bragging rights for 17-0 in 1972. But what about '73? A lot of people forget that we went 15-2 that year. The two games we lost were to the Raiders in Oakland (week two) and to the Colts in Baltimore (week thirteen). We beat the Bengals 34-16 in the divisional play-offs and the Raiders 27-10 in the AFC championship. Then it was on to the Super Bowl for a third straight year.

There are times when an athletic event transcends the boundaries of sport, and becomes embedded in a nation's consciousness. In eight seasons, the Super Bowl has become such an event. The Minnesota Vikings had come this way before, only to suffer a shocking loss to the underdog Kansas City Chiefs in Super Bowl IV. Now, four years later, they stood on the threshold again— but this time, they were the underdogs. In those same four years, the Miami Dolphins had risen from the dregs of the sport to a world championship. Today they would defend that championship amid the celebration of Super Bowl VIII.

—JOHN FACENDA, "SUPER BOWL VIII:
MIAMI DOLPHINS VS. MINNESOTA VIKINGS"[3]

Bob

I was confident, going into Super Bowl VIII. This was my third consecutive trip to the Super Bowl, and we had plenty of time to prepare for Fran Tarkenton and the Minnesota Vikings. It was a foggy Super Bowl Sunday morning as the team boarded the bus for the ride to Rice Stadium in Houston. On the way to the stadium, I fell asleep in the back of the bus. I had never done that before, not even before an exhibition game, let alone a Super Bowl—that's how relaxed I was. Usually before a big game, I spend time worrying, thinking, checking plays, and generally preparing myself mentally for the game ahead—but on this particular Sunday, I was loose and confident. Not overconfident, but confident.

My biggest concern as I walked up to the line of scrimmage for the first play of the game was this: We'd had two weeks to study the attack of the Purple People. We had watched hours of film. We had broken down all sixteen games they played during the season and postseason. We had analyzed the Viking defense to death. Now the question was: Are they going to do what we think they will do? Are they going to do the same things they've done all year? Have they changed anything? Will there be any surprises?

I knew that if the Vikes played the same game they had played all year, we would be okay. But if they threw something new and unexpected at us, then we'd have to adjust. I don't like the unknown; I like to see all the pieces on the chessboard, right where they belong. So I was relieved when I stepped up to the line of scrimmage and looked at Minnesota's defensive set. *Well*, I thought, *there they are. Everything's in place, no surprises here.*

The Vikings' famed Purple People Eater defense had a reputation for coming off the ball fast, so our offensive line would have to be even faster and tougher in order to contain them. Vikings defensive tackle Alan Page was probably the best player in the league at his position. All Page wanted to do was go upfield and get to the quarterback—but fortunately for me, we had Kuechenberg right in front of him. Kooch was one of the smarter linemen to ever play the game, and Shula had drilled left tackle Wayne Moore and Kooch in a number of brilliant blocking schemes to keep Page contained. Kooch would take off running and Page would follow him and we'd trap him. I didn't spend any time that day worrying about Page or the rest of the Purple People Eaters.

Shula had also prepared some surprise plays that started out as inside traps, designed to suck the Viking defense to the inside—then I would whirl around and toss the ball to Mercury Morris, who would carry the ball around the end. We also used misdirection, with our offensive line pulling the defense in one direction while Zonk took the ball in the opposite direction, against the flow. As the first quarter developed, we used those plays numerous times to good effect, confusing and frustrating the Minnesota defense. Our opening drive consumed 62 yards in ten plays for a 7-0 lead.

Next, the Vikings got the ball—but they just couldn't move it against the now-notorious No-Name defense. In the first twenty-four minutes of the game, the Viking offense was only able to get one first down.

I had great pass protection in that game, giving me all the time in the world to throw. I completed 4 of 4 in the first quarter, including a pass to Marlin Briscoe inside the Vikings' 5-yard line. From there, it took Jim Kiick just two dives over the middle to get us our second touchdown. At the end of the first quarter, the Dolphins dominated, 14-0.

Bob Matheson anchored the 53 defense against the pass-heavy Viking offense. Matheson and the No-Names completely controlled the deep zones. Though Fran Tarkenton set a Super Bowl record for completions in that game, all of his completions were quick dunks and screen passes. He was completely unable to break the game open with the long pass. All of his deep receivers were completely covered, and every Viking drive ended in disappointment and a punt.

Our last drive of the half was a rumbling, thundering train ride behind the grinding wheels of Larry Csonka. When the drive sputtered at the Viking 28, just short of a first down, Garo Yepremian stepped up, hit the chip shot, and increased our lead to 17-0.

The Vikings showed some life in a last-gasp final drive of the half, moving the ball all the way to our doorstep. With just over a minute left in the half, the Vikings found themselves with a fourth down and inches situation. Should they kick a field goal—or go for it? They decided to go for it.

On the snap, the Viking offense split the Dolphin defensive line. Minnesota guard Ed White took off through the hole, Tarkenton handed off to running back Oscar Reed, and White led Reed toward the goal line. But the No-Names were ready for them. Nick Buoniconti came flying in, hitting Reed and popping the ball free. Our safety, Jake Scott, smothered the ball and recovered the Viking fumble. Despite a valiant effort in the closing moments of the first half, Minnesota had come up empty.

Paul Warfield was playing with a pulled hamstring, so we used him sparingly in the first half. But on our first possession of the third quarter, Warfield went streaking down the left sideline. The corner rolled up and the safety went over to double the coverage. I put everything I had on that ball, and Warfield had to dive headlong for it, grabbing it with his outstretched fingertips as he sailed through the air and skidded onto the turf just inside the sideline, with a frustrated Purple People Eater riding on his back.

That 27-yard completion got us within spitting distance of the end zone—and it was the last pass I threw in the game. In all, I threw only seven passes all day. I threw them early in the game, then after that completion to Warfield early in the third period, I didn't throw any more. People have asked me why I didn't throw more. The answer is simple: The Vikings couldn't stop the run, and we wanted to keep the clock running. If they can't stop our run, why pass? Should I throw the ball because I've got an ego? Because I want to add some yardage to my stats? All we want to do is win the game. So I completed 6 of 7, and they were all big completions. We dominated the line of scrimmage, we made big plays, we scored a lot of points—and after that, we were just gonna sit on the ball, simple as that.

After calling the play in the huddle, the quarterback has to call something else: the snap count.

The quarterback will say "on one," or "on two," or "on three," sometimes even "on four." When he's up at the line of scrimmage, he will yell, "Hut . . . hut . . . hut." If the snap count had been "on three," the center will snap the ball on the third "hut." Some quarterbacks prefer to yell "hut-hut" quickly, but that usually counts as one "hut," not two. As simple as a snap count is, players occasionally forget it. That's why a lineman jumps offside. Sometimes the center forgets it. Sometimes even the quarterback forgets it, as Bob Griese of the Dolphins did in . . . Super Bowl VIII.

—JOHN MADDEN, *ONE KNEE EQUALS TWO FEET*[4]

This was a day of destiny for the Miami Dolphins, a day when even their own mistakes could not defeat them. As he drove his team toward another TD, Bob Griese realized he had forgotten the snap count. He turned to ask his backfield, but they didn't know either. So he turned back to take his chances . . .

—JOHN FACENDA, "SUPER BOWL VIII: MIAMI DOLPHINS VS. MINNESOTA VIKINGS"[5]

Bob

A couple of plays after the completion to Warfield, we had moved the ball to the Minnesota 5. We knew what kind of defensive plays the Vikings liked to do inside the 5. They had two different kinds of goal-line defenses they usually employed in this situation—and we didn't have any plays in our arsenal that were good against both kinds of defense. All we could do was call a play, then go to the line of scrimmage and see which defense the Vikings chose.

In the huddle, I called the formation, the play, and the snap count. "All right," I told them, "be alert—I may have to check this play off. The play is brown left, eighteen straight, on one. Break!" So everybody broke.

As we went to the line of scrimmage, I was thinking about what play I was going to check to if the play I just called was not a good match for the defense they threw at us. I got to the line of scrimmage and the guys got down. I checked the Viking defense and thought, *All right. They're in the defense that's good for this play, I don't have to check this off.* And then it hit me: *What's the snap count?* I forgot.

Actually, this happens more often than you'd expect. But I didn't want to burn a timeout for something like that—not in the Super Bowl, not with 71,882 people in the stands and millions more watching at home. That would have looked really dumb. I knew the center, Jim Langer, knew the snap count, but I sure didn't want to ask him with Alan Page, Carl Eller, Jim Marshall, and the rest of the People Eaters in earshot. My next thought was, *I know—I'll ask Csonka* (Zonk, the fullback, was lined up right behind me). To this day, I don't know what I was thinking of—Csonka *never* knew the snap count. He just moved when everybody else did.

Anyway, I turned around and said, "Hey, Zonk! What's it on?"

Well, Csonka had his head down, counting the blades of plastic grass in the artificial turf. He slowly raised his head and said, "It's on two!"

So I turned back around and began to call the cadence. "Set! Three-ninety!"

Just then, I heard Jim Kiick, who was lined up next to Csonka, say, "Zonk! It's on one!"

And I heard Zonk (he's a hardheaded guy) insist, "It's on *two*!"

Well, I couldn't wait any longer. The 30-second clock was running down. I said, "Three-ninety!" And I looked to my left, and Marv Fleming, my tight end, was asking the tackle, "What's it on?" I looked to the right, and all those helmets were turning, and guys were asking one another, "What's it on? What's it on?" It was like that all up and down the line.

"Three-ninety, three-ninety, *hut*!" And the ball came up—center Jim Langer was the only guy on either side of the ball who knew it was on one—but nobody moved. The Vikings didn't move, either—they'd been listening to Zonk, and they thought it was on two!

I turned around with the ball in my hands, and there was Larry Csonka, still in his stance. But then he saw me holding the ball out, so he lumbered forward, took the handoff, and crashed over the right side, plowing a Zonk-sized furrow in the end zone, next to the goalpost.

Despite the confusion (or because of it—the Purple People Eaters were just as baffled as we were), the play worked. We added another touchdown and padded the score to 24-0.

After that, we made sure we had code words for the snap counts—red, white, and blue, A, B, and C. When in doubt, I'd ask the center, "Hey Jim, what's it on?" He'd say, "Blue," or whatever, and we'd be in business.

As the game wore down to the fourth quarter and the Vikings hadn't been able to put anything on the scoreboard, their frustration came to a full, rolling boil. The Minnesota offense finally mounted a scoring drive early in the fourth quarter, scoring on a 4-yard run by Fran Tarkenton. After the touchdown, Minnesota kicked a successful onside kick, but it was negated by an offsides call against Ron Porter of the Vikings. Resigned to the inevitable, their next kick was deep.

I could feel the game take on a visceral intensity during that drive. Completely routed, the Vikings were mad and ready to take it out on anybody in a Dolphin uniform. I remember getting buried on one play. Three People Eaters climbed off me and I sat up with my helmet torqued halfway around my head. As I twisted it back on straight, I heard someone yelling at me, "Come on, Griese! Get up! We're coming at ya again!" So I got up, went back to the line, and sure enough, they came at me again.

We went three and out on that drive, and Larry Seiple punted it to the Minnesota 3-yard line—the Vikings couldn't get a single break all day. The Viking drive ended with an interception by Dolphin cornerback Curtis Johnson.

Time ran out. The game was over. Larry Csonka deservedly collected the Super Bowl MVP for his 33 carries, 145 yards rushing, and 2 touchdowns. After that game, the sportswriters were talking about a Dolphin Dynasty, like the dynasty from Green Bay, Wisconsin that had once ruled the NFL. But it wasn't to be. Two months after winning Super Bowl VIII, the World Champion Miami Dolphins were picked apart by the fledgling World Football League, which lured Csonka, Kiick, and Warfield out of Miami. Though the WFL only lasted one season, it punched a big hole in the Miami lineup.

I played with the Dolphins for seven more years and never got to another Super Bowl.

Brian

I admire what my dad did, playing in three Super Bowl games, and winning two in a row. I want to be the kind of football player he was—poised and confident, the kind who plays within the system, the kind who wins games. I think a quarterback should be measured by whether or not he gets his team in the end zone, simple as that. And it's an amazing accomplishment—not just for Bob Griese, but also for Larry Csonka and Jim Kiick and the offensive line and the No-Names and everyone else on the '73 Dolphins team—that they were able to win a Super Bowl with only six completed passes. That's an accomplishment that doesn't get the respect it really deserves.

That's not to take anything away from guys who can throw all the way down the field, the John Elways and Dan Marinos of the game, because they've shown that they can get their team in the end zone as well—they just have a different way of doing it. But there is a lot to be said for the intelligent, low-turnover, ball-control approach to winning football games.

So I admire my dad for the kind of football player he was. But even more, I admire the kind of person my dad is. At the end of the day, I would rather hear people tell me I've got the kind of *character* my dad has than to hear I've got his scrambling ability, or throwing ability, or approach to the game. If I had to face the challenges he's faced in his life, I hope I'd be up to it.

Bob Griese is a football hero to a lot of people. But he's a very different kind of hero to me.

6

KODAK MOMENTS

One year after training camp, Bob Griese and my husband, Howard, decided to surprise Judi and me with a vacation. The Grieses and the Twilleys almost always spent Christmas together, and on our Christmas tree the guys had left a note that said, "Judi and Julie—Pack for a week, destination unknown. We will leave on such-and-such a date." I was still teaching at that time, and the date they picked was during Christmas break—perfect!

So we packed for a week, we got in our car, Bob and Judi got in their car, and we started driving. Judi and I didn't know where we were going, but Bob and Howard took us over to Marco Island on the west coast of Florida. They rented a lanai, and we spent a week over there.

Judi and I were both athletic, and our first day there we played golf, tennis, and shuffleboard. We swam and we sang golden oldies till two in the morning. It was a wonderful vacation.

Bob and Howard were very competitive. Judi and I enjoyed athletics, but we weren't fiercely competitive like they were. Those guys were do or die. Sometimes when Bob and Howard would play, they would dive for shots and come up with skinned elbows and bloody knees. Honestly, they looked like they had just played in the Super Bowl instead of a friendly tennis match! Judi and I would watch them play like that, and we'd just shake our heads.

The first time Judi and I played doubles with Bob and Howard, they were just as competitive as ever. I remember the final score of that game—but for the life of me, I can't tell you who won! But I bet you Bob and Howard remember—they were each determined in their own way to win at whatever they did.

—FAMILY FRIEND JULIE TWILLEY

Bob

Sometime after Super Bowl VIII, I was asked to serve as the national chairman for the Muscular Dystrophy Association. Howard Twilley and I went out to Las Vegas with our wives to play in a tennis tournament to benefit the MDA, and after that we went on to San Francisco for a vacation. Judi and I did a lot of things—like holidays and vacations—with the Twilleys.

We had booked a couple of rooms at the Hyatt Regency on Union Square, but when we arrived, we found that the hotel was putting us in the penthouse suite as a courtesy because of my involvement with the Muscular Dystrophy Association. Judi and I had never been in a penthouse suite, and neither had Howard and Julie. It was the most incredible, lavish place we had ever seen, and our eyes were as big as saucers as we took our tour of the huge, luxurious suite. We and the Twilleys had always split expenses right down the middle, and I don't think they knew at first that we were getting the regular room rate—they both looked at me as if to say, "What is this going to cost us?!"

After the bellman left, Judi and Julie jumped around the room, oohing and ahhing, and calling out, "Look at this vase full of flowers!" or "Look at that view!" They were ecstatic.

After a few minutes of this, there was a knock at the door. I answered it, and a man walked in and said, "Hello, I am Jacques the butler. Would you like any afternoon refreshments?" I'm not kidding, the butler's name was Jacques!

I had never been served by a butler in a hotel suite before. Afternoon refreshments? Sounded great to me. "Oh, yes, of course," I said, trying to sound like ordering afternoon refreshments from the butler was an everyday occurrence.

The butler walked out, and as soon as the door closed, Howard, Julie, and Judi all collapsed in hysterical laughter.

"What?" I said.

They just kept laughing.

"What's so funny?" I said again.

"Oh, Bob!" said Judi, still laughing so hard she was in tears. "'Of course'? It's hysterical watching you play the big cheese!"

In those early football days, I was tapped to do a number of community relations and public relations events. Some, like helping out the Muscular Dystrophy Association, I was glad to do. Others, like schmoozing the big-shot Dolphin boosters—well, I wasn't all that crazy about those things, but I did them. I remember there was one big booster in the West Palm Beach area who wanted me to hunt quail with him on his private game preserve. Well, this was my first time quail hunting, and I'd never even used a shot-gun before.

So this guy showed me how to load the shotgun, and he told me, "When the dogs flush the quail out of the brush, just take aim and fire." So we went out to hunt quail. Pretty soon, the dogs came to a bush and they flushed out the quail. I did everything the guy told me—the quail came out and I shot at them. But the first quail I hit just exploded into a cloud of feathers. There wasn't anything left of the bird to pick up.

The guy turned to me and said, "Uh, Bob, that was a great shot—but we generally let them get into the air before we shoot them."

Bob Griese is a great practical joker. He loves to call his mother and disguise his voice and put her on. One of the best pranks he pulled was at a Halloween party we all went to in 1972, after Bob broke his leg playing football.

—FAMILY FRIEND RON CORDES

Bob

Two weeks after Deacon Jones and Ron East broke my leg in the Orange Bowl during our perfect season, the University Club held a Halloween masquerade party. The University Club was a Miami social club that Judi and I belonged to. We were trying to figure out what kind of costume I could wear with a big plaster cast on my leg. Then Judi—being a nurse—came up with an inspired idea. We roped our friends into the gag, too—Ron and Becky Cordes, and Jean and Bill McNamee. The six of us went as a hospital operation.

Judi was able to get us green surgical gowns and a gurney from Doctors Hospital, and we all had Halloween masks under the surgical masks. Judi was the anesthesiologist, and she administered anesthesia to the patient with a rubber hammer that squeaked when she bopped him on the bean. Then she put a rubber toilet plunger over the patient's mouth and nose. Bill and Ron were surgeons, and Becky and Jean were nurses, and they worked furiously on the patient with saws and pliers, wrenches and butcher knives, and they were yanking big steer bones and spaghetti and all kinds of innards out of the patient. The disguises were so good that nobody in the audience could figure out who the operating team was. It was hysterical.

Finally, the operation was declared a success, and the patient—me, of course—sat up on the gurney. We all unmasked and got a big laugh and a standing ovation.

Judi and I became good friends with Marabel Morgan when we took her "Total Woman" course in the 1970s. One of the things Marabel stressed was that men love to buy nice gifts for the women they love. She said that the worst thing a wife can do is to return a gift or criticize a gift in any way. That takes all of the pleasure out of the gift-giving for your husband.

When I heard that, I instantly knew it to be true. I had learned that very early in my own marriage. Howard is so generous to me, and Bob was always so generous to Judi. They loved to give us nice things.

Judi and I had amazingly similar tastes on everything. On many occasions we would show up at some function wearing exactly the same outfit—that's how similar our tastes were. I guess Bob and Howard knew this about us, because sometimes they would go shopping for us, and they would come back with two of the same item. It was as if they went into a shop and said, "Hey, that's a great dress! We'll take two of those!" They would buy us exactly the same thing and be very proud of themselves.

—FAMILY FRIEND JULIE TWILLEY

Bob

I remember one time that Howard and I went shopping for our wives, and we bought them each a red velvet cocktail dress. We figured, *Julie and Judi have the same tastes—let's not complicate things. We'll pick out one dress and buy the same one for each of them.*

When Judi and I were engaged, I was still finishing my studies at Purdue, and I couldn't afford a big ring. After playing for the Dolphins for a few seasons, I was making better money, and I wanted to get Judi a nice diamond band for her wedding ring. I gave it to her one Christmas. I think Howard Twilley was taking home movies that Christmas morning. Judi opened the present while our boys, Scott and Jeff, were running around the room—Brian hadn't been born yet. When Judi opened that jewelry box and she saw that diamond band, her face lit up and her eyes glistened. It really made her happy, not the gift itself, but what it meant to her. I always enjoyed giving her things like that, just to see that look on her face.

Material things were never all that important to Judi. She never expected me to shower her with gifts, she never asked for it, and luxury things were never a high priority to her. The only things that really mattered to Judi were family and faith and friendships. But she always enjoyed the things I gave her—I think because she knew it was my way of showing her how I felt about her.

> Mom loved kids. She was crazy about babies. I was surprised she had three babies after reading what she wrote in the baby book she kept for me. There's a line that says, "Describe your labor and delivery." She wrote, "Real rough!"
>
> —ELDEST SON SCOTT GRIESE

Bob

Brian David Griese was born by cesarean section on March 18, 1975. During the pregnancy, Judi went to the obstetrician for a checkup and she came back and said, "The baby's going to be born March 17, a Monday." Since it was a C-section, the doctor could just choose a date on the calendar and schedule the birth.

"Well, that's interesting," I said, "but on St. Patrick's Day, we're going to be on Marco Island with your dad, playing golf."

"You can't do that," Judi said. "I'm having this baby. You and my dad will just have to change your plans."

I called Judi's dad and kiddingly told him, "Elmer, Judi's doctor is messing up our golf game. Are we gonna put up with this?"

So we talked to Judi's doctor and had him move Brian's birthday to Tuesday, March 18. I didn't want him born on St. Paddy's Day anyway, because then we'd have had to name him Sean or Patrick or some such thing.

So Judi's dad and I got to play golf on Marco Island, and the next day, Brian was born. I remember driving home with Judi and Brian a few days after he was born. Judi had Brian wrapped in a blanket, holding him in her arms. As we pulled up in the driveway, Scott and Jeff ran out of the house and crowded at the car window to get their first glimpse of their new brother.

Judi was an excellent athlete, a terrific golfer and tennis player. In fact, I got acquainted with Bob because Judi used to come to our house and play tennis with my wife, Becky. Of course, we knew of Bob before that—everybody in Florida was a Dolphin fan and a Bob Griese fan. But we got to know Judi personally before we got to know Bob.

All three of Bob and Judi's boys are great athletes. Scott, Jeff, and Brian were all football players in college. We used to kid Bob that the boys' athleticism was genetic—it came through Judi! When I play golf with Bob and his sons, I tell the boys to be glad they got their mother's golfing talent—not their dad's.

Judi was such a great match for Bob—for his love of sports and his love of family. She was the best thing that could've happened to Bob, in terms of his life and his career. She worried about him and prayed for him throughout his playing years, and she was so supportive of him while he was playing with the Dolphins.

—FAMILY FRIEND RON CORDES

Bob

I've never had a hole in one in my life, and neither has Brian—but Judi had a hole in one. She was also the Fort Wayne Junior Girls champion in high school. Judi and I enjoyed competing with each other on the golf course. For years, she saved a golf card from a game we played in North Carolina one summer—she shot a 78 and I had an 80.

Judi was a good softball player, a good tennis player, a good bridge player; she was very competitive. I really believe that Scott, Jeff, and Brian get their athleticism and competitiveness from Judi as much as me. She was just as competitive as the rest of us. She had to be—it was a matter of survival in the Griese household.

In the summertime, Judi and I would organize softball games with some of our friends, and we have home movies of those games. We'd choose up sides and mix up the teams so there were equal numbers of men and women on both sides. Judi was by far the best of the women players—and she was better than some of the guys. It was slow-pitch softball, so the goal was not to get strikeouts, but to get a lot of hits and action, to make the game more fun. Judi was a good pitcher, a good hitter, and she could run well. She was just a great all-around athlete.

Brian

She used to play tennis with Scott and Jeff all the time—I was a little too young. It would be Scott and Jeff against Mom, and she would just whip the two of them. I think she would deliberately tire them out on the court so they wouldn't cause so much trouble in the house.

Bob

Sometime in the mid-seventies, I was on a team plane with Don Shula, returning home after the last game of the season, and he asked me, "What are you going to do after the season?"

"I dunno," I said. "I haven't really given it much thought."

"Well," he said, "you oughta go skiing. It's a great family vacation. Our family just started skiing last winter, and we love it."

"But we don't ski," I said. "I don't, Judi doesn't, and the boys don't."

"Then it's high time you learned!" he said. "Take the family skiing!"

I thought about it for a moment, then I said, "I thought the team didn't want me to go skiing! What if I break my leg out there? Hey, Shoes—are you trying to tell me something?"

Well, we tried skiing, and Judi and the boys picked it up right away. Old Dad took a while longer to get it, but eventually we were all on the slopes, and it turned out to be one of our favorite ways to vacation. Skiing is a great family sport. When we'd come in off the mountain, the kids would be tired, we'd have a big meal together, and the kids would go right to bed. Judi and I would always have some time to ourselves. The next morning, we'd feed the kids and send them back out onto the slopes. It was great.

When we were in California, Judi's favorite places to relax were Carmel-by-the-Sea and Pebble Beach, south of San Francisco. We would play golf at Pebble Beach, then go out on Seventeen Mile Drive with some friends. We'd take pictures and laugh and talk and look at the tide pools and the Monterey cypress trees growing out of the rocks. Those were the best of times, and I remember those days as if they were yesterday.

When we were in Florida, Judi loved to go to Marco Island. We went there often when the kids were small, and we stayed in a place right on the Gulf beach. They had a little pitch-and-putt golf course there, and we took some great home movies of the boys playing golf. I remember one time in particular when Scott was about nine, Jeff was seven, and Brian was three. They went out on the golf course with their swimming suits on, and they played with one club and a putter. While they were playing, the sprinklers came on—and as far as they were concerned, there was nothing better than playing golf in the sprinklers.

We had our share of Kodak moments while the boys were growing up. We have home movies of the boys out on the green. Scott shows off his proper putting technique, then Jeff hams it up, walks into the camera or bumps into the flag, then little Brian drags the ball into the hole with his putter. I got one shot of Brian standing in the sprinklers, swinging at the ball with all his might—and shanking it straight into a sand trap.

Brian

That club was bigger than I was. I remember one time I swung that club and it spun me around in the sand trap—the club went flying and I fell facedown in the bunker.

And there's that movie Dad took of the three of us on the green—Scott holding his 9-iron, Jeff with his wedge, and me with a putter. I raised that putter over my head and swung it down, *wham!* And the head of that putter sank about four inches into the green. And Scott started yelling at me, "Oh, no, no, no! Don't do that!" And I yelled, "Hi-yah!" and *wham!* I sank that putter into the green again. After all the holes I dug in that green, I'm sure the greenskeeper was glad to see us leave.

> Brian used to follow us everywhere. We lived on a golf course in Miami, and Jeff and I would go running off to play football on the golf course. We tried to leave Brian in the dust—we thought he was too little to tag along with us.
>
> But pretty soon, he would show up on his little yellow bike with the training wheels. He'd get off and want to get in the game with us big guys. We'd let him in the game, and a lot of times he would get beat up in the game and run crying home to Mom. But he was tough, and he always came back for more.
>
> —BRIAN'S BROTHER SCOTT

Brian

The only times Mom ever lost her cool were when we three boys fought. She never could understand why brothers fight. Usually, it was just a case of teasing that went a little too far. You know how it goes—I poke you, then you punch me, then I punch you back, and you bite me, and it just escalates. Brothers tease one another and fight. That's normal, but my mother could never understand that.

Don't get me wrong—it wasn't like we fought all the time. Fact is, we were very tight as brothers, and we always stood up for one another when the chips were down. Since I was the youngest, Scott and Jeff were always looking out for me, always taking care of me. I've seen the home movies that show Scott and Jeff pushing me around in a baby carriage, picking me up and playing with me, making sure I was all right. I remember those guys as being very concerned that I was okay. But as I got older, of course, there was more teasing and roughhousing. They started beating on me a bit. Actually, I'm glad they did, because they beat on me and made me tough. And I got the last word—I'm bigger than they are now!

Bob

I really think that's why Brian has gotten to be so good at different sports—he had to be tough and good just to survive as a kid with two older brothers. It happens all the time, the youngest of the brothers plays with the older brothers, and he learns to compete with the big guys. That was the way it was for me when I was a kid, playing football on the library lawn in Evansville with my big brother, Bill, and his friend Ted Temple. I'd get a bloody nose every time I played, but I learned not to be afraid of the big guys and not to worry about a little blood or a little pain.

And Brian? Same thing. He was out there playing with Scott and Jeff and their friends, competing with them as an equal, trying to be as good as they were, trying to be as tough as they were, even though those guys were two, three, or four years older than he. Because he learned to compete at that level, when he competed against other boys his age, Brian always seemed to be the best.

Brian

Scott and Jeff used to jump on top of me. We had this couch with leather cushions, and they would pile the cushions on top of me, then

Scott would jump on top of the cushions, and Jeff would jump on top of Scott—and there I was, stuck on the bottom, and I wouldn't be able to breathe. Those guys would hear my muffled screams and mock me—"I can't breathe! I can't breathe!" I would be all red in the face when I got out from under that dogpile. That probably prepared me for football and surviving a dogpile of big defensive linemen.

Though Scott and Jeff were bigger than I was, I devised my own defense mechanisms and held my own. I had a collection of little Matchbox cars, and those things are made of die-cast metal. So when they would come after me, I would grab a handful of Matchbox cars and start throwing. When those metal cars started pelting them, they would run screaming for cover. Man, that was cool! I could keep the big guys at bay—they wouldn't come near me as long as I had a handful of Matchbox cars. Maybe that's one reason I'm a quarterback today, because of all that practice I had with those little cars—I really had a lot of opportunities to work on my aim!

Along with the roughhousing and good-natured competition, we had a lot of love in our family. To this day, we're all very close, and we still compete with one another—only now we compete on the golf course or a basketball court.

I remember a fort that Scott and Jeff built in a tree on the golf course. Actually, it wasn't much of a fort. It was more like a lot of pieces of wood randomly nailed into the branches. One day I fell out of that tree and broke my forearm. I got on my bike and rode home. Mom took one look at my arm and said, "Oh, you've got to go to the hospital." Scott and Jeff and I were always getting banged up, cut up, bruised, and what have you, and Mom would either patch us up or toss us in the car and rush us to the hospital. She was very calm and professional about it, because she was a nurse. With all the scrapes, lacerations, and broken bones in our family, it was a good thing Mom was a nurse.

Every Christmas, Judi made the house look like a fairyland. She and Bob always had a beautiful tree, and the boys would decorate it so lavishly. They would have their home decorated with Christmas villages and snow—Brian would set that out every Christmas. Judi did a lot of needlepoint, and she would frame them and put them up

---

around the house. She put decorations in all the rooms and up the staircase. There would be Christmas lights, Christmas pillows, and Christmas stockings with everyone's names on them. Judi loved Christmas, and she had a special touch that made Christmas a really magical time in the Griese household.

—FAMILY FRIEND JEAN MCNAMEE

Brian

We have a lot of home movies from Christmases over the years. There's one video—I think we had just bought the video camera and Scott was playing around with it. He set it up on the tripod, turned the recorder on, then jumped on the couch in his pajamas and went into his routine. The video camera had a microphone, and he'd put the mike up to his mouth and launch into a perfect impression of his favorite sports announcer: "Hello, this is Howard Cosell. Welcome to the Meadowlands in New York, where we're going to have a big game for you today between the Giants and the Chicago Bears—" And he'd go on for fifteen minutes, giving the starting lineups, calling the kickoff and the play-by-play. He had Howard down to a tee.

Bob

When Brian opened his presents, the other boys thought he was too slow. "Open it, open it!" they'd yell. Then Scott just ran over while I was taking the movie, and he snatched the present out of Brian's hands— "Here, lemme show ya how to do this!"—and *riiiiip!* He tore the thing open with one motion, with Christmas wrapping paper flying everywhere.

Brian

Yeah, Scott was definitely the hyper one. He was always running around, always impatient, always had to be doing something and burning off energy. We called him "Scrambling Scottie."

Another thing I remember about Christmas when we were growing up was that Dad always had extra presents he pulled out for all of us. After we had opened all the presents under the tree, he'd bring out the presents he had stashed away in the closet or the trunk of the car or back in the guest shower. He had a different hiding place every year. There'd be something for Mom and something for each of us boys. But Mom always came first. When she opened that extra gift from Dad, she always had a look of genuine joy and appreciation on her face.

I especially remember the year Dad got her a black fur jacket for Christmas. She opened it and it brought tears to her eyes. I'll never forget that.

Bob

One problem we had every Christmas was the old problem of kids shaking gifts and figuring out what was inside. Scott was the biggest offender, but all three of them did it. It was always a challenge to surprise the kids at Christmastime, because they were so good at figuring out what was in a present without unwrapping it. Brian was too young to be as sly and sneaky as his older brothers, but they would help him look for his gifts: "Hey, Brian! Let's check and see what this is! Here, give it a shake!"

So I came up with a code system to keep the boys from figuring out which present was theirs. Instead of writing "To Scott" or "To Jeff" or "To Brian" on the tag, I'd write "28601" or "65912." Every year, I'd pick one digit as the actual code digit—the rest were just camouflage. If I picked the middle digit and the code was "74359," then I'd know that the 3 stood for the number three boy, Brian. If the number was "42105" then I'd know that the present was for the firstborn, Scott. Only I knew the code, and— simple as it was—the boys never did break that code.

Brian

The only problem was that sometimes we'd get to Christmas morning and you'd forget the code.

Bob

Yeah, that happened a few times. We bought the gifts three or four weeks before Christmas and had them stored away, so sometimes I'd look at the code on the gift and think, *Let's see—was it the first digit this year? Or the last digit? Or the second digit? Or—?* Finally, I'd give up and say, "Just take your pick and open one of the presents . . . Okay, Brian, you've got Scott's present, you switch with him, and you switch with him," and so on. We'd just sort it all out in front of the tree.

Brian

And then there was Holly.

Bob

Oh, yeah! Holly was a little Maltese, a little white furry dog. Judi brought home that dog for the family as a surprise one Christmas.

Brian

Why are you making a face like that?

Bob

Well, number one, I don't like surprises. And number two, I wasn't all that crazy about that little dog. Let's just say it wasn't my favorite Christmas present that year.

I mean, a house full of boys needs a big roughhousing dog, like a seventy-pound Lab, to flop around with and wrestle with on the ground—not a five-pound Maltese. Those boys treated that little furry dog like an old football. They would get that dog in a small room with a door at either end, and they would tease that dog and make her try to get past them and out of the room. The boys had a lot of fun with that little dog—but I don't think the dog enjoyed it much.

Scott: Remember that year you threw more interceptions than touchdowns?

Brian: Did you, Dad? I didn't know that.

Bob: More interceptions than touchdowns? I never had a year like that.

Scott: Sure you did. Just that one year. I think it was in 1978 or 1979.

Jeff: Yeah, we looked it up.

Bob: Are you sure? That can't be right.

Scott: I remember, the last couple of years before you retired, sometimes there were hecklers in the stands. Mom would sit there at the games, and she would never lose her composure. I'd get really mad, though. I'd hear them yelling at you or yelling at Shula to take you out, and I'd get mad and throw peanuts at those jerks. I mean, that's my father out there. So I'd just unload on them.

Brian: I don't remember that—but I was only three at the time. I was five when you retired.

Jeff: I don't know if those guys knew that your family was sitting just a few rows down, but sometimes they were really obnoxious. But Mom wouldn't say anything to them. She had her face set, and she ignored them and watched the game.

Scott: She would just be very dignified and noble, you know?

—CONVERSATION BETWEEN BOB, SCOTT, JEFF, AND BRIAN

Bob

Judi planned a surprise birthday party for me one time while I was with the Dolphins. I had just turned thirty—the big three-o. Well, that surprise party didn't go over too well with me. I don't like surprises.

Brian

You can dish it out, but you can't take it.

Bob

That's right! I guess I just like to be in charge—it's the quarterback in me. A quarterback doesn't like surprises; he doesn't like to see any new defenses out there.

I showed up at the house, and there were all these people there. Judi had organized all the neighbors, and they all yelled, "Surprise!" After it was over, I told her, "I appreciate what you tried to do for me, but I just don't like surprises." Well, that was all right with her. She understood. She didn't spring any more surprises on me . . .

Until ten years later, and the big *four*-o.

Judi and I, along with the Cordes and the McNamees, went out to Carmel, California, for a vacation. I was playing in the Bing Crosby Pro-Am, and Ron Cordes volunteered to caddy for me during the three-day tourney. The night before the first round, all three couples went out to dinner together, then we went back to Ron's hotel room. I brought the golf bag over. "Here," I told him, "I just want to make sure you're up to the job of being my caddy. See if you can carry this thing."

Ron gripped the bag—and almost yanked his back out of whack. I had loaded it up with golf clubs, horseshoes, a boat anchor, a couple of anvils—the usual things you find in a golf bag. "You expect me to lug this around all eighteen holes?" he asked.

"There's a fifty-cent tip in it for ya," I said.

"Oh, well, in that case—"

The next day Ron and I went out to the first tee, and I was just getting limbered up and taking a few practice swings when I got my first shock of the day. There, walking across the grass toward me, were my wife, Ron's wife, Becky, and Jean and Bill McNamee—and they were all wearing the ugliest bright-yellow T-shirts you ever saw in your life. Each one of those T-shirts had big black lettering across the front that read:

BOB GRIESE IS 40 TODAY!

I groaned and turned to Ron. "Well," I told him, "at least *you* had enough class and good taste not to be involved in this!" And that's when I got the second shock of the day. Without a word, Ron unzipped the side pocket of the golf bag, pulled out another one of those ugly yellow shirts,

Father and son leading their teams to the Rose Bowl—
Brian (left) as a senior at Michigan in '97, and Bob
(right) as a senior at Purdue in '66.

Bill, "Slick," and Bob Griese
(1945)

Bob at age two with his mother, Ida (1947)

Bill (age eight) and Bob (age six)
playing football in their backyard

Bob Griese at age seven all dressed
up for his Confirmation

Bob Griese on the run at Purdue.
He is a two-time All-American and Heisman trophy runner-up.

Fort Wayne *News-Sentinel* Photo

Judi and Bob Griese in 1967

Judi congratulates Bob
on being selected by
Miami in the first round.

Brian and his mom in Snowmass,
Colorado (1983)

Bob and Judi on a cruise in 1985

The Griese family in the mid-1980s:
Scott; Bob; Judi holding their dog, Holly; Brian; and Jeff

Brian's favorite picture of his mom

Brian at age eight, playing youth
league softball.

Brian at age ten,
posing for his youth league
football picture.

Brian in eighth grade, playing
for his school team.

Bob scrambling in his early days with the Dolphins.

Photography by Bob and Sylvia Allen

Miami Dolphins quarterback Bob Griese prepares to take the snap.

Bob, Jeff, Brian, and Scott
on Caribbean island cruise (1990)

The Grieses at Jeff's college graduation (1993)

Pro Football Hall of Famers in 1990
First row: Bob, Don Shula, Larry Little
Second row: Paul Warfield, Jim Langer

Brian led the University of Michigan Wolverines
to their first national title in fifty years.

Rose Bowl bound! Brian acknowledges the
Wolverines' 20-14 win over Ohio State.

Bob and Brian in Pasadena, December 31, 1997,
the day before Brian's team won the Rose Bowl.

Brian as quarterback for
the Denver Broncos

Bob as quarterback for
the Miami Dolphins

Bob and Shay Griese

and put it on. He wore it all day. And he didn't get that fifty-cent tip, either.

> After Griese retired in 1980 and moved to TV, he let young Brian tag along at the games he broadcast. "He enjoyed being in the press box and getting hot dogs for us," says Griese. "For a kid, that was pretty exciting."
>
> —*PEOPLE* MAGAZINE, DECEMBER 1, 1997

Brian

After Dad retired from football, he became a broadcast analyst, covering pro football games for NBC, and later doing college games for ABC. As any kid would, I really enjoyed going to the games with my dad. I liked to ride in the airplanes, sleep in the hotel rooms, order room service, and watch TV. That was my favorite thing to do.

During the games, I would go to the concession stand, buy hot dogs, and bring them back to the broadcast booth for my dad and some of the other guys. When I was a bit older, I went down and watched the games from the field, and sometimes I would help the guy who would send the game into commercial. I'd hold cables or tell the players that the commercial was still going, that kind of thing. It was a lot of fun, and it was a great way for me to see a lot of football, close-up.

One time we were in L.A., and Dad was calling a game between USC and Notre Dame. I went down to the field and stood at the entrance where all the players came out. I remember watching the Notre Dame offensive linemen coming out of the tunnel, and I thought they were the biggest guys I had ever seen in my entire life. I just came up to the belt buckle of the players—they were immense. Things like that make a big impression on a kid.

Bob

I remember covering an NFL game for NBC—it was a Raiders game in L.A., an afternoon game. This was probably around 1985. Brian went with me to the game, and then we went back to the hotel. The game was over at four, and there was no flight to Miami until the next morning. I said, "Hey, Brian, guess what! I got two tickets for the Lakers-Knicks game! We're gonna watch Kareem and Magic and all those guys! Won't that be great?"

But his nose was glued to the TV. He said, "I dunno, Dad. I think I just wanna hang around here."

I couldn't believe my ears! Lakers! Knicks! Kareem! Magic Johnson! And all Brian wants to do is hang around the hotel and watch TV? He's got to be kidding!

So I said, "Tell you what. Let's order room service right now, and then we'll go to the game, okay?"

"Okay, Dad! That's great!" Instant enthusiasm. All you had to do was mention room service, and he got all excited. There was nothing Brian loved more than a hotel TV and room service.

Judi was crazy about her three boys—there was nothing she wouldn't do for them. She had such patience and devotion to them. Each of those boys has a very different and unique personality, and she was very careful to raise them as individuals and to foster their unique talents and character traits.

One day when I talked with her on the phone, she said, "Today was my day to take Brian to lunch, and we just had the best time together." She always had a day each week to spend a special time with each boy. Brian was the youngest of the three, and Judi liked to take Brian to this cute little restaurant where they had tables that were covered with glass, and miniature railroad trains would be running on tracks under the glass. They just talked and enjoyed each other's company. It was one of the great joys of Judi's life to spend individual time with each of her boys.

—FAMILY FRIEND JEAN MCNAMEE

Brian

I made a science project for a school science fair when I was at St. Thomas Elementary School. We had to make a science experiment and display it in the school gymnasium. There were all these smart kids with their weird-looking projects—they had electricity arcing around and planets circling around lightbulbs and big colorful displays with flowers and vegetables and all kinds of fascinating things to look at. And me? I had an experiment where I ionized some water. I separated all the dirt and nutrients out of the water on those little filters, and then I would lay out the filters on the table. I had a jar of water with an ionizer sticking out of it, and that was it! I had the worst project in the whole school, and nobody would come look at my project because it was so boring.

But my mother came and sat there with me the whole time. And all these people would come by and look, then walk away. And then the judges would come by and look, and I would be so nervous. The judges asked me about my project, why I did it, what I learned, and all that stuff. And the fact was that my project was terrible, I did it because it was an assignment, and I didn't learn anything.

But my mother was totally supportive. She smiled and squeezed my hand and said, "Don't worry, Brian. You did fine. I'm proud of you."

I have a picture of my mother and me standing in front of that science project. I love her smile in that picture, even though she wasn't well at the time. She had been sick for a while, and you can see in the picture that her eyes are watery and she has gained some water weight because of the cancer treatments, but it meant so much to me that she came out and helped me with my project. To me, that's a picture of how much she loved me.

Of all the things I miss about my mother, the thing I miss most is her smile. She had a great smile. My dad, my brothers, and I all have this fake TV sports announcer smile. But my mother's smile was genuine—you could tell it came from within. She was the only one in the family with a decent smile.

She had a lot of love to give. She was totally unselfish. Even near the end of her life, when she was very sick, she told us to keep going to school, to work hard at our studies and our sports, and not to worry about her. She'd be all right. She wanted us to keep moving forward in our lives, and she didn't want her illness to get in anybody's way.

My mother always put everybody in her life ahead of herself. Everybody else needed to be taken care of, but she would be okay. That's what she always told us, and sometimes we would fall into the trap of believing her. If there's one thing I regret about her illness, it's that she was always doing so much for us, and I think we could have done more for her.

I have my mother in my mind all the time, because I have a lot of pictures of her. One of my favorites was taken in her kitchen in Miami. She has her apron on, and she's got a big smile on her face and her eyes are beaming. It's much different from the pictures that were taken later, when she was sick.

But I remember all the times with my mother—not just the good times. I remember the times when she was healthy, and we'd be out on Marco or someplace, having a picnic or playing golf or tennis. And I remember the times when she was sick. And in all those times, I can't remember a single time she ever talked about herself. I don't remember even one time that she ever complained or said she needed something or said she wasn't feeling well. She always seemed content.

Mom was very gracious, very compassionate. She was always pitching in and helping out. That was her personality—always giving, always looking out for others, always doing everything with dignity and grace. She would spend hours helping at our schools, helping to make the costumes for the All Saints' Day pageant or the nativity pageant. She was very involved with the church and our schools and in the neighborhood.

She was a friend to everybody, and people always called on her and looked to her for help. Everybody knew they could count on Judi Griese. That's just who she was.

—BRIAN'S BROTHER JEFF

Brian

Mom taught my CCD class. CCD stands for Confraternity of Christian Doctrine, and it's a program they have in Catholic churches to teach children about the Bible and the Christian faith. I was very young when she taught the class, about seven or eight. I really enjoyed being taught by my mom—and if she hadn't been there, I think it probably would have been the most boring thing I ever did in my life, because the material they used in those classes was really dull. But my mother knew how to bring the material to life and make it interesting.

I respected that instruction more and came to really believe in the reality of God because my mother believed in it so sincerely, and because she lived what she believed. She took the time to teach me and the other children the stories about Jesus. If she hadn't been the teacher, I probably never would have done any of the CCD work. In fact, I probably wouldn't even have gone to the classes.

Bob

Judi's faith was very important to her. She was raised as a Catholic in Fort Wayne, and while I was still with the Dolphins, she became very involved with a nondenominational Bible study class. She had a number of Christian friends who went to that Bible study, and it was very important to her. She loved the Bible, and it was very real to her—not just a book of abstract teachings or Sunday school stories. She was always finding ways to apply what she learned in the Bible to everyday life.

Judi was always praying for us, for her family. She prayed continually for me while I was with the Dolphins, that I would stay healthy and not get hurt. And she prayed for the boys all the time. I know she's watching over her family still.

We have a lot to be thankful for. The boys and I have a lot of great memories, a lot of photographs and reminders of some very good days when Judi was with us.

In 1983, a shadow came over our family. That's when Judi was diagnosed with cancer.

7

INTO THE SHADOW

When Brian was 7, Judi was diagnosed with breast cancer, and after treatment, she went into remission. But, one day, without warning, the cancer came back. Bob wore himself out trying to hold things together, often flying home on late-night flights from ABC games to be with Judi and the boys, organizing a team of friends to watch over them while he was out of town, and personally caring for Judi in the hospital when she was gravely ill. Bob never shared his heartache or his fears, not even with his closest friends, preferring to carry the emotional load himself.

"Bob gave back everything that Judi had given to him," Vicki Dennis, a family friend, says. "He never once thought she couldn't beat it. He never, ever gave up hope."

—USA Today, April 21, 1998

Judi was the most selfless person I ever knew. She always thought of others before herself.

One day a couple of years after she was diagnosed with cancer, she called me and wanted to take me out to lunch for my birthday. So we went to a beautiful restaurant, and she gave me a lovely gift. We talked and had a wonderful time. Afterwards, we walked out of the restaurant and I said, "Would you like to do a little shopping before we go home?"

"Oh, I wish I could," she replied, "but I have to go to Baptist Hospital for a treatment."

"My goodness!" I said. "Why didn't you tell me? We could have skipped lunch, and I could have taken you there."

"Oh, no," she said, "I wouldn't have wanted to miss this lunch—we had such a wonderful time! Besides, I feel pretty good today, and I wanted to see what I can do without help. I wanted to see if I could handle this treatment by myself." And she did.

That's just the kind of person she was.

One time in 1980, before she was diagnosed with cancer, Judi was in the middle of cooking dinner for her family when a friend called and told her that my father was in the hospital and not expected to live. And wouldn't you know? Judi dropped what she was doing, called a neighbor to stay with her boys, and rushed to the hospital to be with me at my father's bedside.

When she walked into the hospital room, I said, "Judi, you've got a husband and three boys to take care of! You shouldn't be here!"

She said, "I want to be here!" Well, that was her nature. She was just a totally giving person.

—JEAN MCNAMEE

Brian

I was seven when my mother found out she had cancer. At that age, I didn't understand anything that was going on. Over the next few years, I realized that my mother was very sick, but I always thought she would get better.

On Mother's Day 1987, when I was twelve, I gave her a Mother's Day card. I wrote in it, "I love you, Mom. Keep this card because I'm going to be famous someday." That was her last Mother's Day.

Bob

Being a nurse, Judi was very health-conscious, and she took good care of herself. She was careful about diet and exercise and regular checkups. In 1983, she found a lump—a very small lump—in her breast. She immediately went to her doctor, and he performed a biopsy. When the test came back positive, the next step was a lumpectomy.

"What are the chances the cancer has spread?" Judi asked.

"Oh, very slight!" the doctor said reassuringly. "The tumor is small, and we caught it very early. When we do the lumpectomy, we'll also check the lymph nodes to make sure the cancer cells haven't spread. Odds are, the nodes will come back negative."

But when they did the lumpectomy, two or three of the lymph nodes came back positive. That began a five-year battle.

Judi went in for chemo and radiation, and she went back every six months to be checked. For the next two years, she'd have these check-ups and everything would be fine. But one day she went in for a checkup, and there was a spot on a rib. So there would be more chemo, more radiation, more checkups—and eventually more spots. From then on, it was a constant battle. Judi fought it hard, and the doctors did everything they could. Every treatment worked for a while, but then the cancer came back.

After each disappointment, Judi would be down and discouraged for a while—and then she would say, "Okay, let's fight this." I went with her to the appointments with the oncologist, and the doctor would say, "Here are the different treatment options. There's a new form of chemotherapy we could try." And Judi would say, "Well, let's do it." She was a fighter, and she wouldn't give up.

In time, though, it became obvious that nothing was working. The cancer had spread to her liver. At that point, being a nurse, she knew that there were no more options.

I don't think Scott, Jeff, and Brian knew how bad it was until very near the end. Judi didn't think it served much of a purpose to inform them of every up and down during her therapy. By 1988, Scott was at the University of Virginia, and Jeff was getting ready to leave home for North Carolina. Brian, of course, was home. Judi never wanted to be a burden to me or the boys. Whenever the boys were around, she was happy. She put on her best face and carried on. She didn't want anybody worrying about her.

Judi was what I would call a very quiet Christian. She was very comfortable with her faith, but she didn't feel she needed to talk about it a lot.

I'm probably one of the few people with whom she felt comfortable sharing that side of herself. Because she shared that with me, I can tell you that her faith, her relationship with God, was the most important thing in her life. I could see her becoming even more open about her faith in those closing days of her life.

When Judi was in the hospital, she didn't want to talk about everyday matters. She

---

wanted to talk about her Lord. She would point to some passage in the Bible and say, "What do you think about this?" And in that quiet way of hers, she was a real example to other people of the reality of God and the love of God, even in the most terrible circumstances. People were attracted to the Christlikeness they saw in her—not so much in her words as in the positive, loving way she lived her life.

One thing that always impressed me so much about Judi was that she had such a balanced spirituality. She never got things out of order. She had her priorities straight.

Judi's first priority was always to God. Her second priority was always to Bob. Her third priority was always to her children. I admired that quality in her, and she was a great inspiration to me.

—JULIE TWILLEY

Judi took her faith very seriously, and she sometimes expressed to me that she wished she had learned more about the Bible when she was growing up. When she heard of a women's Bible study near her home in Coral Gables, she was eager to join—but she was very shy about going into a roomful of strangers. She was uncomfortable because she didn't know anyone in the Bible study, but they would all instantly know her as the wife of football star Bob Griese—so she asked me to go with her.

Well, I wanted to know more about the Bible, too, so I was glad to go with her. We went to the Bible study every Wednesday for eight months during 1986 and 1987. It was a group of about fifteen to twenty-five women from the local area, and it was led by a fascinating woman teacher. Judi was amazed at how interesting Bible study could be, and it was a great comfort to her, because she was curious about many things in the Bible.

I think it says a lot about how important that Bible study was to her in that she made an effort to be there every week, no matter what she was going through, what treatments she was undergoing, or how she felt. She gained strength from having this direct connection with God, and I think she learned a lot from the Bible about how to handle the crises of life.

I think people don't realize how much the Christian faith applies to everyday life until they really begin to study the Bible for themselves.

—JEAN MCNAMEE

Bob

Judi's faith was strong—stronger than the cancer, stronger than the fear of death. Throughout the chemotherapy and radiation, the raised hopes and the disappointments, she never once doubted the reality of God. She continued to study the Bible and to pray—and she didn't so much pray for herself as she prayed for me and the boys. She worried about how we would get along without her.

I was glad that we had good friends like Jean and Bill McNamee, Ron and Becky Cordes, Dick and Vicki Dennis, and many others. By the time Judi was diagnosed with cancer, I was retired from football and working as a broadcaster, so I had a lot of freedom in my schedule and was able to spend time with Judi and the boys. But there were also many times when I had to be out of town covering games, and I always knew I could count on our friends to look after Judi and the boys when I was away. Besides helping with a lot of the practical details—meals and transportation and that sort of thing—they also helped put Judi's mind at ease.

On one occasion, when I was out of town, Judi was scheduled to receive some treatment for the cancer, and Ron volunteered to drive her to the hospital. During the drive, Judi became a little teary and told Ron how worried she was about leaving me with the responsibility of caring for the boys after she passed away.

"Those boys are always going to be Bob's first and foremost concern," Ron reassured her.

"I know," said Judi. "That's why I worry about him so much. I hate to leave Bob with such a burden to carry all by himself."

"It'll be tough on Bob, that's true," said Ron. "But you know, you've done a fine job as a mother, and you've started those boys in the right direction. Besides, there's enough of you in Scott, Jeff, and Brian that Bob's not going to be able to mess them up too badly."

Well, that was just what Judi needed to hear. She laughed—but she realized that what Ron had said was true. She had been a good mother to her boys, she had given them a good start in life, and they were going to be okay. Even I couldn't undo all the good she had done in their lives.

On another occasion, when I was out of town for a game, Ron was supposed to take her for a treatment, but she took a turn for the worse and the doctors decided she wasn't strong enough and canceled the treatment. I called Judi and said, "Honey, I'll catch a plane and come right home."

"No, Bob," she said, "you've got a job to do. Our friends are here, and I'm in good hands. I'll be fine."

And she was right, of course.

On another occasion, when Judi was in the advanced stages of her illness and confined to her bed, Jean McNamee was visiting with Judi at her bedside. Again, I was out of town at the time, covering a game. "Judi was very ill, but not complaining," Jean recently told me, recalling that day. "Even when she was bedridden, she looked lovely. She always had on just the right colors, and her hair was always so pretty."

As Jean was sitting at Judi's bedside, Judi said, "We had a little problem last night. I guess I'm going to have to talk to Scott about it." It seems our eldest son, who was home from college, had invited some friends over the previous night, and there had been some beer-drinking—nothing wild, but Scott and his friends had put away a few beers. So while Jean was there, Judi called Scott to her bedside.

Scott sat down on the edge of the bed and said, "How are you doing today, Mom?"

"I'm fine, Scott," she replied. "I want to talk to you about last night."

"Would you like me to leave?" asked Jean.

"Oh, no," said Judi, "just stay right here." Then she turned to our son. "Now, Scott, you had some boys here last night, and they had a few beers. You know that I'm glad when you bring your friends home—but if anything happened to them after they left our house, we would feel responsible. You can always have your friends here, but I don't want there to be any more beer drinking when they're here."

Scott nodded and said, "All right, Mom, I won't let it happen again." And Scott gave her a big grin and a hug, and she smiled her big, beautiful smile at him, and that was that.

After Scott left, Judi turned to Jean and said, "That was a lot easier than I thought it was going to be." Anybody would love to be talked to the way

Judi talked to Scott. A scolding from her was more pleasant than being praised by most people.

My wife, Becky, was very close to Judi. They had a lot of conversations throughout Judi's illness. Becky had gone through cancer in 1973, and she'd had the same surgery Judi had. So when it came time for Judi to go through those treatments, Becky was able to be a resource and a friend for Judi. Becky went through her trial of cancer, and she beat it. We were hoping that Judi would beat hers too.

—RON CORDES

Marco Island was one of Judi's favorite spots, and we continued to vacation there after she became sick. We often had our friends out to the island with us during the summer or on weekends. I remember one time we were there, and a big storm came up with a lot of wind and lightning. Brian went out on the balcony with his camera and snapped a really incredible picture of a lightning strike. He captured the lightning bolt at the precise instant that it seemed to form stair-steps into the sky. I had that picture enlarged and framed for our family room in Coral Gables.

One time, when Jean McNamee was over at the house, Judi was showing her the picture on the wall. "They look exactly like steps to heaven," Jean said, marveling.

"I hope those steps aren't for me," said Judi.

It was a rare moment that Judi would ever be so somber, even about the cancer and the prospect of dying. She rarely talked about how ill she felt, and she never even looked as sick as she was. You often hear about the ravages of cancer, and how this is such a wasting disease. But the cancer never took away Judi's beauty—neither her inner nor her outer beauty.

During fall of 1987, she wanted to be strong for her boys. She went to Jeff's senior game at Columbus High. When all the parents of the players went down to the field and stood with their sons, Judi and I stood with Jeff, though it was a battle for her to walk out onto the field. In October, she insisted on going to Parents' Weekend at Scott's school, the University of Virginia. She refused to let her illness keep her away. She was a fighter, and she fought that cancer with every ounce of strength she had. She wouldn't yield an inch.

December came, and Judi was pretty sick. In the past, Christmas was always a big deal with lots of gifts and celebrating with friends and family. But that year we downplayed it because Judi didn't have a lot of strength at the time. We kept our Christmas gathering small, just the five of us, and we didn't take our usual Christmas card photo that year.

Still, we made it a meaningful family time. We read the Christmas story from the Bible, and we were thankful to be together. We knew that God had blessed us, and we were all upbeat and positive—that's just the kind of family we are. We believed Judi could beat this thing, and none of us was thinking, *Is this our last Christmas with Judi?* We just didn't think that way. But, as it turned out, it was our last Christmas with Judi.

I usually go to the Super Bowl in January, but I skipped the Super Bowl in 1988 because Judi's health was not good. As February approached, she was too sick to walk, but she called her friends Jean McNamee and Becky Cordes to her bedside and told them, "Bob's birthday is on February 3. I want to have a birthday party for Bob."

Becky and Jean looked at each other in surprise—but they were willing to do anything, if it would make Judi happy. "What do you want us to do?" they asked.

Judi had it all figured out in her mind—the guest list, the decorations, the menu, everything. So she told Jean and Becky what she wanted done, and they wrote it all down and carried it out. It was just a nice, quiet little patio cookout dinner party with a few of our closest friends. Judi's parents also came down from Fort Lauderdale.

By this time, the cancer had gone to Judi's bones, and she had broken her hip, so she was bedridden. But Jean and Becky had moved her to the chaise lounge on the patio and propped her up with pillows so she could be a part of this celebration she had planned for me. She was so happy to be there. For the rest of us, of course, it was a very bittersweet occasion. It was as if Judi was there, but receding from us, almost as if she were watching my birthday party from another world. We could talk to her, we could see her smile, but she was gradually moving away, beyond our reach.

A few days later, Judi had to go into the hospital one last time. I camped out in her hospital room, and when I wasn't there, our friends took turns keeping her company. She was hardly ever alone during those last few days.

Sometime later, Jean McNamee told me about one of the conversations she had with Judi by her hospital bed. "Jean," said Judi, "there are so many things I want to talk to Bob about, but I haven't been able to do it."

"Why, Judi?" said Jean. "You and Bob always talk about everything. Certainly you can talk to him now."

"Well, I just hate to burden him any more than I already have," Judi replied. "He never says very much about it, but I know this whole thing has been very hard on him—all the worries he's carrying, having to care for me, and having to do everything for the boys. He's been so good to me and he never complains. There are some things I wish I could say to him, but I just don't want to add to his burdens."

"Well," said Jean, "what would you like to say to him?"

And Judi told Jean about some of the matters that had been preying on her mind—matters having to do with the final arrangements and the funeral, and matters having to do with her boys or her parents, and matters regarding the distribution of some of her jewelry and other personal effects.

"Judi," Jean said firmly after hearing all Judi wanted to tell me, "let me tell you what you need to do: When Bob comes to the hospital tonight, ask him to shut the door. And while the two of you are alone, you just tell him everything you've told me. Tell him just the way you're talking to me now. You have such a nice way of expressing what you feel, and I know that you won't be adding to Bob's burden—you'll be relieving him of a big burden. Because I'm sure Bob is already wondering about most of the very things you just told me about, but he doesn't know how to ask you about it."

"Do you think so?"

"Judi, I'm sure of it."

"Well, I'll think about it. But right now, I'm feeling kind of sleepy."

"Well, dear, go ahead and sleep."

Judi nodded—and with that, she was asleep.

Jean stayed with her until it was time for her to go. Before she left, Jean took Judi's hand and once again said, "Now, when I come tomorrow, I want you to tell me that you have talked to Bob about all these things you wanted to say."

Judi nodded—and Jean left.

That night, I went to the hospital to sit with Judi, and when I entered the room, she had a determined look on her face. I didn't know anything of the conversation she'd had earlier that day with Jean McNamee. But as I entered the room, Judi looked at me and said, "Bob, please close the door and sit here by me. There are some things we need to talk about."

So I did as she asked, and we talked for a long time. When we had finished talking, we had resolved all those issues that had been bothering her—and just as Jean had told her, it was a big relief to us both. The fact is, many of those matters had been weighing on my mind for weeks, but I never wanted to burden Judi with them.

The next day, Jean walked into Judi's room, and was greeted by her big, beautiful smile. "You did it!" said Jean.

"I did!" said Judi.

[Bob and Brian,] father and son, bonded by football but also by the death of Judi Griese in 1988. That loss, preceded by the departures to college of Brian's older brothers, Scott and Jeff, left Brian shell-shocked. "We had this great big family, and then—bam—it was just me and my dad," he recalls. "I had to rely on him, and he had to rely on me."

—*PEOPLE* MAGAZINE, DECEMBER 1, 1997

Brian

Those last few days, I remember we'd visit Mom in the hospital and she was always asleep. She couldn't do anything, and we couldn't really talk to her. I guess they had her on drugs to control the pain.

Dad prepared us as well as he could. But I was just twelve years old—about to turn thirteen the following month. How could any kid prepare himself to lose his mother? I think there was a denial thing going on, where I tried to avoid the fact that she was really going to die. But inside, I knew I was losing her, and there was nothing I could do about it.

Bob

The night of February 12, I was in Judi's hospital room, along with Bill and Jean McNamee, Ron and Becky Cordes, and Dick and Vicki Dennis. Judi had slipped into either a long sleep or a coma. The doctors said she could go at any time, and she had received last rites. I waited at her bedside until about eleven, and I could hardly keep my eyes open. I felt totally drained—and I guess I looked it. Jean said, "Why don't you go home and get some rest, Bob? I'll stay here with Judi."

Reluctantly, I agreed. I didn't know if Judi would still be there the next morning, so the others stepped into the hall for a few minutes so I could be alone with Judi. I said good-bye to her and kissed her, then I left, and the Cordeses and the Dennises went with me. Bill left sometime later, and Jean stayed alone with Judi. Jean said she couldn't sleep, and she just wanted to be there, watching over Judi and praying for her.

Sometime around three in the morning, the nurse came in and checked on Judi. "I might as well tell you," she told Jean, "it's going to be soon."

Jean later told me that she held Judi's hand and was amazed that Judi looked so peaceful. In fact, she didn't look sick at all—she simply seemed to be asleep. "Her eyes had been closed all evening," Jean recalled, "but as I held her hand, she opened her eyes—she had those beautiful long eyelashes—and her eyes just lit up. She had a slight smile on her face—and then she closed her eyes and she was gone."

My phone rang sometime between three and four, the morning of February 13—just ten days after the birthday party Judi had planned for me. I answered the phone and it was the hospital, telling me that Judi had passed away. Scott was away at college at the time, but Jeff and Brian were both home. I couldn't see any point in waking them up in the middle of the night. I figured morning was soon enough for news like that.

Brian

That morning is kind of a blur in my memory. I don't remember much about it—but I do remember coming downstairs for breakfast, and that's when Dad told me. Even though I knew it was coming, it was like a punch in the stomach. I remember feeling like I couldn't breathe.

I felt that somebody had wrongfully taken something away from me. I was really angry. I was angry with God for letting my mother die. I was angry at society for not being able to cure this disease. I was angry for a long time.

Bob

I understand why Brian felt that way. I can certainly understand people feeling angry in a time of loss like that. Both Brian and Jeff were very quiet when I gave them the news. They both wanted to go to their rooms and be alone for a while. I had felt the same way when my dad died thirty-three years earlier in 1955.

People have asked me if I ever felt angry after Judi died. Honestly, I didn't. Sadness, loss, loneliness, yes—but not anger. I look at it this way: People die every day. People die before they have a chance to live. People die at birth. People die in accidents. Judi lived forty-four years. That's too young to die; that's a tragedy. But it was forty-four years, and they were good years, because Judi knew how to make the most of her time on earth.

One thing is really true: We had better use and enjoy the time we've got while we've got it. We assume we're going to live to be seventy or eighty years old—but there are no guarantees in life. Judi's dad, the boys' grandfather, is over ninety, but most of us won't live to be ninety. So we'd best live our lives as Judi lived—making every day count, and appreciating all that God has given us to enjoy.

I know that Judi was at peace with her own death. We discussed her feelings about death in the days before she passed away. There was no fear in her mind—only regret that she wouldn't be around to see her sons grow up. She was sorry that she wouldn't get to go to their weddings, and that she wouldn't get to hold her grandkids and go to their christenings, recitals, games, and other events. I told her not to worry about that. "You'll get to go to all those things," I said, "and you'll have a better seat than the rest of us." And I know that what I told her is true—she hasn't missed a thing, and she always has the best seat in the house.

Whenever I go to a graduation, a christening, a Rose Bowl game, or a family event, I think about Judi, and I know she's there too. When I go to Scott and Jennifer's and hold our little granddaughter, Reneé Judith, I think about Judi, because I know she would have loved to be there, holding this little kid. But you know, if God is good, and if His promises are true, then the good Lord has some children up there in heaven for Judi to hug and to love. If heaven is what it's built up to be, and if God is good, then she's not missing a thing.

The hospital called Bob and told him that Judi had passed away. I left the hospital, went home, and showered. Then I got in the car and went over to make sure Bob and Brian were okay. I got to the house at about six in the morning, and as I looked at the house, I was overcome by the most awful feeling. The house was beautiful and everything was perfect—just as Judi left it. But something about all that tidy perfection was just devastating, because Judi didn't live there anymore.

I went to the door and Bob let me in. "I don't know what I can do," I said, "but I just needed to come here." He nodded, but he didn't say anything. He was very quiet.

A few minutes later, Brian came down. Bless his heart, he was such a sweet guy at twelve, going on thirteen, and he looked so devastated. Bob took some cinnamon rolls out of the refrigerator—the kind that come in a roll that you break open and bake in the oven. "Here," he said, "could you fix these for Brian?"

Well, I had never even opened one of those things before, and I said to Brian, "I don't know how to open these things." So Brian took it and banged it against the counter, and it popped open. I put the cinnamon rolls out on a cookie sheet and placed them in the oven for Brian's breakfast.

Another thing—Brian wanted something hot to go with the cinnamon rolls. Maybe it was hot cocoa, I don't remember. But I didn't know how to work the microwave. So Brian had to do the microwave himself.

I watched him make his breakfast, and I watched him eat it, then put his dishes in the sink. He was so quiet, and I knew there was no use trying to make conversation.

Nobody needed anyone to talk. Bob and Jeff and Brian just needed some time alone, some quiet time. There wasn't anything else I could give them, so I tried to give them some time to themselves.

—JEAN McNAMEE

Bob

The morning Judi passed away, Jean McNamee came over at around 6:00 A.M. I know she stayed up most of the night with Judi, so I guess she didn't get any sleep at all that night. I let her in and asked her to help Brian with his breakfast, then I went back upstairs for a while. Pretty soon, other friends showed up, and the phone started ringing. It just rang and rang all morning. I asked the people downstairs to just thank whoever was calling, but I couldn't talk to anybody right then.

After a while, someone came up and said, "Don Shula's on the phone!"

I said, "Okay, I'll take it up here—but no other calls, please." So I talked to Don Shula.

A little while later, the phone rang again. I was upstairs at the time, but I'm told that the conversation downstairs went something like this:

"The *Archbishop's* on the phone!"

"Bob says he doesn't want any more calls."

"But it's the *Archbishop*! I can't tell him, 'Bob can't talk to you'!"

So they sent word up to me that the Archbishop was on the phone. So I took two calls that morning—from Shoes and the Archbishop.

Brian

I stayed home from school for a few days after that. We had some friends and grandparents over, and the next few days were taken up with making plans for the funeral. Those first few weeks were horrible. In a way, it wasn't that big a change from when Mom was in the hospital—she had been away a lot while she was sick. But now, I knew, it was permanent. She was not going to come home again. That part of my life was over.

I remember the first few days as being very hectic. People kept coming over and bringing casseroles. We must have had ten or fifteen casseroles in our freezer at one time. We got to a point where we just didn't want to see anybody else. We didn't want friends over at the house all the time. We just wanted to be by ourselves.

Bob

You can only take so many condolences. You reach a point where you don't want anyone coming by. People call you, and they think they have to say something to make you feel better. I didn't need anyone to say anything. I knew how people felt. Nothing anybody said was going to make the hurt go away. I just needed some time to be alone.

Some of our friends were concerned about me, because I didn't seem emotional at the time. They thought I was "stuffing" my emotions. I don't think I ever "stuffed" my emotions. Fact is, I'm a pretty emotional person—I don't think you can play football without being emotional. But I'm not openly emotional outside of my family. When I'm with my family, I show them how I feel, I show them I love them. Judi and the boys always knew how I felt. They would be the first to tell you I expressed my emotions in a healthy way—but I did that in private.

When Judi died, I told the boys, "It's okay to cry, it's okay to show your emotions. When you've just lost a parent, it's normal to grieve." But for me, the place to express emotions is in private, not in front of everybody else. And I just didn't feel I needed everybody else to come over and talk to me. I didn't need that.

Brian

I saw two people in my dad during those days. I saw him with friends and with people who came over to the house after the funeral. With those people, he was always upbeat and positive. He'd say things like, "This is the best thing that could have happened. Her suffering's over, she went peacefully, and she's with God now."

But when he was alone, when he was just around us, like when we would go out to the cemetery together, he would show his emotions. He missed my mother terribly.

It's been more than ten years, and to this day, I cry every time I go out to the cemetery. I cry when I go home for Christmas or an anniversary. We're a private family, but my dad showed me that it's healthy to be honest about our feelings. I think he handled his grief very honestly—privately, but honestly.

Howard and I lived in Tulsa when Judi passed away. One of the hardest things I've ever done in my life was to fly down to Florida for Judi's funeral. We went to the house before the funeral to be with Bob and the boys, and with Judi's parents, Elmer and Madeline. We visited for a while, and as we were leaving to go to our hotel, Bob said, "I want you to sit with us tomorrow at the funeral, but you have to promise that you are not going to cry."

Well, I'm the kind of person who cries at Kodak commercials. "I don't know if I can do that, Bob."

"Well, I can't have you bawling at Judi's funeral," he said. "I need you to hold up for me."

"I'll try, Bob," I said. "I'll really try."

So I prayed before we went to that funeral that I would have the self-control to get through it without crying. I prayed that God would make me strong. The funeral was a beautiful, beautiful celebration of Judi's life, and I got through it. I didn't cry a drop.

Howard, on the other hand, was a basket case. He could hardly breathe, he was crying so hard. Bob had told me not to cry, but I guess he forgot to tell Howard.

—JULIE TWILLEY

Brian

When did I sense that my mother was with me? From the beginning, even when she was in the hospital, before she died. That's the way she lives inside me, in my mind.

I didn't have as many good years with my mother as Scott and Jeff did.

She was diagnosed when I was seven, and she died just before I turned thirteen. So she was sick for half of my life.

There were two services—a private funeral service for the family and a public memorial service for the friends and the community. I vividly remember the private funeral. The four of us—Dad, Scott, Jeff, and I—all sat in the front row while Father Dennison, the pastor of our church, was up there talking. I remember my grandmother, my mother's mother, sat behind us and she was crying. I had the most horrible sense of loss. I felt as if somebody had ripped my throat out, like I couldn't breathe.

Bob

Judi's memorial service was more of a celebration of her life than a mourning of her death—and that's exactly what she wanted. Even though the cancer took her life, it never conquered her spirit. It never robbed her of the beauty, grace, and courage that was Judith Ann. It never shook her confidence in the hope of the Resurrection. She died—but she died undefeated.

It was a Catholic memorial service. Judi had many Protestant friends, such as Julie Twilley and the women in Judi's weekly Bible study group. At the end of the service, Father Dennison offered Communion, which is normally offered only to Catholics. But he made a point of inviting all of Judi's friends, including her Protestant friends, to participate in Communion. Again, that was something that Judi wanted, and it was a testament to the love that Judi had for others, a love that didn't even take notice of such distinctions as Catholic or Protestant or any other boundaries or barriers.

I remember that after the funeral, Scott, our eldest, didn't drive home with the rest of us. He walked home instead. He wanted to be alone with his thoughts for a while, and I think that was good for him.

Before Judi died, she told me, "Don't forget me." I said, "Don't worry about that. The boys and I will never forget you. We couldn't forget you if we tried. You'll always be with us." And she is. A day never goes by that I'm not reminded of her. There are reminders of Judi wherever I go. The boys—the things they say and do—continually remind me of her. There is so much of Judi in all three boys. When I'm in a store, I see things she would have liked. When I'm on a golf course or a tennis court, I remember the times I spent with Judi, playing golf or tennis. I could never forget Judi if I lived to be a thousand years old.

The hardest thing I ever had to do was saying that final good-bye to Judi. It was hard for all of us—for Scott, for Jeff, and for Brian. But we're Christians. We believe in God, in life after death, in the Resurrection. We know we'll see her again, and we're looking forward to that.

8

FATHER AND SON

They were always close, father and son. When Hall of Famer Bob Griese was still quarterbacking pro football's Miami Dolphins, he would take his youngest with him to practices and watch game films with little Brian perched on his lap. And when Brian's mother, Judi, died of breast cancer just before his 13th birthday, he and his father became even closer. "I wanted to make his life as normal as it could be," says Griese, now 52. "I'm no great cook, but I'd get up and make him breakfast every day." Despite his own hectic schedule as a TV football commentator, he made a point of showing up to watch nearly all of Brian's high school games. "I didn't want him walking out after a game and having no one there," says Griese.

—*People* Magazine, December 1, 1997

```
Bob
```

A week or two after Judi died, it was really something of a relief when the well-wishers and phone calls tapered off, and we were able to get back into the rhythm of living. The boys and I were still strong as a family, and we were okay. Our faith was strong, and my understanding of the way life works is pretty simple: These things happen. We don't want death and loss to come into our lives, but they do. For some reason, this happened to us. Judi fought the cancer courageously, and this was the outcome. When it happens, you deal with it, and you go on.

I had one son, Scott, already in college. I had another son, Jeff, about to leave for college. And I had my youngest son, Brian, who was almost to his thirteenth birthday, and he needed a lot of my time and attention in order to get through this thing.

Having lost my dad when I was ten, I had some idea of what Brian was going through. I thought back to what my mom did for me to keep my life on an even keel, and I tried to do the same for Brian. He had already gone through a life-shattering loss for a boy his age, and I didn't want him to have to go through any more changes or losses. I wanted his life to go on as normally as possible—his schoolwork, his athletics, his daily routine.

Brian

Dad really swept everything aside and focused on the job of being a full-time parent. Maybe that's a lot of the reason why my schoolwork and sports never suffered after Mom died. I know that a lot of kids, when they lose a parent, go into a kind of slump. Emotionally, it was hard for me, of course—but the loss didn't affect my performance in school or playing sports, and that's probably because my dad was so careful to keep my life as normal as possible, given what had happened.

Scott was away at school, so Dad and Jeff were my main emotional support during those first few months after my mother died. But then Jeff graduated from high school and took off for college in August. So it was just Dad and me. It was a tough adjustment, going from a family of five to just the two of us in the space of about a year. But we held on to each other, and we got each other through it.

The most important thing my dad did during that time was lead by example. He showed me how a man responds to a crisis or a loss. He taught me a lot about how to handle life. And it just happens that all those things he taught me about life can be applied to football. What he did in raising me after my mother died was not easy. It was far more difficult than winning a Super Bowl—but he did it, and he did it well. And that's why I admire the kind of man he is, and why he's had such an impact on my life.

We had a lot of friends, of course, and they were always stopping by in those first months—friends like Dick and Vicki Dennis, Ron and Becky Cordes, and Bill and Jean McNamee. They looked in on us and made sure we were eating well and getting along all right. A lot of my mother's friends seem to feel a responsibility to look after us and give us a woman's perspective on things. We also had a housekeeper—actually, she was more of a house manager and a friend. Her name was Isabel Saint-Gaudens, and she looked after us and did the grocery shopping and cooking and the like. Dad was there most of the time, but if he had to be out of town and miss one of my games, he'd always have some of our friends there to support me. I never played a game without a rooting section.

I think one of the best things any person can do after suffering a loss like that is to get back into a routine—to regain a sense of a normal life. Dad knew I needed that. So that was his focus—making sure I had a routine in life, something I could count on every day. It began with breakfast.

Bob

I'd get up every morning at 6:30 and wake Brian up for school. He'd shower and get dressed, and be downstairs for breakfast at 7:20. That gave him ten minutes to eat breakfast, then we would jump in the car at 7:30 and I'd drive him to school. I knew within a minute or so when he would come down the stairs and into the kitchen. So I knew exactly when to put the frozen waffles in the toaster or when to break the eggs in the pan. We had it down to a science.

I made sure his breakfast was hot and steaming on the plate for him when he sat down to eat it. I didn't get it on the plate thirty seconds too early or thirty seconds too late. Every morning, I set the plate on the table and boom!—Brian would slide into his chair and start eating. We were like two cogs in a well-oiled machine, and everything went like clockwork.

Brian

Exactly. It was just like he said. Dad was a perfectionist, even in making breakfast. Not that it *tasted* perfect—but the *timing* was perfect. He took it as a challenge, as if he were managing the clock in a big game.

Bob

Yeah. It was a challenge. I'd always try to do it better the next day than I did the day before. And I had a regular menu, so Brian always knew he could count on breakfast. Monday was frozen waffles with butter and syrup. Tuesday was bagels and cream cheese. Wednesday, we had eggs—either scrambled or sunny-side up. Thursday was cinnamon rolls with cream icing. Friday was potluck, surprise-me day, so it might be cereal with fruit or whatever.

Brian

He was not a great cook, but he was dependable. He had some weird ideas about how to cook an egg. He'd pour water in the pan when he cooked them over-easy, and they came out runny.

Bob

But you ate 'em.

Brian

I ate 'em. I liked the routine. I liked knowing what I was going to get when I sat down. No surprises. Something to depend on, something that never changed.

Bob

And if I ever did change it—boy, did I hear about it! "Hey, what's this? Where are my scrambles?!" I think the routine was good for both of us. Maybe we were in a rut, but that rut gave us both a sense of order. He was helping me and I was helping him, and we were getting through a tough time together.

Brian

People look at the way I play football, and they say I play the game a lot like my dad did. They figure he probably spent a lot of time training me and teaching me the game. But he really didn't. Fact is, we almost never talked about football when I was growing up. But we talked a lot about life. We'd take flowers to the cemetery. On the way there and back, we'd talk about my mother and about life and death, and how we felt about things. We talked a lot, and that made us close and helped us understand each other.

We were father and son, but we were also best friends.

Christmas had always been such a special time in Bob and Judi's home. After Judi passed away, Bob made sure that the family Christmases were still special. He always saw that there was a big, beautiful Christmas tree for the boys to come home to. He continued all of Judi's Christmas traditions, and he included Judi's parents in all the celebrations. He was very good to Judi's mother and father.

I don't think Bob really had his heart in celebrating Christmas the first couple of years after Judi died. I know that when my husband, Bill, passed away, I just turned off everything—I didn't care about Christmas trees or decorations or celebrating the season. It's hard, when you are suffering and you have all these memories, to pull down the boxes and go through all the things that remind you of happy Christmases past. So I'm sure it must have been hard for Bob to do that. But he did it for his boys.

He made sure that the traditional Christmas stockings were out with the boys' names on them, along with all the pillows and decorations that Judi had made. Bob thought it was important to keep everything normal and traditional, so that, as much as possible, the boys would be able to have the same life they had before Judi passed away. That was very wise, and I admired Bob for that.

—JEAN McNAMEE

Bob

The first Christmas after Judi died, I tried to keep up Judi's traditions. There again, it was a case of not wanting the boys to experience more losses and more change than they had to. So we got down the decorations and we put up the tree—but it was obvious that things were just not going to be the same without Judi in the house. I pictured Christmastime at the house in Coral Gables—just me and the three boys exchanging gifts, and all of us sitting around thinking about her. And I thought, "That's no way to spend Christmas."

I was supposed to do the Aloha Bowl that year, but I asked ABC if I could have it off. I told them, "This is the boys' first Christmas without Judi. I want to spend that day with them." They said, "Fine, take the day off." So we took off for Colorado and went skiing in Snowmass, near Aspen. We still missed Judi, but we also had a good time.

Brian

I don't remember much of that trip except a lot of skiing. Christmas Day came around and we went to church, then we came back to the lodge and the four of us guys just hung out together, gave one another a gift or two, and that was it. It just wasn't the same without Mom. In some ways, it didn't even seem like Christmas.

For sure, it wasn't like the Christmases past, when my mother would go through the Christmas story with us, and gifts were all laid out. It was obvious to us all that the glue that held everything together was missing. Once we lost that, we had to find other ways to make the season meaningful.

And we did. Over the next few years, the relationship between my father and me, and between Scott and Jeff and me, grew a lot stronger. Before, we had always depended on my mother to bring us together. Now it was totally up to us, and we had to depend on one another.

Bob

We really did pull together. Even though Scott and Jeff were away at school most of that time, I think in many ways we actually grew closer as a family. We had to. We were all in this thing together, and we had to help one another get through it.

Because we were depending on each other daily, Brian and I seemed to be especially close. I was aware of Brian really trying to be a friend to me and looking after me. One time, about three years after Judi died, he said to me, "Dad, you've got to find yourself somebody, a lady friend. You gotta stop hanging around this house with me." He said it kiddingly, but I knew he meant it.

Brian

Of course I meant it. I mean, it was obvious that I could only do so much as a son. He needed somebody different from himself—he and I were so much alike, it was like talking to a mirror. He needed a different perspective, a different point of view. I was only a teenager, but I could see that very clearly.

For one thing, I wanted to have a life. I was a normal high school kid, and I wanted to have a normal social life. But I'd see my dad at home with the newspaper and the TV set, and I'd think, *Gee, he gave up so much so he could be here for me—I need to be here for him, too.* So I'd stay home and watch TV with him, even though I wanted to get out, because I felt guilty leaving him alone. Except for me, he just didn't have anybody to talk to or share things with. He just had his work and me—that was it. I knew I was going away to school in a few years, and I didn't want him to be lonely.

> Bob and I met on a Miami to Dallas flight in early 1990. I'm very outgoing and talkative, and Bob is just the opposite—very quiet, very reserved. So he was sitting there in his window seat, hiding behind his copy of *USA Today*, and I sat down next to him

and started talking. "Hi, my name is Shay! How are you? What's going on? What are you reading? Do you play gin? I bet I can beat you at cards!"

I didn't know who Bob Griese was, but I knew I was going to be sitting next to this guy for the next couple of hours, and I didn't think we should sit there not speaking, like strangers on an elevator. So I was doing everything I could think of to get him to open up a little—but he wouldn't talk! Everything I said to him, he answered back with a monosyllable, and he'd raise his newspaper a little higher.

Finally, I talked him into a little game of gin—he reluctantly agreed to play cards with me. Well, he was sitting in a window seat, and when he held his cards up, I could see his entire hand reflected in the window. I knew every card in his hand. So I cheated my brains out, and he couldn't win a hand!

And maybe that's how I won him over. Bob is so competitive, he just hates to lose at anything—yet there I was, beating him at cards all the way from Miami to Dallas! Maybe he was thinking to himself, *Someday I'm going to find a way to beat this woman!*

In any case, we became friends. And for the next few months we'd call each other every once in a while, or maybe have lunch together. It wasn't a romantic thing at first—we were just friends. Brian was still at home, and Bob was very focused on being a full-time dad. I thought that was very nice. I admired Bob's devotion to his boys.

It was a long time, months and months, before I told Bob that the reason I kept beating him at cards was that I cheated!

—SHAY WHITNEY GRIESE

Bob

I met Shay on a flight in 1990, and we became friends. We'd talk about things over lunch or on the phone. I liked her, but I wasn't ready to start dating again. Judi had passed away just two years earlier, and I wasn't in the market for a new relationship just yet. But Brian kept prodding me to get out more, to "get a life." So, seven or eight months after meeting Shay on that flight, I asked her out for our first after-dark date—Shay calls it "coming out of the closet."

Brian

I was still around, still in high school, and Dad was very cautious about the whole dating thing. Before she passed away, my mother had told him she wanted him to remarry. She didn't want him to be alone after she died. But for a long time, he just said, "I don't want to date anybody." He didn't want to bring anybody in the house until he knew it was all right. Dad and Shay dated some while I was home, but for a couple of years, she was mainly a family friend. Dad and Shay started dating seriously only after I left for college.

Bob

Shay and I were married on July 9, 1994, four and a half years after we met. We chose to be married in one of our favorite places in the world, at the Church of St. Bernadette's in Banner Elk, North Carolina, in the shadow of Grandfather Mountain. It was my favorite kind of wedding—small and private, just nine people.

We had the reception in one of the smaller, more intimate rooms at the Elk River Country Club. There was a fire in the fireplace, and the room was lit by a soft glow from the crystal candelabra. We ate lobster and sipped champagne around one big square table, so everybody could face one another and take part in the conversation. We had a pianist playing old show tunes, Broadway stuff, and the nine of us got up and danced and had a great time. Afterward, Shay and I honeymooned right there in Banner Elk, and we played golf and dined at our favorite restaurant. It was a great way to start our life together.

Shay has been incredibly good for me and the boys. The boys were grown when we got married, so they didn't need someone to come in and be a mother to them—and Shay never tried to take that role. But she's been very kind to my sons, and they know that she's been good for me. I think they're glad that she's here, keeping an eye on their old man. She keeps the house in good order, cooks for the boys when they come home, and even competes right along with the rest of us on the golf course. Shay's mother passed away some years ago, and she knows what the boys have gone through. She knows that to this day they think about their mother a lot. When she comes across a memento or a reminder of Judi that Scott or Jeff or Brian might want, she makes sure to get it to them.

At Christmas, I bought a Foosball game for the family. It's a table soccer game with rods and little men, and it's a very big game in Europe and Canada. I grew up in Ontario, Canada, and they play it a lot up there. It's a really fast, fun game, and all three boys picked it up quickly. Brian is very good at it. I'm pretty good at it (for a girl!), because I played it for years in Canada. There's a lot of defensive and offensive strategy to it, a lot of bank shots and trick shots, and it's hard to make a goal. Well, the four of us, the boys and I, played a lot of Foosball at Christmastime, and they hit me as hard as I hit them. Nobody let up on me because I'm the girl. In this household, it's competitive to the max.

It's the same thing when I play tennis with these guys. If I hit a good shot to them, they will return it right at my head. Nobody in this family ever lets up on you because you're the girl, or because you're the old man, or because you're the youngest, or whatever. Nobody ever thinks that way in this family. We all play as hard as we can, and we play to win. They've done it that way all their lives—and I'm sure that's why Brian is such a good quarterback. Nobody ever went easy on him, so he learned to be tough in order to hold his own in this competitive environment.

Same thing with golf. They get me on the golf course and they won't give me as many strokes anymore, because I'm getting to be a little better player. They used to give me handicap strokes—1 stroke on a par 3, 2 strokes on a par 4, 3 on a par 5. Now they tell me, "If you want us to spot you a stroke, you have to play from our tee."

And we have to negotiate these matters before I tee up. We banter and we argue—and it's fun. It's really entertaining to watch Bob and his sons compete against one another and argue with one another in that good-natured way they have.

They find a way to compete in everything. They even shoot hoops to see who washes the dishes. They play H.O.R.S.E. in the backyard after dinner, and whoever gets eliminated has to wash the dishes. They've been shooting hoops for dish duty since long before I married Bob.

We are "game people." There's a game attached to everything we do. We're talking about healthy competition. It's all good-natured and fair. I would sure rather see the boys shoot a basketball after dinner than sit in front of a TV.

—SHAY WHITNEY GRIESE

When Bob was inducted into the Hall of Fame in 1990, a lot of his friends went to Canton, Ohio, to be a part of the celebration. But before we went, Bob told us, "Now, please don't embarrass me. I don't want you people going crazy and waving signs and all that. This is an important moment for me, so let's keep it dignified, okay?"

We all agreed to be on our best behavior. We went to the Hall of Fame and it was a wonderful celebration. When the other inductees' names were called, they each had a cheering section filled with people whooping, hollering, and waving banners—doing all the things Bob had asked us not to do. But we were determined to honor Bob's wishes and be dignified.

When Bob was introduced by Don Shula, we politely applauded, just as Bob had asked us to. Then Bob got up and gave a speech—a short and very heartfelt and dignified speech in which he referred to Judi in the most lovely way. He said he knew that Judi was looking down on the celebration and she was very pleased that he had been inducted into the Hall of Fame.

That night, after it was all over, we all got together with Bob at a restaurant. And Bob looked around at all of us and said, "What's the matter with you people? All the other inductees had cheering sections—but you guys just sat there!"

—JEAN MCNAMEE

In 1982, two years after I retired as quarterback of the Miami Dolphins, I was honored at the Dolphins' annual award banquet with the retirement of my jersey, number 12. That was the only jersey ever retired in the first 34 years of the franchise, and I think it was the decision of Joe Robbie, the Dolphins' owner at the time, to do that. Joe had a reputation as a cantankerous guy, and there were a lot of people he didn't get along with, but Joe and I always got along fine. I always felt that if I was playing for a coach or an owner, it was my job to get along with them, not their job to get along with me. Over the years I played for him, Joe was always fair to me.

Ten years after my retirement, I was honored to be inducted into the Pro Football Hall of Fame. Though I was happy to be inducted, I was saddened because Judi wasn't at my side when it happened.

A player becomes eligible for induction five years after retirement, so the first time I made the ballot was in January 1986. I made it again in '87 and '88, and each time I made the ballot but didn't get inducted, Judi would get upset about how dumb those guys were—she wanted to go grab them by the neck and shake them up. But me? Well, I just thought it was an honor to be considered, to even have my name on the ballot. When I got into pro football, I certainly never thought I would ever end up in the Hall of Fame. Judi passed away two years before I was finally inducted.

Brian

Do you remember how you found out you'd been inducted?

Bob

Do I!

I was on a business trip in Las Vegas at the time. I remember I was sitting in one of the public areas in the hotel, reading the morning paper. Just then, I got a page over the hotel intercom. This was the Saturday before the Super Bowl, and I knew the sportswriters were voting that morning. My first thought was, *I must have been elected to the Hall of Fame. Why else would somebody be paging me here?* I'd gone through this for five years— being nominated but not elected—and nobody had ever tried to get hold of me before. In fact, nobody even knew where I was except my family. I figured that if I was being paged, this must be big news. That was my first inkling that I might have been elected.

So I went to the hotel phone, and it was Brian. He said, "I just saw it on TV, Pops. They had the Hall of Fame ballot, and you didn't make it. Sorry."

Well, I suspected something was up. Brian's always pulling something on me, and it was a little out of character for him to call me just to tell me I didn't get elected. My suspicions were confirmed a short time later when I got another call—this time from a sportswriter. He told me I had just been inducted and he wanted to interview me. So Brian's little scheme was foiled—but he still had another scheme or two up his sleeve.

Back in Florida, Brian and some of my most trusted friends were conspiring against me. I flew back from Las Vegas, and as soon as I got off the plane in Miami, I was surrounded by TV cameras, plus a lot of family and friends. "How does it feel to be a Hall of Famer?" asked the reporters. What could I say? "It feels great!"

Then they put me in a car and drove me back to my house in Coral Gables. When I got there, my jaw dropped into my lap. Our friends had spent the whole day fixing up the place for my arrival. My once-beautiful house now looked like a used-car lot. There were signs and strings of those tacky triangular flags everywhere. A huge sign was plastered over the garage door, and it read, WELCOME TO THE HALL OF PAIN.

Ron Cordes had gotten some sawhorse-type road barricades and blocked off the street, and the whole neighborhood turned out for the party. Brian stood at the barricades and collected a 12-cent toll from every car that went by—12 cents because of jersey number 12. The sign on his collection bucket read: FAMOUS PERSON SHRINE—TOLL BOOTH, 12 CENTS. Inside the house, there was a sign that read: HAVE YOUR PHOTO TAKEN WITH MR. BIG TIME, 12 CENTS. The interior of our beautiful home was "decorated" all around with bouquets of weeds—that's right, weeds.

We all went inside and had a party. That was some party—they made me, the guest of honor, make all the food! If I do say so myself, I make some of the best Cuban sandwiches anywhere outside of Tampa, so they stuck a white Panama hat on my head and put me in charge of the sandwiches. (A Cuban sandwich, in case you've never had one, is a big loaf of hard-crust Cuban bread, sliced lengthwise and layered with pork loin, ham, Swiss cheese, dill pickles, mustard, and mayo. You butter the bread and either grill it or brown it in a frying pan until the cheese begins to melt. A good Cuban sandwich contains at least 1,500 calories and no less than 45 grams of artery-clogging fat. The secret is not so much the ingredients themselves, but the order in which you stack them and the way you smash it all down.)

After a while, I said, "Hey, this is supposed to be my party! How come I'm doing all the work?" They just said, "Keep working! We need more sandwiches, pronto!"

```
( Brian )
```

And you remember how I used to rag on you about those eyeglasses in the Hall of Fame?

```
( Bob )
```

Oh, I remember! Here's the story about the glasses:

In the 1980s, before I was inducted, the only thing of mine on display was a pair of glasses I wore while I was with the Dolphins. They were special glasses fitted with a head strap, and I started wearing them on the field in 1977 (the placard by the glasses said something about my being the first QB in the game to play the game with specs). Until 1990, that was my entire legacy to the Hall of Fame—an old pair of eyeglasses. And all three of my boys would kid me about that, but Brian was the worst; he was merciless. "Face it, Dad," he told me, "that's as close as you'll ever get to being in the Hall of Fame!" Well, finally, I got my revenge. I was going to be inducted—and I wasn't going to let Brian forget it!

I went up to Canton for the ceremony, along with my three boys and a lot of friends and family. It was like going to my own funeral and living to tell about it. Wayne Huizinga gave us a plane to fly up there and back, and the ABC network, which broadcasts the Hall of Fame Game, threw a party for us. The ceremony was held under a big awning in front of the entrance to the Hall. There was a huge audience and lots of media coverage.

It was my privilege to have Don Shula present me at the ceremony. Shoes is the only guy I ever considered for that honor, because if he had never come to Miami, there would have been no world championship, no perfect season—and no Hall of Fame for Bob Griese. In fact, if not for Don Shula, *five* Dolphin Hall of Famers—Larry Csonka, Paul Warfield, Jim Langer, Larry Little, and Bob Griese—would today be known as "Huh? Who?" (I take that back—Warfield probably would have made it anyway; he was that good.) Shoes turned that franchise around, molded the '72 Dolphins into a legend, and made it possible for a guy like me to be enshrined in Canton, Ohio.

While Shula was introducing me, there sat fifteen-year-old Brian, grinning up at me. I had some notes for my prepared remarks, but looking at Brian with his great big grin, I had to make a slight departure from the script. I said, "My three sons are with me today, and my youngest, Brian, used to tell me that the closest I would ever get to being in the Hall of Fame was an old pair of glasses in an exhibit case. So there's something I'd like to say to my youngest son . . ."

And I looked down at Brian and said . . .

Brian

He said, "In your face, Brian!"

Bob

And the whole place roared with laughter. Brian had been kidding me for years, and in all those years I had no comeback. Now I had a comeback!

Brian

The best comeback of all. Yeah, I kidded him all right. But I was proud of him, too. I've always been proud of him.

This Florida high school quarterback attends classes past 2:30 in the afternoon. After taking tests on the practice field and pop quizzes on game days, he goes home to study. Brian Griese does his homework in front of the television, with consent and help from his in-house tutor, of course.

You read the surname correctly. Brian's tutor is Bob Griese, former Miami Dolphin, current NFL Hall-of-Famer and Quarterback Professor. Father and son are best known for their physical and mental talents, for their diligent work habits, and for calculating how to pass the next exam.

Of Griese's three sons, Brian is the youngest and the only one to inherit the play-caller position. As a senior at Miami's Christopher Columbus High School, 17-year-old

---

> Brian could be one of the premier recruits in the city, if not the state, according to some Miami high school coaches. If that proves true, Griese might just be planting new footsteps on his father's path—steps that could be larger and deeper than his father's.
>
> —*ST. PETERSBURG TIMES*, TUESDAY, OCTOBER 13, 1992

Brian

Though my brothers and I all played football in school, my father never pushed it. And he certainly never pushed us to follow in his footsteps as a quarterback. Scott and Jeff both played defensive positions in college, and I specialized as a linebacker until seventh grade, when I made the switch to quarterback. I played on the JV squad my first year at Christopher Columbus High, a Catholic high school in Miami (a school that also fielded Mike Shula and Alonzo Highsmith). I got my big break my sophomore year when I was subbed in after the starting quarterback was injured. I threw a TD pass in my first game.

Those high school years were important learning years. That's when I learned how to read defenses, how to avoid the blitz, and how to find open receivers and throw the ball away from the defense. I watched a lot of college game films with my dad, and he would point out various nuances of the game. He didn't give advice or say, "Now here's what you should do in this situation." What he did for me was a lot better than that—he taught me how to study the game. He trained my eyes so that I could see things for myself, so that I could learn as I went. He never tried to prod me in this direction or that direction. He let me find my own way, and make my own mistakes.

Even though my dad never tried to mold me in his image, I think I learned a lot and absorbed a lot just from growing up under the same roof with the man they called "The Thinking Man's Quarterback." That gave me a certain edge over a lot of other guys who played my position. A lot of quarterbacks go out and just play the game. They concentrate on physical skills and coordination. I learned early on that the great quarterbacks don't win a football game in the air or on the ground. They don't win it with their arms or their legs. They win it inside their helmets. They *think*. Without really meaning to or trying to, my father taught me how to *think* about the game of football. He'd always say, "The more you know, the better you'll play."

I played other sports in high school—I lettered in basketball and golf—but football was always The Game. Yet Dad always made it clear that my number one job was my schoolwork, not sports.

Bob

You bet. Brian was a class-A athlete all through high school. His junior year at Columbus, he racked up almost a thousand passing yards and eight touchdowns; his senior year, he completed 101 of 183 for 1,387 yards and seven touchdowns, breaking the school record (despite the fact that Hurricane Andrew shortened the season to seven games!). On the basketball court, he averaged 10 points per game. But all along, he understood that his most important stats were the ones he racked up in the classroom. During his high school years, Brian maintained at least a 3.7 grade point average, scored 1,170 on the Scholastic Aptitude Test, and was in the National Honor Society.

I told all three of my boys as they were growing up that they should get a good education—no dumb jocks in this family! And I made it clear that they should not plan on a career in the NFL. When you plan your life, you plan to get a degree and a good job, period. If you happen to get to play pro ball for a few years along the way, well, then you can consider yourself very lucky.

The older boys had played at Christopher Columbus High in Miami, and each had played in college as a walk-on, but neither had tried quarterback. Both played defense. It was the youngest son, the one who hadn't witnessed the father's football career, who decided to become a quarterback.

"[Brian's] the type of kid who'll say, 'I'll be a better quarterback than you were,'" the father says. "That's how he is. He's bigger than any of us. Notice I didn't say faster, but bigger. He was a high-level tennis player as a kid. He's a six-handicap golfer. He played basketball and baseball. He's the athlete."

—*Sports Illustrated,* Monday, October 13, 1997

Brian

When I was playing football at Columbus High, my father would always try to help out the team. He'd talk to me on the sidelines and say, "Why don't you guys try this route or that play? Go ask your coach what he thinks." So I'd talk to the coach, and the coach would say, "Is that what your dad said?" And I'd say, "Yeah, that's what he said." And the coach would say, "I'll think about it—maybe we can work it into the game plan." I don't know how much of Dad's stuff he actually used—not because it wouldn't work, but because we weren't the Miami Dolphins and we didn't have the athletes to pull it off.

Bob

You guys could do those plays. I kept it real simple. All you had to do was spread out four wide receivers, two on each side. That way, you spread out the other guy's defense, and if your quarterback has an arm, he'll complete some passes.

Brian

But we didn't *have* four wide receivers.

Bob

No problem. You just send four guys running upfield. If two of them are receivers and the other two are decoys, you've still spread their defense out. They don't know which of your guys can catch and which can't. It's philosophical, more than anything.

And what about all those little slants and hitches I came up with? You guys used to get some touchdowns with those plays.

It's just like dealing with Coach Shula. You have to make it sound like it's the *coach's* idea, and then he'll think it's a *great* idea.

The only route we ever threw that you gave us was the circle-square-in. I think we threw it maybe twice.

What about the four-verticals?

You're saying you gave us that play?

Yup. The four-verticals, straight up the field.

I think you should know that when you gave me those plays and I passed them on to the coach, I sort of put my own little spin on them. And sometimes if I wanted to put an idea of my own in, I'd say, "Hey, Coach, my dad says we should run this one."

Oh, now it comes out!

By the end of his senior season the son had broken the school record for career passing yardage and had been noticed by college scouts. Texas wanted him, as did Purdue—the school the father led to its only Rose Bowl appearance, in 1967. The son wasn't sure what to do. The father offered an alternative: Pick a school and join the football team as a walk-on. The father would pay the tuition. The son picked Michigan.

—*Sports Illustrated*, Monday, October 13, 1997

Bob

The recruitment of college athletes sure has changed since I got out of high school in '63. My mom's boss, Ferris Traylor, a big-time Purdue alum, had gotten me an interview for an athletic scholarship to Purdue, and Indiana also showed a lot of interest in me. So I got together with Tom Neimeier, one of my buddies from Rex Mundi High School in Evansville, and we loaded up a 1955 Ford Valiant and followed the snowplows across Indiana in the dead of winter. Tom was a heavily recruited 6'8" center on Rex Mundi's basketball team—I played guard, and just fed him the ball. Outside of Purdue and Indiana, I wasn't being recruited at all. We visited Purdue one weekend and Indiana the next. That was our big recruitment tour.

Today, of course, college athletics is a big deal, and the top high school athletes are flown all over the country, all their meals and hotels and other expenses are paid, and the universities have hosts who squire you around to parties and clubs and ballgames—they really wine and dine you and roll out the red carpet. Tom Neimeier and I never got any of that stuff in '63.

It was a whole different world for Brian thirty years later. He wasn't the most highly recruited high school football player in the country, but there were plenty of schools that were interested in him. During his junior year at Columbus, he attended Bill Walsh's quarterback camp on the Stanford campus (the coaches at the camp rated him one of the top QBs of all the kids who attended), and he liked what he saw at Stanford. It would have been a good fit for Brian's strong academic ability, as well as his football ability. Brian also took a good, hard look at Virginia, Duke, Georgia Tech—but when it came to my old alma mater—

Brian

Purdue was never on my list. Scott and Jeff were the same way. We all told Dad early on, "Anyplace but Purdue!"

Bob

Yeah, all three boys used to rib me all the time. I had all this Boilermaker memorabilia all over the house, and these guys were always telling me they would never, ever go to Purdue. It was a running joke with all three boys.

Brian

It was no joke, Dad.

Actually, Purdue really worked hard to recruit me. They did a good job, stressing academics as much as football. And they understood the pressures I felt, having the Griese name to live up to. They promised me they would not play up the father-son comparisons. I listened to them, but I never considered Purdue. Part of the reason I didn't want to go to Purdue was that I didn't want to invite those comparisons.

Scott and Jeff and I all dealt with those comparisons all through high school—being the son of a famous dad, a Miami quarterback. You start playing on the junior varsity team in high school, and everybody expects that you'll be another great quarterback because your dad is Bob Griese. And the comparisons never stop. You get to be a good player on your high school team, and the newspaper writers start asking, "Well, how does he compare with the best high school players in the country?" Then you go to college and it starts all over again. The pressure of those comparisons was never detrimental to my game, but they got to be a nuisance, an annoyance, all the same.

So I figured, *There are a hundred universities where I could go and play football—why go to the school my dad attended? Why go out of my way to invite comparisons?*

I also never considered any schools in Florida. I really wanted to leave home and have the whole college experience and see a different part of the country. Dad supported me in that. He thought it would be good for me to get out of Florida. Jeff told me to make a list of the schools I wanted to go to and the pluses and minuses of each one. Then, he said, I should just keep researching each school and narrow it down from there.

But in the end, it just came down to the fact that I had visited Michigan and I liked it there. I didn't find any school with a better combination of academics and athletics than Michigan. And at that point, they had just won five Big Ten championships in a row—and that was a very big draw for me, a school that was the best in the Big Ten conference for half a decade.

The irony, of course, is that once I got there, Michigan went four years without a championship. Mine was the first class in a decade to go all four years at Michigan without a championship ring. I had to go back for a fifth year to get one.

Bob

In some ways, I think the Griese name hurt rather than helped Brian's chances with some university recruiters. I think some schools looked at Brian as the son of an NFL Hall of Famer and thought, *Well, what if this kid doesn't pan out? Who's going to get blamed for that? The school!* I think a lot of recruiters just didn't want to take that chance—so they gave Brian a pass.

I remember there was one school that showed some interest in Brian, and Brian had interviewed with the coach of the school's football program in November, but by January, as we were getting close to the February cut-off dates, Brian hadn't heard anything from them. They didn't say yes; they didn't say no. Brian called the school to find out where he stood, and I made some calls, but the coach wouldn't get back to us. He was always in a meeting or out of the office or one thing or another, and he'd never get back to us. I figured this guy was just dodging me.

I thought, *Now this is crazy behavior for a college coach. I'm an ABC college football broadcaster, and I know this guy. So why is he blowing me off? It makes no sense.*

I was sitting at home with Shay, complaining about the runaround I was getting from this coach, and she said, "Give me the phone. What's the guy's number?"

"What are you going to do?" I said.

"I'm going to get him on the phone," she said. "I know how to deal with these guys." And she really does. She used to be an automobile finance manager, and she knows how to get through to people who are trying to avoid your phone calls. So she dialed up the coach's office and said, "I'm calling for Bob Griese."

They told her the coach was in a meeting.

"I'll hold until the coach can come to the phone," she said.

They told her it could be quite a while.

"Look," she said, "I'll hold for as long as it takes."

Well, it didn't take long and the coach came to the phone. And Shay handed the phone to me with a grin, and I talked to him. It turned out that he had taken his quarterback way back in November, right after Brian came to visit, and he never even told Brian or me. Well, I was torqued off about that and I told him so. Why wasn't he straight with me and Brian? If the answer was no, why couldn't he just say no? Why leave Brian dangling like that? Brian had decisions to make before the cutoff date in February, and it was irresponsible of that coach to string him along like that. It's hard to respect people who can't face things head-on—who duck your phone calls and won't give you a straight answer.

So now we were down to January. Most of the schools had snapped up their players, and most of the scholarships had been handed out. All along, I had wanted Brian to make his own decision, so I had never given him much advice beyond the suggestion that he find a school that was strong in both football and academics. I told him that twenty or thirty years down the road, when football was no longer part of his life, he should still be proud to say, "I'm a Duke man," or "I'm a Stanford man," or "I'm a Michigan man." I also told him, "If there's a school you want to go to that doesn't offer a scholarship, then you can walk on, the same as your two brothers did."

Duke had offered him a scholarship and pursued him, but he said, "No, that school's not for me. Duke is too preppie." I'm not sure what he meant by that, but there were a lot of guys he knew who were going to Duke, and his attitude was, "If they're going to Duke, I ain't going to Duke." There were other schools that pursued him, but I think he considered those schools to be too easy. He craved the challenge and competition of a school that had a dominant tradition in college football, a school where he would really have to gut it out and compete for the starting quarterback position.

Finally, late in the process, he said, "Well, I thought it over, and I want to go to Michigan." This was 1993, and Michigan had been in six of the last ten Rose Bowls, so I could see what the attraction was up in Michigan. I also knew that in a program like Michigan's, the competition for starting quarterback would be fierce—but Brian had never shied away from competition. So I called up to see if Michigan was interested, but they had already committed their scholarships. They had depth in the QB position and had already taken a quarterback that year.

Brian sent some tapes of his Columbus games, and the Michigan coaches liked what they saw. They came down and visited with Brian, and he went up and visited the school. Since there were no scholarships left, they wanted him to walk on, which is what I had told him he should do. So he went to Michigan and started working out with the team, and I think the coaches were surprised at how good he was. They were surprised that a guy who was offered scholarships to other schools would really just walk on at Michigan—there's gotta be something wrong with this kid. But it turned out that Brian was better than some of the players they already had on scholarships.

Brian

Before I was accepted at Michigan, I was in suspense—big-time. When I graduated from Columbus High, Dad and Shay threw a big party for me. My girlfriend and all our family and friends were there. Even though I didn't know whether I would be accepted, the party had a University of Michigan theme and Dad passed out Michigan hats and jerseys for everybody to wear. They gave me a bunch of terrible gifts, like stationery that read DON'T FORGET TO WRITE HOME ON THIS CRUMMY STATIONERY. And they took my picture with a sign that read WRITE HOME ONCE IN A WHILE—GET BIG BROWNIE POINTS.

During the party, the phone rang, and Shay answered it and said, "Brian! The phone's for you! It's Coach Moeller from Michigan!"

Yeah, right. The Michigan coach just happened to be calling during my grad party. "Sure, Shay!" I said. "Get out! I'm not falling for that one!"

"No, really!" she said. "It's Gary Moeller! He says he has some news for you!"

"Nice try," I said, "but it won't work! Give it up, Shay!"

But she finally coaxed me to the phone. I took it and said, "Yeah? Who is this?"

And the voice on the line said, "Brian Griese? This is Gary Moeller at the University of Michigan. I just wanted you to know that you have been accepted into our program, and we're looking forward to seeing you in the fall."

It was true! I was on my way to Michigan.

9

DAYS OF MAIZE AND BLUE

During his five years at Michigan, Brian Griese helped establish a program in which athletes would read to elementary school children. He helped form IMPACT, a service designed to help athletes struggling to adjust to college life. Griese also was an active participant in From the Heart [Foundation], which sent athletes to Mott Children's Hospital to visit sick children . . . "I think he understands how lucky he is and how blessed he is," said [Brian's friend, Anita] Bohn. "And I think part of it is just genuine compassion and kindness. He's got a great heart."

—*DENVER ROCKY MOUNTAIN NEWS,* SUNDAY, MAY 3, 1998

(*Brian*)

In the fall of 1993, I enrolled at the University of Michigan. When I started out in the football program, I figured, *If I'm good enough and a scholarship opens up, I'll get one. If I'm not good enough, then I shouldn't have gotten a scholarship in the first place. Either way, I'll go and play as much football as they'll let me—and the worst that can happen is I'll get a good Michigan education.* As it turned out, after I was there two weeks, a guy dropped out of the program. Coach Moeller came over to me after practice that day and told me, "We've got a scholarship for you." So everything worked out fine, and I redshirted my freshman year.

During my second year of wearing Michigan maize and blue, I actually got on the football field for a few games—as a placekick holder on field-goal attempts. So the first two years of my Michigan football career were not much to write home about.

But one thing happened during my freshman year that affected my whole Michigan experience. I remember it was a Thursday, and I was driving with Jason Carr and some other players. Jason was a backup quarterback and the son of Lloyd Carr (who later succeeded Gary Moeller as Michigan's head football coach). Jason was going to drop me off someplace, but he said, "Why don't you come with us? We're going to the hospital."

"The hospital?" I said. "Why? Who got hurt?" Sometimes we'd have a player over at the University of Michigan Hospital for knee surgery or something, but I hadn't heard of any injuries on the team.

"No," he replied, "we're going over to Mott Children's Hospital to visit the kids." Mott's is a branch of the University of Michigan Hospital.

"Okay," I said, "I'll go, too."

So we went and just walked around to the different rooms and visited with the kids, especially the ones on the seventh floor, in the cancer ward. Although these visits were organized by a group called From the Heart Foundation, which was founded by Ed and LeAnn Bouillon, there was no agenda or program or anything—we just played with the kids or talked to them or chatted with their parents. Some of the kids and parents were big Michigan fans and wanted us to sign autographs.

There were some difficult moments, too—kids who just tore the heart right out of my chest. I saw kids who couldn't get out of bed, kids who couldn't talk, kids who couldn't focus their eyes on me, kids who probably were not going to walk out of that hospital. In spite of all that—or maybe because of it—I was glad I went. Before I went there, a part of me thought, *Gee, this is going to be hard; this is going to be painful to watch.* But I came away feeling good that I had gone, and eager to go again the next week. It was therapeutic for me as well as for the kids.

So that became a weekly thing for me, going with Jason and the other guys to the hospital to visit the kids. I saw kids who didn't have the opportunities I had, and were not in the fortunate situation I was in, and I would try to help them out a little. Maybe the only smile they had all day was when a bunch of football players dropped in to say hi. And maybe we helped make those kids feel good for five minutes—but it made my week. I looked forward to our Thursday night at the hospital every week.

When I say it made my week, I mean that literally. It gave me an emotional recharge right when I needed it. Monday, Tuesday, and Wednesday, I'd study film and practice with the team and concentrate on my academics—and then Thursday came and I would say, "It's time to take a break from all this." And I'd go to the hospital and be with the kids and be refreshed and recharged. It restored my perspective about what I was doing and why God put me in the world—not just to help myself, but to help people who were not as fortunate as I am.

Then Friday would come and I'd be ready to go, ready to get back into the grind, and Saturday would come—game day—and I'd be at my mental and emotional peak. I knew what was going on for the game, and I was in a charged-up, positive, focused mind-set to play the game. The hospital visits were a large part of that emotional rhythm that kept me "in the zone."

Those visits changed my life. When you go to a children's ward in a hospital, you see a lot of things that break your heart. But you also see a lot of kids who are fighting hard to get well, and to beat their injury or disease. There were kids I developed a relationship with over the five years I was at Michigan. Some who were there my freshman year were still there when I left. Scott Loeffler and I got to know one girl named Emily who came down with cancer during my freshman year. She went through treatment and remission, and I didn't see her for a while.

Then, in my junior year, she was back because the cancer came back. I watched her fight the cancer through my junior and senior years. I came back for a fifth year, and in the middle of my fifth year, she died. And that was hard, that was painful, because I had gotten to know her, and I had watched her every week, fighting, fighting, fighting that disease.

Sometimes I would think I had it hard, keeping up my studies, writing papers, cramming for exams, going through grueling practices, getting up early, staying up late—and then I would think of Emily. I thought, *She's a tougher competitor than I am! She's fighting harder than I am—and about something more important than a grade or a football game*. Emily, and a lot of other kids like her, helped me keep my perspective.

I think there is a sense in which I took my mother into the hospital with me. She was a nurse, a very caring and compassionate person, and she knew what fighting cancer was all about. She was always caring for other people—and that's why she became a nurse, to make other people feel better. So I think that a part of her was there with me—her caring and her compassion for others.

My experience with these courageous kids gave me a college experience that was more than just football, more than just academics. I got to experience what life is really all about. And I wouldn't trade it for the world.

The similarities are striking, from the smooth way in which each delivers a pass to the intelligent yet guarded responses to reporters' questions. From 1964-66, Bob Griese quarterbacked Purdue to a 22-7-1 record, including a 1967 Rose Bowl victory over Southern California . . . And now, Brian Griese, one of Bob's three sons, has been thrust into college football's national spotlight as the University of Michigan's starter . . .

"It's not tough at all to play in my father's footsteps, because I don't look at it that way," Brian said. "I look at it as playing my own career."

—GANNETT NEWS SERVICE, FRIDAY, NOVEMBER 10, 1995

Bob

In September 1995, Brian's third year at Michigan, he got his first chance to play when starting quarterback Scott Dreisbach suffered a mild concussion in a game against Boston College. Brian finished the game, and Michigan won, 23-13. A few weeks later, Dreisbach injured his throwing hand during a drill in practice, and Brian got his first start in a game against Miami of Ohio. In that game, he completed 14 of 24 passes for 192 yards and two touchdowns—and Michigan won.

In a game against Northwestern, Brian took a really hard hit that left him with a painful separated right shoulder. He finished the game, playing hurt—and his shoulder continued to bother him for weeks thereafter. Northwestern won it, 19-13.

Brian

The shoulder bothered me during practice the next week, and the trainers and Coach Carr weren't sure about playing me in the next game against Indiana. But I kept working out the shoulder and throwing the ball, and Coach could see I was throwing pretty well by the end of the week, so he started me—and we beat Indiana, 34-17.

ABC wouldn't let my father cover my games because of a so-called "conflict of interest," but I always talked to him on the phone after a game. He was concerned about me after I got hurt in the loss to Northwestern, and he celebrated with me after the big win over Indiana. Sometimes he had advice for me, which I listened to. Even though he couldn't be there, covering the game, I knew he was there for me in every way that really mattered—and there was always someone from the family there to greet me after a game, either Shay or my father's brother, Bill.

Bob

When I first heard that Dennis Swanson, then president of ABC Sports, had excluded me from covering Wolverine games, I thought it was a mistake. I understood the thinking, of course, but I knew I could cover those games fairly. I had earned the trust of the coaches of the teams we covered, and I knew I could do the job fairly and impartially if given the chance. Besides, I thought the network should hype it, not shy away from it: What is Bob Griese going to say when he's covering his son's games? How is he going to handle it when Brian has a great game or an off game? I thought that would have made great copy in the media, and it would have been great for ratings.

But I could see ABC's point. Even if I did the job well, there could easily be a perception (however mistaken) that I was playing favorites. And of course, there was the opposite possibility, the more likely possibility, that I would bend over backward to be fair to the opponents, and in the process I'd be unfair to Brian and the Wolverines. So that was the decision, and I understood it and I didn't fight it—even though, as a father, I would have given anything to be at my son's games.

It was inevitable and understandable, I guess, that a lot of people would make comparisons between Brian and me. But there was one game during that 1995 season—a game against Penn State—in which he seemed to be making a statement: "I'm not my old man!" In contrast to Super Bowl VIII, where I only threw 7 passes in the whole game, Brian completed 24 of 46 for 323 yards and a TD. That 46-throw performance is the third highest single-game performance in Michigan history. I wish I could have seen it in person.

The "conflict of interest" rule also kept me away from another great Michigan game—a 52-17 win over Minnesota in which Brian completed 4 touchdown passes. He was named Chevrolet's Player of the Game in that one, and I would have given anything to be there. Since I couldn't, I did the next best thing and made sure that a number of our close family friends could be there to cheer for Brian.

Brian

We finished the regular season and went to the Alamo Bowl, where Texas A&M beat us, 22-20. That was a game where I wish we'd had more time to throw the ball, but the Aggies had one of the best defenses in the country. We hit some big plays, but I got my head beaten in.

During my last three years at Michigan, Scott Dreisbach and I were in a seesaw competition for the starting quarterback position. It was a friendly competition, and Scott and I maintained our friendship through-out our time on the team. Sportswriters talked about a "quarterback con-troversy" at Michigan, but there was never any controversy—just a healthy, friendly competition.

Scott and I had the same goal: to get our team to the Rose Bowl. I wasn't in it for Brian Griese, and Scott wasn't in it for Scott Dreisbach. We were both in it to do what was best for the team. It was about winning, not about ego. I was glad I got the chance to play in '95. It's hard standing on the sidelines with your helmet in your hand. I was there to play, and after two years on the bench, I finally got my chance.

Every Saturday, there was a Mass before the game. There were about a dozen Catholics on the team, and we'd go to Mass before the pregame activities. Every Saturday morning, I would pray, and I'd talk to my mother, and that helped me remember what was important. I always thought about how proud she would be, whether we won or lost, whether I did well or not. Praying and talking to my mother kept me calm and centered. Even in the big games, I never felt a lot of pressure and I was rarely nervous on game day, mainly because I remembered what was really important.

Bob

That's the key to Brian's play—that ability to stay poised and unpressured. That's where poise in the pocket comes from. Brian never lost his composure if he threw an interception or if the first series or the first quarter didn't go well for him. If something wasn't there for him, he'd try something else. He'd let things develop. He never panicked or made desperation plays just to make something happen. He kept his wits about him, and he used his intelligence. Brian is a very intelligent quarterback, a thinking man's quarterback. That's his strength. He is a leader, he plays within the offense, and he makes good decisions.

Brian

People have asked me where the confidence to play quarterback comes from—especially when you're thrown into a situation as a backup. Obviously, there's a lot of pressure in a situation like that. A lot of people are depending on you. The guys on the team are looking to you for leadership. And the fans in the stands are looking for you to make plays and make something happen.

A lot of guys get rattled under that kind of pressure. But some guys feed on it. I can't answer for anybody else, but the way I handle it is like this: I say to myself, *All right, there's pressure here. Everybody's waiting for me to do something—but after all, it's just a game*. I always play the game best when I take that kind of attitude. I don't live and die by any one game. I just tell myself, *I'm gonna go out and do my best, and if it's good enough, it's good enough. If it's not, I'll live to fight another day.*

Brian couldn't have had a better coach than Lloyd Carr. He was the perfect match for Brian's temperament—steady, poised, a thinking man's coach. Plus he is just a wonderful guy—loyal and dependable.

I remember one incident the first year Brian played as a starter, there was a sportswriter for the *Detroit Free Press* who wrote a column about one of Brian's games. The guy just tore into Brian and said, "The kid is downright awful," or words to that effect. Well, maybe Brian didn't play well in some of his early games—but he was a backup quarterback and he was there to learn the game. Is that any kind of criticism to print in a newspaper?

Shortly after that column appeared, I was in Ann Arbor and I went to a Michigan press conference that Lloyd Carr held, and this same sportswriter stood up and asked a question. And Lloyd just ripped him up one side and down the other.

"Let me tell you something," he said. "The kids in this football program aren't pros earning a million bucks a year. They're playing for nothing. They're here because they want to be here. They are trying to get a good education while working overtime to play in this football program, and it's a very tough program. How you can sit there and write in your newspaper that somebody's kid is 'downright awful' is just beyond me!"

Oh, it was great! But that's the kind of guy Lloyd Carr is. When I saw the way he stuck up for Brian, I became Lloyd Carr's biggest fan.

—SHAY WHITNEY GRIESE

"If you have the name Griese, the expectations are going to be there," Michigan coach Lloyd Carr said. "And at Michigan, the coaches and the players understand the expectations. You aren't going to please some people no matter what you do." . . . Carr is bothered when fans criticize the quarterback who rarely makes mistakes.

—GANNETT NEWS SERVICE, FRIDAY, NOVEMBER 10, 1995

Bob

Brian, what about the media? During your time at Michigan, you took your share of flak from the newspaper and broadcast pundits. Did those guys ever get under your skin?

Brian

No. I never worried much about the things they said and wrote. That's probably because I grew up around you and all the media guys you work with. I spent all those years hanging out around the broadcast booth and the TV cameras, so I was never very impressed with the media. I've known guys who haven't had a lot of exposure to the media, and they were intimidated by that stuff. But that was never a problem for me.

The media are there because of the athletes who play the game, not the other way around. Teddy Roosevelt once said, "It is not the critic who counts . . . [but] the man who is actually in the arena, whose face is marred by dust and sweat and blood." I'm good if I play well—not because the media says I'm good. So I never worry about the media or the critics. I never let their assessments affect my thinking about myself or my performance.

A backup quarterback is in a kind of catch-22 situation. You get thrown into a game and you've got to perform like a starter. But the only way you learn how to do that is through experience, and that's one thing a backup rarely has. You get thrown in there and you hope you don't make any mistakes until you can sense the flow and pace of the game. There's a flow to every game, and as a quarterback you've got to find out what that is.

My first year, I was thrown in there and I didn't know exactly what I was doing. I made a lot of mistakes and I didn't look good out there. We went 5 and 4 in the games I started, but I gained some experience in the process. The next year, 1996, I didn't play much, but I still knew what was going on in the game. I knew what the quarterback should and shouldn't do, and that's what made that year so frustrating. I'd be on the sidelines, and I'd watch the ball being snapped. I'd see the defensive set, I knew what was going on and where the ball should go—but the ball would go somewhere else. We'd lose yardage or get picked off or something, and that was frustrating for me. I'd look in the faces of those seniors who were out there busting their tails, trying to get it done—and I couldn't do anything about it from the sidelines.

Throughout my Michigan career, I always tried to remember the fortunate position I was in—first, for just being there at a great school with great traditions; second, for being a good student with prospects for a good future, whether or not football would be a part of that future; and third, for the privilege of being a quarterback on the football team. I always tried to focus on the things in my everyday life that would remind me of how fortunate I was, and not get wrapped up in the urgencies of the moment— "Oh, man! I've gotta study for this test, and I've gotta read those chapters, and I've gotta study Iowa's film, and I've gotta look at the defensive line and break down the linebackers' strengths and weaknesses, and I've gotta go over the coverages"— You can go crazy with all the pressure. I decided that instead of getting so caught up in those things, I would try to do the routine things that would let me lead a normal life and keep my perspective.

I was able to do that pretty well during 1995. But there was a moment in the spring of 1996 when I lost sight of all that. I screwed up—and it cost me.

Michigan junior quarterback Brian Griese, suspended indefinitely from the football team, stood mute at his Washtenaw County Courthouse arraignment Tuesday on the charge of malicious destruction of property . . .

Coach Lloyd Carr has not publicly commented on the situation, but he did release a joint statement with athletic director Joe Roberson.

"I have met with Brian and with the team," he said in the statement. "You have to realize that an incident such as this has an effect on the entire program, not just on one individual . . . We have indefinitely suspended Brian Griese."

—GANNETT NEWS SERVICE, TUESDAY, APRIL 9, 1996

Brian

It was Easter break, and my friend Scott Loeffler and I got some friends together for Easter dinner. I cooked the turkey, and it took a while to cook—maybe four hours or so—and I'd been drinking some wine while it was cooking. It wasn't a wild party or anything—just a quiet dinner party with friends who weren't able to get home for Easter because of spring practice.

After dinner, Scott and I went out to a sports bar in Ann Arbor. I had a little more to drink while I was there, and I started messing around with some of the people who were playing pool in the bar. The manager came over and kicked me out of the bar, which he should have, because I was out of line.

So they pushed me out the door, but my friend Scott was still inside and I didn't have a ride home. I was out on the sidewalk by myself, trying to figure out how to get Scott to come outside and give me a ride home. I went to the door and said, "Look, I don't want to make any trouble. I just want to get my friend."

"Forget it," said the bouncer, "I'm not letting you in."

"Well, at least get on the P.A. and call my friend for me," I said.

"Okay," the guy grudgingly replied. He made the announcement, but when Scott heard it, he thought it was a joke and he didn't come. So I went back out on the sidewalk and stood around for about half an hour. The bouncer kept watching me, and I could tell he didn't like me hanging around. At the same time, I was getting madder and madder because I had no place to go.

So finally Scott came out and he said, "Hey, Brian—I didn't know you were still out here! I thought you got a ride home!"

The bouncer looked at the two of us and said to Scott, "Are you with this guy?"

Scott said, "Yeah."

Well, that was all the bouncer needed to hear. He gave Scott a shove out the door, and Scott went down on the pavement and hit his shoulder. Scott was another backup quarterback for the Wolverines, and he'd just had surgery on that shoulder. He jumped up, madder than anything, and he wanted to fight. Well, I didn't want to fight anybody, so I grabbed Scott and said, "Let's go, let's go."

I was mad, too—mad because I had been thrown out, mad because I'd had to wait half an hour on the sidewalk, and mad because of the way the guy threw Scott on the sidewalk for no reason other than that he was with me. I knew if I got into a fight, it would mean trouble for me, but as mad as I was, I wanted to do something. Just then, I had a crazy impulse—and I turned around and kicked the big plate-glass window in the front of the bar. The window just shattered.

Instantly, I thought, *Why did I have to go and do that?* I had pulled Scott away because I didn't want trouble. I had avoided getting into a fight because I didn't want trouble. And then, on a stupid impulse, I had kicked in a window.

And now I was in trouble.

I turned around to walk away—and right across the street was a police car. The cop inside was looking right at me. I don't know when he arrived, but he was sitting right there, watching as I kicked the window in. Well, there was nothing to do but stand there while the cop walked over and put the handcuffs on me. Then he led me to the car, and we were off.

All of which is a perfect illustration of why drinking is stupid. Alcohol dulls your ability to see the consequences that are right in front of your face. Sober, I never would have kicked that window. I wouldn't have done half the things I did that night. It was really dumb.

I spent the night in jail, and I called Dad the next day—I wanted to get to him before it hit the newspapers, but I didn't dare call him from jail. He answered the phone, and I said, "Dad, I'm sorry, I really messed up—but I promise you, I'm going to make it right, no matter what it takes." Then I told him what I had done.

Dad didn't say all that much about it. In fact, he didn't really seem angry with me. I almost wished he had been angry—that would have been easier to deal with. The thing that hurt the most was hearing the disappointment in his voice. Having your dad angry with you is one thing; you know he'll get over that. Disappointment, though, lasts a lot longer.

Bob

I didn't see any point in jumping all over him—he was already as sorry as he could be. He had screwed up, and he was accepting the consequences. There wasn't much I could add to that. Besides, it came as such a shock. Brian had never done anything like that before.

I've always told my kids, "I'll stick by you no matter what happens," so I told him, "Okay, we'll talk tomorrow. Find out what's going to happen, and keep me posted." I was disappointed, but the bottom line was that he had broken a window. He wasn't hurt, and neither was anybody else. When the police came, he didn't run and he didn't smart off to them. He hadn't been involved with drugs, and he didn't beat up anybody. He had messed up, but it could have been worse.

Brian

One of the first things I thought of was the fact that what I had done was going to affect a lot of people—my dad, my family, my coach, my teammates, my school. When you do something like that, you don't even think of the consequences to yourself, much less others—but soon you start to realize all the other effects of a decision like that. The story went out on the newswires, and they carried it on ESPN—it was a big, public mess. My girlfriend was in Spain at the time, and she even heard about it over there on CNN.

Most of all, you think of what you've done to the family name. You only have one family name, and soon all the people who share that name—your father, brothers, grandmother, aunts, uncles—are having to answer questions like, "Hey, what happened to Brian? I always thought he was such a good kid." I could deal with the consequences of my own actions. I had that coming. It was only natural that people would question my character and judgment after something like that. But I didn't want my family, my friends, and my school to go through all this pain and embarrassment because of something I had done.

The first couple of months after the incident, I put up with a lot of jokes. Whenever I threw a ball, someone would say, "Don't throw it through a window!" I had to hear the same dumb jokes over and over again—and every time someone made that joke, he thought he was the first to think of it. But I couldn't get mad at the jokes. I had done this to myself.

> I think the way Brian handled the incident earned everyone's respect. He didn't hide. He didn't make excuses. He took everything that came with it.
>
> —MICHIGAN COACH LLOYD CARR

Bob

The one thing that made me mad about this thing was when they charged Brian with a felony. What he did was wrong, and he was willing to take his lumps. But they had this quirky law that if you destroy private property valued at more than $100, you can be charged with a felony (the window would cost more than $500 to replace). This law dated back to 1936, when $100 was a lot of money, and even though it was rarely enforced for something like breaking a window, it was still on the books. Normally, an offense like this would have been a misdemeanor, punishable by a fine and a suspended sentence—especially with a first offense. But the assistant prosecutor was under pressure to make an example of Brian because of previous incidents involving athletes from the university.

Brian had to pay for what he did, and I wanted him to pay the full consequences. He was suspended from the football team, and Coach Carr was right to do that. It was a major public embarrassment for Brian, and it was all over the newspapers and the TV. But it wasn't a felony.

So I was there for him, I supported him, and I told him, "Keep doing what you have to do to make this right. One day, you'll put it behind you."

Brian

I was ready to plead guilty and make it right—but I wanted to plead guilty to the right charge, not a felony. I didn't rob anybody or hit anybody over the head. I kicked in a window; I wanted to plead guilty to kicking in a window. Eventually, we got it sorted out with the prosecutor's office. I paid a fine, made restitution, and got probation.

I made up my mind that I was going to see this thing through without complaining, because over the years I've seen a lot of athletes who do something wrong—they get caught with cocaine, or they are stopped for drunk driving and refuse a breath test, or they beat up their wife or girlfriend. They blame other people or buy their way out of it and avoid responsibility for their actions. People like that don't give themselves a chance to learn from the experience, grow from it, and become a better person. I decided a long time ago that I would never be that kind of athlete.

The next hardest thing I had to deal with, after telling my dad about it, was facing my coach. Like Dad, Coach Carr was disappointed—and that was hard, because I had so much respect for him. Coach Carr had to be tough in order to maintain discipline on the team. So he told me I was suspended from spring and summer practices—I couldn't work out with the team during my suspension. It was certainly fair, and I accepted it.

At that point, I made a commitment to reestablish myself and keep my nose clean. I was going to do everything the right way from then on. I was going to take this wrong I had done, and I was going to put it right. It's amazing when you think about it—it took me only a fraction of a second to kick in that window and make a mess of things—but it took me a whole year and a lot of hard work to recover from what I had done and to put things right again.

Mentally, I had to put it behind me. I decided I wasn't going to focus on something I did in the past. I was going to focus on the future. I was going to earn back the trust of my coach and my teammates. That wasn't easy, because I was no longer able to work out with them. I was barred from going down to the athletic complex and working with the team for the duration of my suspension.

But I made up my mind that I was going to work harder than ever to get myself in shape and get ready to play. I made a decision to do everything my teammates were doing, so I would still feel a part of the team. I built myself a training regimen that was exactly like training with the team. My training schedule was always exactly one day behind the team's, because I would ask the guys what they did, and I would do the same thing the next day. The day after they ran the track in the athletic complex, I was running the track in the intramural building. The day after they ran the stadium stairs, I ran them. I kept up with my weight training and conditioning.

Eventually, my suspension ended, I was back with the team, and I was a stronger person for having dealt with that situation. But I was still a backup quarterback, sitting on the bench.

Bob

This is when I had those long-distance talks with Brian, when he was chomping at the bit, wanting for a chance to play. Week after week, I'd tell him, "Be patient, your time is gonna come—"

Brian

And I'd say, "Yeah, yeah, yeah—but when? I've been pacing these sidelines for four years—"

Bob

And I'd say, "I know, I know, I know. But you can't let down. You have to be ready to play in every game, because you never know when your chance is gonna come." And I was right, because on Saturday, November 23, in Columbus, Ohio, Brian's chance finally came.

10

FROM SETBACK TO COMEBACK

As it will for most American households, Thursday's holiday meal at the home of ABC college football analyst Bob Griese will be a chance for the family to give thanks for all the good things that have happened since this time last year.

But the elder Griese, a Hall of Fame quarterback for the Miami Dolphins, claims to be a little less thankful for the conduct of his son Brian, a Michigan quarterback who came off the bench Saturday to lead the Wolverines to an upset road win over Ohio State.

The Michigan victory spoiled the prospect of having two unbeaten teams, the Buckeyes and Arizona State, meet in the Rose Bowl, which—surprise, surprise—will be seen on ABC on New Year's Day.

"When I see the kid, I'm going to kick his butt. He just ruined the Rose Bowl and he might have cost the network a lot of money. Why couldn't he have beaten somebody else?" said Griese, jokingly.

—LOS ANGELES TIMES, THURSDAY, NOVEMBER 28, 1996

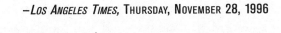

Dreisbach left after a bell-ringing hit. The son trotted onto the field. The father didn't flinch. He reported that news as he would have reported any news. He didn't say that his son was playing. He said that Brian Griese was now at quarterback. The son was a neutral X playing against a team of neutral O's.

The father broadcast with remarkable detachment that day . . . At one point the father even said that the Buckeyes had to get after the quarterback, send some blitzers, confuse him. I'm telling them to attack my son, the father thought later, as he watched the tape of the game. I can't believe it.

Not until the final moments, with a Michigan victory assured, did the detachment disappear from the ABC booth. Griese remembers Jackson, his partner for a decade, finally saying, "Whoa, Nellie, I guess there are going to be some good stories to tell around the dinner table in the Griese household this Christmas."

—Sports Illustrated, Monday, October 13, 1997

Bob

The 1996 season brought a welcome change. Tony Tortorici came aboard as ABC's coordinating producer of college football coverage, and he reversed the policy that kept me from covering Michigan games. "The possibility of a conflict of interest is a valid concern," he said, "but maybe we take ourselves too seriously. Let's just loosen up and see what happens. A situation like this doesn't come along very often—let's take advantage of it." That change in policy came just in time for me to be there for one of the best games in college football—and certainly one of the best games of Brian's career.

Brian

Ranked twenty-first in the nation, we went to Columbus to play the second-ranked, unbeaten Ohio State Buckeyes, who were rolling their way to the Rose Bowl and a national title. We had lost our previous two games, and had a record of 8 and 3 (5 and 3 in the Big Ten). The Buckeyes had won 10 straight games. The Michigan-Ohio State game would be our season finale.

I started that game where I had started every game that season—on the bench. But late in the second quarter, Scott went out of the game with a concussion. At that point, we were down 9-0, thanks to three field goals by the Buckeyes' Josh Jackson. I came into the game with only enough time left in the first half to run the two-minute drill—but that can be a pretty important two minutes for a backup quarterback.

When you're up against a tough defense, it's important that you come off the bench and not make any mistakes. This was our last game of the season, and I hadn't played a snap all season, so those two minutes got me in the game, got the butterflies out, and scuffed up my pants a bit. That's important, because a quarterback needs to get a feel for the game and what the defense is up to. I threw a few passes and moved the ball a bit before intermission, and when I came out for the second half, I could say to myself, *All right, I've already been out here, I know what's going on. Let's play.*

Bob

When Brian came into that game, I thought, *It's about time.* I had seen him over there warming up, and the other guy was having problems getting it done. I'm a big believer in using more than one quarterback, especially in college games. In the pros, where you've got a guy like Dan Marino or John Elway established, that's one thing. But in college, I think it's good to change it up, use more running backs, more receivers, more tight ends, and two quarterbacks—at least early in the season.

I'm not saying a coach should mix it up on every series or every other play like Steve Spurrier of the Florida Gators sometimes does. But I think it's healthy to change it up after a few series. A change may help the guy who's in there. You get him out for a couple of plays, then let him look at the game from the sidelines while you send somebody else in to see what he can do. The game looks different from the sidelines than from the trenches, and I think it can improve a quarterback's overall perspective to stand back for a few plays and get the big picture.

So when Brian went into the game, I thought, *Well, this is an opportunity for him to do something*—and early in the third quarter, he did.

> Brian came to me in the locker room and said, "Coach, they're playing a lot of man-to-man coverage. Let me throw the slant." He said if we'd call it, it would be a big play. He had a vision that he was going to throw a slant and the guy was going to run in for a touchdown. On the second play of the second half, he threw a slant and Tai Streets went 69 yards for a touchdown. Then Brian pointed up to the coaches' box as if to say, "I told you so!"
>
> —MICHIGAN ASSISTANT HEAD COACH FRED JACKSON

Brian

We were one minute into the third quarter. I really had nothing to lose, the team had nothing to lose, and we needed something, because we hadn't gotten anything done in that game. I hit Tai Streets on a short slant, and he took it in for a touchdown. Instead of 9-0, it was 9-7, and that really fired us up. It gave us momentum. Even though they still led, we had done something the Buckeyes hadn't—we had scored a touchdown. Suddenly, it was a 2-point game. At that point, we knew that this game was ours if we wanted it bad enough.

But at the same time I'm down on the field trying to win a ballgame, Dad's up in the ABC booth, making like a cheerleader for the Buckeyes.

Bob

What are you talking about? I called that game right down the middle.

Brian

I watched the tape of that game, remember? I heard you say, "Ohio State had better get after that quarterback." Dad, that quarterback was *me*!

Bob

That's exactly what I mean when I say I was calling that game right down the middle. That was the first game of yours I ever called, and I wasn't going to have anybody saying I was playing favorites because my kid was in the game.

The way I stay neutral is that I just naturally tend to root for the offense because I identify with them; that's my side of the ball. And that's why I'm able to be fair in covering Brian's games—each team is on offense about half the time, and I can always get behind the offense, no matter whose offense it is.

Brian

But when you said, "The Buckeyes had better get after that quarter-back," you weren't rooting for the offense.

Bob

Don't be too sure. Maybe I said that because I knew what a threat that particular quarterback could be.

Brian

Nice try, Dad.

Fact is, people were more worried that my dad would be too supportive of Michigan—but he was actually more critical of Michigan. I don't think he was really prepared for me to come into that game. I had been on the bench all season, and I think he just figured I wouldn't see any action against Ohio State. He tried to prepare himself for the possibility that I would play, but when I actually came into that game, he was like, *Oh boy! Now everybody's gonna be scrutinizing everything I say, so I'd better not say anything favorable to Brian and Michigan.*

Bob

Hey, I was prepared to be fair! Problem was, nobody else was prepared for me to be fair. The moment you came into that game, everybody was asking one another, "Oh, no! What's Bob Griese gonna do now? What's he gonna say? How's he gonna be objective when his own kid is in the game?"

Brian

Objective! Here's an example of how objective you were: I threw that touchdown pass to Tai Streets. Remember what you said after that pass?

Bob

I said, "Michigan needed a big play—and Tai Streets stepped up for them."

Brian

Who stepped up for them?

Bob

Hey, I told you a long time ago that you would never get a fair shake with me in the booth, and I stuck to my word.

Brian

You sure did!

But seriously, it was fine with me. I was just glad my father could be at my games. And every sports reporter who commented on that game, from *Sports Illustrated* to ESPN, agreed that he really did call it without a hint of bias.

Bob

I'll admit that there were a couple of times during that Ohio State game when I allowed myself to think like a father. I'd catch myself doing that and I'd think, *Boy, I'd better jump back and stay on the fence!* I didn't let myself do that very much, because I didn't want it to come out in the broadcast. But after the game was over, and we'd put Brian on the hookup and talked to him on-camera, well, that was different. That was okay. I could relax and be a proud papa again.

> A lot of people are amazed at how cool Bob and Brian are under pressure. They step into a tough situation, like Brian stepping into that Ohio State game at the end of the

season, with a 9-point deficit—and they never get rattled, they never get rushed, they never panic. They just patiently stay with it until they turn things around in their favor.

When I married into this family, one of the first things I observed was that these guys get stronger when the chips are down. I don't just mean Bob and Brian, but Brian's brothers, Scott and Jeff, as well. They're all like that. Adversity makes them stronger. You see it when they are playing football or golf, and you see it in the way they respond to life.

These four guys took a big emotional hit when Judi died. They were sad and hurting when they lost her, and that's only right—you should be sad and hurt in a time like that. It's tragic when anyone dies, and especially when a wife and mother dies so young. But that loss didn't defeat these guys. They got stronger.

I play golf with Bob and the boys, and I see this special quality they have when we're on the golf course. When I've got a six-foot putt, I walk over to it and I talk myself into every way of missing it. But they talk themselves into every way of making it.

You come up to a hole where there's water in front of the green and bunkers on each side and an elevated green, and you don't dare hit it too long or too short, and you'd better not hook or slice or you're dead. I look at that hole and I freak out—I'll never make this shot! Bob and Brian consider that a fun challenge. I would psych myself out, but those guys never psych themselves out because they don't fear anything. They are just levelheaded people, level and steady.

Bob and his three boys are different from you and me. They have a completely different mentality. When they are losing, all they can think about is winning. And they make it happen. They are different.

Where does that mindset come from? Where do you get that kind of poise when the pass rush is coming at you? You go into the half, and you are down by a couple of touchdowns, and what do you do? A lot of people are just defeated at that point. But Bob and his boys just battle back and win. They don't get scared. They don't get rattled. Nothing intimidates them.

I once heard an illustration that makes the point. You take a two-by-four and lay it down on the sidewalk, and it's easy to walk back and forth balanced on that board. A child could do it. But put that same board across a gap between two ten-story buildings and it becomes a whole different situation for most people. Ask someone to walk that board and they'll say, "No way!"

But what's changed? It's still the same board, just as long and just as wide as it was when it was on the sidewalk. The only difference is what's going on in your mind.

But for Bob and Brian, it doesn't make any difference whether the board is ten stories up or just sitting on the sidewalk. They wouldn't be intimidated by it.

People ask me, "Is it genetic?" I don't know, but I do know that all three boys have the same confidence as their dad. Brian's probably the most like that, maybe because he spent the most time with his dad, because they were alone together for so long. I don't know if you can breed confidence, but I think you can teach it by a combination of words and example. I think Brian and the other boys just absorbed it from Bob because Bob was such a good father, and he invested so much of himself in them.

—Shay Whitney Griese

Brian, you looked really cool and confident coming off the bench in the Ohio State game. Did you feel as calm as you looked?

Brian

Yeah, I did. Once I got on the field and sized up the situation, I knew we could turn things around. The Ohio State defense was tough, but kind of overanxious, you know? They were thinking, *This guy's just a backup quarterback. We're gonna chew him up and spit him out.* I mean, they would have just loved to get in there and bury me. So I thought, *Fine, let's have some fun with this.*

Anytime a defensive lineman or a linebacker blitzes and comes free, he's so excited he's finally gonna get a sack, and he wants to hit you so hard he can taste it. It's kind of like the way my brother Jeff plays golf—he wants to hit the ball so hard that sometimes he just wiffs. It's so funny when these defensive guys come free, and they're coming at you so fast that any slight movement you make, man, they're going right by you. And it makes them look terrible.

And as long as you can keep your head about you and stay calm, you can have fun with it. You say to yourself, *All right, I see him coming this way, and when he gets close enough, I'm just gonna take a step forward or to the side*—and whoosh! There he goes like a big freight train, right past you. And it's funny.

Bob

Did you ever say anything to those linemen or linebackers when they sacked you or tackled you?

Brian

Not when they sacked me—but when they missed me, I'd say, "You can't be so excited when you get back here, man. You've got to learn to lay back, man, 'cause you'll never get me that way."

Bob

You didn't say that to those guys!

Brian

Against Ohio State? Sure, I said that to them.

Bob

What did they say back?

Brian

They'd say, "I'll get you next time, Griese! Next time I'm coming from your back side!" Didn't you ever talk to those guys when you were with the Dolphins?

Bob

Nah, I never used to say anything to the defensive linemen. When they'd come through and fall all over you, they'd be yelling and trying to intimidate you. Some of those guys were real talkers, like Jack Youngblood of the Los Angeles Rams—but I never said anything back.

I didn't want them getting in my head and getting me distracted—and I sure as heck didn't want to say anything back to them that would make them mad. I didn't want to give them any extra motivation to come after me.

Sometimes, if I was feeling real sportsmanlike, I might slap them on the backside and say, "Good play." But not very often. I didn't want to boost their confidence, either.

Brian, that Ohio State game was a big turning point for you, wasn't it?

(**Brian**)

It really was. I think my teammates saw something in me when I came off the bench in the biggest game of our season and we won that game. I had spent the whole season on the sidelines, and they didn't know what to expect. The fact that I came in and we were able to come back and win the game showed them that they could depend on me. At that point, I had the confidence of my teammates, and that's the most important thing for a quarterback to have.

I think it had a lot to do with what I did in the off-season, working out and training, even when I was suspended from the team. After the suspension was over, I was always the first one to every meeting, the first one in conditioning. I wanted everyone to know that I was serious about the team and serious about winning. I would try to get everyone together to do the little things, and I worked hard to make sure my attitude and everyone else's attitudes were right.

You have to win as a team, and if the team doesn't believe in you, then you're just one guy flailing around out there. The quarterback is the guy who says, "I need you to do this, and I need this guy in position here and that guy blocking there." If they don't have confidence that you know what you're doing, then nothing's going to work. That Ohio State game really set up a confidence factor that carried over into the following year— the year we went undefeated, won the Rose Bowl, and took a national championship.

Bob

By the time it was over, the Wolverines had upset the Buckeyes 13-9. Brian completed 8 of 14 for 120 yards, and Michigan's Remy Hamilton sealed the win with a pair of field goals. In the second half of the game, the Buckeyes were outgained 237 to 84 yards, and their six second-half possessions yielded five punts and an interception. In short, the Buckeyes' game was over by halftime. Ohio State still went to the Rose Bowl—but the loss to the Wolverines cost them an undisputed conference title and an undefeated season.

Michigan, meanwhile, went on to play Alabama in the Outback Bowl. The Wolverines narrowly lost that game, 17-14, but Brian played well against a tough Crimson Tide defense, completing 21 of 31 for 287 yards, one touchdown, and one interception.

Brian

In the Outback Bowl against Alabama, I played well but we lost the game. I had a totally different attitude at the end of 1996 from when I started those games in 1995. I went to the Outback Bowl with a kind of "I'll-show-'em" attitude. I played as if it were my last game, as if I had to show everybody that I should have been playing all year. I was really getting some frustrations out in that game. I went out and threw the ball all over the place and tried to make some plays. I wanted to send our seniors out the way I thought they should go out—with a win. It didn't end up that way, but at least I showed people I still had some football left in me, that I hadn't just been sitting on the sideline all season, feeling sorry for myself.

It was a tense, hard-fought game all the way, and we had a 6-3 lead going into the fourth quarter. On one play early in the final quarter, I went back to pass and I saw an Alabama lineman coming at me. I didn't want to take the sack, so I hurried a pass and got hit just as I was releasing the ball. It sort of floated up, and an Alabama linebacker snatched it out of the air and ran it in for a touchdown. At that point, I was kinda thinking that I should have taken the sack.

The Crimson Tide scored again just before the two-minute warning, and we answered back with a scoring drive that consumed only 1:01, plus a 2-point conversion. Down 17-14, we just needed a field goal to send it into overtime—but Alabama recovered the onside kick and ran out the clock. Our season was over.

It was like a prince and princess. Almost.

The athlete scooped the girl out of her wheelchair in his strong arms. They danced and he held her up. She ain't heavy, she's my friend.

There were 200 pairs of eyes in the room and most of them were wet by now. His biceps were burning at the end of the music, the way a cross-country runner's lungs burn going the last 100 yards.

"Let's do this one song at a time," Brian Griese said.

—NANDO.NET NEWS, THURSDAY, JANUARY 1, 1998

Brian

I met Jayne Uber in 1995 during one of my regular Thursday visits at Mott Children's Hospital. Jayne was sixteen at the time, and had just been admitted a day or two before with a spinal cord injury. She had always been very athletic before her injury—she was on her high school ski team and soccer team, and she was an avid horseback rider. But a horse had thrown her, and the fall broke her neck, leaving her paralyzed from the neck down.

I walked into her room, and two of her high school friends were with her. Her friends were actually big Michigan fans and knew who I was, and they were real excited to see me. But Jayne had no idea who I was. To her, I was just another guy who was coming around to cheer her up when she felt like her whole life was over. When I came in to say hello, her attitude was, "Oh, whatever . . ."

I asked the other girls to step out in the hall, and Jayne and I talked for about five minutes. As we talked, something just clicked. Because the injury had happened just a short time before, she was very emotional at that point. I think she was looking for someone outside of her family, outside of her friends, that she could relate to.

She ended up being in the hospital a couple of months, just going through rehab and trying to survive. I would visit her every Thursday, and I began to feel a real bond with her. Even though what she was going through and what I went through when I lost my mother were very different tragedies, I think we both sensed some common ground. When I lost my mother, I was faced with a totally new situation, and I was going to have to grow up a lot faster than a twelve-year-old was supposed to. Now Jayne, at sixteen, had lost the use of her body, and she faced a totally new situation, and would have to grow up fast, too. She'd have to decide how to react to her new situation—whether she would adjust to this loss, accept it, and try to make a new life for herself, or whether she would sink into bitterness and despair.

I tried to help her sort out those feelings and issues—issues of maturing, taking responsibility for her attitude, and accepting her new life. We talked a lot about her experiences, her feelings, her fears. And we talked about my own losses, even the trouble I got into at the sports bar, and the isolation I felt as a consequence of a poor choice I had made.

One of the toughest things Jayne had to deal with was the loneliness of her struggle. She had parents who loved her, friends who visited her, hospital staff who helped her and consoled her—but the reality was that she was going to have to deal with this injury all by herself. Other people could come and visit and talk with her and sympathize, but afterward they could get up and walk out of that room. Jayne couldn't—and she never would. This was the way her life was going to be, and it was only natural that she had a lot of trouble dealing with that.

So when she and I would talk, I couldn't pretend that I or anyone else could help her walk again. I was just there to be a friend to her, to listen to her, and to share my own experiences, which, I hoped, might give her some idea of how she could react to her new life.

I continued to visit her while she was in the hospital. If she was in therapy when I came, I'd leave her a note. I remember going there one Halloween night with Scott Loeffler. It was her birthday, and I took a present to her. It was after visiting hours, so we had to sneak past the nurses' station. That night, Jayne and I talked for about two hours. After she was discharged, I'd sometimes go by her house and visit her there.

So Jayne and I got to be good friends over the next couple of years. And in May 1997, around the same time I was set to graduate from Michigan, she called me on the phone with a request that really blew me away: She asked me to take her to the senior prom at Pinckney High. "You don't have to answer right away," she said, "and I'll understand if you say no."

"Well, let me think about it, okay?" I replied. "I'll call you back."

I talked it over with my roommate, Scott Loeffler. Scott was recruited to Michigan the same year I came, and he and I were bitter rivals our first few years on the team, but in our last couple of years at Michigan, we had become good friends. Scott had been really involved in the hospital visits, and he knew all about Jayne's situation. At first, I didn't think I should take Jayne to the prom, because I didn't want to create a situation where people would talk to Jayne only because I was there. I wanted people to talk to Jayne because she's a terrific person, period—and I thought my presence there might be a distraction.

But Scott said, "Just do it. This will be a night she remembers the rest of her life." He convinced me, so I called her back and said, "If your offer's still open, let's go."

Getting Jayne to the prom was a production. Her family had just gotten a big custom van that could accommodate a wheelchair. In the same van, we took five of her girlfriends. She had already promised to take them and she didn't want to leave them out, so I said, "No problem, I'll take all of you." So I drove the van and we all went to the prom.

On the way, Jayne kept saying, "I want to dance, but how are we going to do it?" She was really nervous about it. The last two years of therapy had helped her regain some limited mobility in her arms, but she was totally paralyzed from the waist down, and mostly paralyzed from the neck down. I didn't know, either, but I said, "We'll think of something."

After a while, a slow song came on—it was "Lady in Red"—and Jayne looked at me and said, "I love this song." Well, I knew this was the song, and it was time for us to go out and dance. I still didn't know how we were going to do it, but I went over and lifted her out of her wheelchair. I took her out on the dance floor, and she put her arms around my neck. I just cradled her and held her, and we moved around the floor. I looked at Jayne and her eyes were glistening, and all around us people were watching out of the corner of their eyes and smiling. She had a lot of friends, and they were happy for her. We danced three or four times that night.

That was quite an emotional event for Jayne and for me. I was happy that I could do that for a friend—a friend who had done so much for me. Jayne helped me put things in perspective. She showed me I should never take anything for granted in life.

Jayne Uber is going through the toughest battle anyone could ever face. She's a champion, she's a fighter, she's the toughest competitor I've ever met. If anyone can claim the title "undefeated," it's Jayne Uber. To take the kind of hit she took and to come back determined to remain active, determined to go to her high school prom—her spirit defines what it means to be undefeated by the battles of life.

Jayne, if you're reading this, I want you to know that you're someone special. You've inspired me and a lot of other people.

11

THE MIRACLE SEASON

This time, everything went right for Griese. He won the starting job back from Dreisbach; Michigan roared to an undefeated season and a No. 1 spot in the rankings . . .

It's incredible, in retrospect, how close Brian Griese came to not being the star quarterback on Michigan's undefeated and No. 1-ranked Rose Bowl team; how close he came to chucking this once-in-a-lifetime moment away.

—GANNETT NEWS SERVICE, TUESDAY, DECEMBER 30, 1997

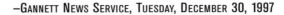

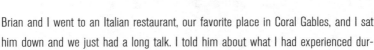

Brian and I went to an Italian restaurant, our favorite place in Coral Gables, and I sat him down and we just had a long talk. I told him about what I had experienced during the couple of years I'd been out of school and working in the real world. I'm a banker, and I like it, but working in a bank is not like playing in the Rose Bowl.

I said, "Brian, there's no rush for you to get into the real world. You've got another year of eligibility at Michigan. Use it. Enjoy it. Play football. Take another year and see what happens. You'd be crazy to pass that up."

We all knew that Brian had real talent, maybe enough talent to get into the NFL. I thought he could spend a couple of years as a backup quarterback, and even go on from there. For him to just graduate and join the workforce, to miss out on a chance at the Rose Bowl, and a career with the Broncos—that would have been such a waste. He came close to throwing it all away.

—JEFF GRIESE

```
  Brian
```

For weeks, people had been telling me, "Brian, you ought to go back to Michigan for another year." I mean, everybody was telling me that. My dad was telling me that. My brothers were telling me that. People who didn't even know me were telling me that.

One night, Dad, Shay, Jeff, and I went out to Abracci's, a restaurant in Coral Gables. We sat down for dinner, and Loris, our waiter, came over. The first thing he said to me was, "Brian, you ought to go back to school and play football another year." Even the waiter was trying to decide my future!

```
  Bob
```

Brian graduated in May of 1997 with a B.A. in environmental policy, but because he had redshirted his freshman year, he still had a year of football eligibility left. Brian was discouraged about spending most of the previous season on the bench, and he didn't want to go through another year of frustration at Michigan—he was ready to begin his postgrad work in international affairs at George Washington University.

I tried to persuade him to stay at Michigan. "You can always go to grad school or get a job," I said. "If you pass up this year and Michigan goes to the Rose Bowl, you'll be kicking yourself for the rest of your life." I don't know if he was listening to me. I sure didn't seem to be getting through to him. I guess he had to hear it from someone who was more of a peer—his brother Jeff.

```
  Brian
```

I valued Jeff's opinion because he'd played college football, and he'd graduated and gone out into the workforce. He'd been there. He told me, "I made a decision to give up football, and for me it was the right thing to do. But that's not for you, Brian. You've got the rest of your life to start working, if that's what you want. But you don't have the rest of your life to go back to college and play football and maybe go to the Rose Bowl. You've only got right now, this year, and when it's over, it's over."

That's almost exactly what Dad had told me. But somehow when Jeff said it, it made more sense.

At that point, leaving school would have been the end of my football career. I had only played in two games—a win and a loss—during 1996. And though I had played pretty well in those two games, I knew the NFL scouts weren't going to be beating down my door. So if I left school, that would mean the end of my football career—period, finis, end of story.

To a large degree, it was the frustration of the 1996 season, my sideline season, that made me want to leave school. I didn't want to go through a fifth year of just sitting on the bench, watching my team lose another four games (we'd had a 4-loss season each of my first four years at Michigan). I didn't want to sit there, feeling miserable while my team lost, thinking I could do something about it if I were in the game.

But ironically, it was that same frustration that tugged at me and made me think real hard about what everyone was telling me. I didn't want my football career to end like that. What if we really *could* go to the Rose Bowl? How could I turn my back on even a long shot at the big game?

The more Jeff talked about it, the more sense he made. Finally, I said, "Jeff, you're right. I'll give Michigan another year, and if it works, it works. If it doesn't, then I'll take my degree and get a job."

I look back on that decision and how close I came to walking away from everything—from the Rose Bowl, the national championship, the NFL, everything—and I think, *Man, life turns on a dime! I can't believe all I would have missed if I hadn't gone back for another year.*

The fact is, my life has turned on a lot of dimes; it has taken a lot of unexpected directions. The choices you make at any given moment can steer the course of your life like a little rudder steering a big ship. I made a really stupid choice when I decided to kick a window in—and it set me back a lot. I made a really smart choice when I listened to Jeff and stayed at Michigan for an extra year—and it was magical.

When you make these choices, you don't really know how it's going to turn out. There are no guarantees in life. I had no guarantee that I'd get the starting quarterback position. For all I knew, Dreisbach would still be the starter and I'd be the backup for another year. I had no guarantee that we would have an undefeated season and go to the Rose Bowl—the odds were way against it.

But I wasn't looking for guarantees. I was just going to enjoy my last year and help my team any way I could. And the result of that choice was beyond anything I could have imagined.

"I found myself calling [Brian] by his last name just to make sure nobody thought I was favoring him," Bob Griese said, laughing.

Griese . . . has spoken to Brian about not taking what he says too personally. "You talk to your son, you're honest with him and say, 'Hey, you've got a job to do and I've got a job to do and I've got to call it the way I see it,'" Griese said. "That's no problem, because I'm fair and objective anyway. This just happens to be my son, and I've told him, 'If you throw a bad pass or an interception, you did that. And if you throw a touchdown, I taught you all you know.'"

Ah, just like a father.

—*THE DETROIT NEWS,* THURSDAY, SEPTEMBER 11, 1997

Brian sent me a University of Michigan sweater with a big block letter M on it. I wear that sweater when I watch his games on TV, and whenever I've worn that sweater, he has won the game. So I'm going to keep wearing that sweater.

—BRIAN'S GRANDMOTHER, MRS. IDA GRIESE

Brian

Going into the 1997 season, I sensed that something was different about the team. Each of my first four years at Michigan, we had been expected to do well, and for whatever reason, we did not do well. We had lost to Northwestern two years in a row. We had lost to Penn State two years in a row. But as we were in training during the summer, getting ready for the '97 season, I sensed a different spark, a different attitude on that team.

The difference was this: Each guy on that team felt a responsibility to the next guy. During the summer practice, each player worked out as hard as he could—not so much for the coaches or the fans, but for the guy next to him on the line. It was the first time I had ever experienced that, and we carried it on throughout the season.

I've heard that it's like that in wartime. Soldiers are shipped to a war zone in some foreign country, slogging through rice paddies or deserts, shooting and getting shot at—and if you ask them what they're fighting for at that moment, they won't say, "I'm fighting for the flag or freedom or the Constitution or the girl back home or Mom and apple pie." They'll say, "I'm fighting for my buddy. I'm fighting for this guy right here. We look out for each other and watch each other's back." It's that intense. I saw that same kind of spirit on our team that year.

Nobody on the team that year was selfish; nobody was a glory hog. Charles Woodson, who got the Heisman and a whole shelf-full of individual awards, never let it go to his head. All season long, he was focused on the team effort, not his own ego, doing things that he probably didn't want to do—but he did them because that's what playing for your teammates is all about.

Bob

In the years before Brian got to Michigan, the Wolverines usually had a good season and went to the Rose Bowl. But Brian's first four years at Michigan, the Wolverines lost four games each year—and no Rose Bowl. I think the frustration the team felt was a lot like the frustration we built up on the Dolphins before we went undefeated. That kind of frustration is a powerful motivator, and can really get guys to pull together toward a goal.

Michigan had a Rose Bowl tradition and belonged in the Rose Bowl. Just as the frustration of losing Super Bowl VI set up the Dolphins for a 32-and-2 run and back-to-back Super Bowl wins, I think the frustration of four 4-loss seasons at Michigan ignited the Wolverines for a storybook run in 1997. When you are frustrated, you take out that frustration on your opponent. You take care of business. That's what Brian and the Wolverines did that year.

Brian

My first year on the team, I sensed complacency there. Michigan had been to the Rose Bowl a dozen times since 1970, including 1987, 1989, 1990, 1992, and 1993. We were the perennial Big Ten champions, and the team's attitude was, *This is our due—it's an annual event. We win the Big Ten and we go to the Rose Bowl.*

When I came to Michigan, I was part of a class of around twenty-five guys. Over the next four years, that class shrank to just five guys. I became tighter with those five guys—Ben Huff, Glen Steele, Zach Adami, Colby Keefer, and Rob Swett—than any other five guys I've ever known. We had been through the wars, and we had endured the criticism of four straight 4-loss seasons. We all felt the same frustration, and we were determined not to let this team fall into that same trap for another season.

We talked about it; we were wide-open about it among ourselves. We didn't talk to the media about it. We didn't even talk that much to the coaches about it. This was between us and the other guys on the team. We had team meetings, and when things weren't going the way they should during the summer practices, we sounded off. We said that every man on that team should take it personally when other guys were slacking off, not showing up for practice, not showing up for conditioning, not caring whether this team won or lost. "Look," we said, "it's obvious who wants to work hard and who doesn't, who wants to win and who doesn't. Everyone on this team has a choice: You can get by, or you can get better. Now what's it gonna be?"

We were looking at the toughest schedule in the nation: Colorado, Baylor, Notre Dame, Indiana, Northwestern, Iowa, Michigan State, Minnesota, Penn State, Wisconsin, and Ohio State. Coach Carr told us to look at it as if we were climbing a mountain. That summer, when we gazed up at that schedule, no one thought, *Hey, let's go undefeated!* How could you ever dream of going undefeated? Impossible. But Coach Carr said, "Just look at each game on that schedule. Is there any game on that schedule that we are not capable of winning? We can beat Ohio State, right? And we can beat Penn State. And we can beat Colorado." At that point, we understood that we would have to take the schedule one game at a time. We would play each individual game on that schedule, and we would focus on that one game.

Then Coach Carr brought in a mountain climber, Lou Kasischke, who was with Jon Krakauer on the ill-fated Everest attempt described in the best-seller *Into Thin Air*. Kasischke described what it was like on the mountain, and that gave the whole team a powerful emotional metaphor to visualize the challenge we faced. Step by step, as we moved farther up the schedule, we were moving higher up that mountain. And the higher you go, the easier it is to get knocked off. By the time we got to Penn State and Ohio State, we were going to be at a very high elevation, breathing rarified air with little oxygen. It would be harder to breathe, harder to play, and there'd be a temptation to quit, to slough off, to turn around and go back. The mountain climber described all these emotions to us, and sure enough, that is exactly the way we felt when we reached that part of the schedule.

He told us, "There's a point where you want to say, 'All right, we've come this far. We now have this window of opportunity to reach the summit.' On Everest, there's a period of only two weeks when the weather is good enough that you can make a charge at the summit. That's the moment that makes or breaks your adventure. Either you take advantage of your opportunity—or you lose it; you turn back." That talk seemed to clarify the issue in the minds of all of us on the team.

I think a lot of guys get into college, and they think, *Hey, it would be fun to play football. That's just one of the things I'll be doing, along with my schoolwork, my girlfriend, my partying, my skiing.* I think that's especially true of freshmen—you get into college, into the football program, and don't really understand what you've gotten yourself into. But the fact is, football is a really tough challenge, and every man on the team needs to give 110 percent—anything less is unacceptable. Faced with that challenge, a lot of our guys made a decision to step up.

Ranked fourteenth in the nation, we opened the season September 13 in Michigan Stadium, hosting Colorado. Our defense completely smothered the Buffaloes' offense, holding Colorado to 224 yards versus our 426.

The Michigan defense collected three sacks and four interceptions, and Colorado's only score was a 52-yard field goal.

Bob

Brian completed 21 of 28 pass attempts, including two touchdowns. Keith Jackson and I were in the ABC broadcast booth for this game, and though it was a laugher rather than a really great contest, it was fun to see Brian so confident and dominant in the game. It was definitely one of those games where I taught him all he knows. Lloyd Carr had shown his team the mountain, and they had firmly set one foot upon the slope. The Colorado Buffaloes fell, 27-3.

Brian

The following week, September 20, we beat the Baylor Bears, 38-3. That win moved us from fourteenth to sixth in the AP and Coaches' polls. Our offense had been underrated by the media. We had started the season with three new guys on our offensive line, and a lot of the pundits were saying that these new linemen wouldn't keep anybody out of our backfield. But our front line handled Colorado, they handled Baylor, and the following week, they handled Notre Dame. The first few games of the season were valuable because they gave our new guys some battle seasoning against some rugged opponents—and it was only going to get rougher as the season went on.

We faltered but survived game three, September 27, against Notre Dame. Leading by only a single touchdown, we got sloppy and fumbled away three consecutive possessions in the fourth quarter. Fortunately, our defense rose to the challenge, and the Fighting Irish weren't able to capitalize on our mistakes. We hung on to win it, 21-14. It was an ugly win—but it was a win.

The following week, October 4, we defeated Indiana in game four. We had run up a 31-0 lead by halftime, and in the second half we sent in the second string and sat on the ball until the clock ran out. In game five, on October 11, we beat the Northwestern Wildcats, 23-6. Our defense was so dominant in that game that Northwestern never got into the end zone.

Bob

At this point, Michigan was 5 and 0. But the next game on the schedule threatened to blow a hole in their undefeated season. A lot of people think game six against Iowa was Brian's worst game of the year. Looking back, I think it may have been one of his best because he got a chance to display something in that game—something called *character*.

Griese looked like a leader, shaking off a terrible first half and playing a phenomenal second. Not many quarterbacks could have pulled that off, and they are the ones who are able to usually end their seasons on New Year's Day.

"That was the toughest game I've ever had to play," Griese said. "But I knew sooner or later I was going to have to play in one of those games. Everything wasn't always going to go right for me."

—*MICHIGAN DAILY* (UNIVERSITY WIRE),
MONDAY, OCTOBER 20, 1997

Brian Griese is one of the greatest leaders I've been around. He shows so much composure and so much confidence as a leader. It definitely rubbed off on the team. He keeps us so relaxed, and one of the prime examples was the Iowa game. He had one of the worst first halfs of his career, and you would never have known by the second half. He was a totally different quarterback in the game, and not too many people could have done that.

—MICHIGAN TAILBACK CLARENCE WILLIAMS

Brian

I threw five interceptions during the entire 1997 season—and I threw three of those picks in the first half of a single game—game six, October 18, against Iowa in Michigan Stadium. Our entire offense struggled in that first half. We had a blocked punt, a fumble, a lot of penalties, and a man down on the field—Chris Howard was carted off to the hospital with a rib injury. But most disastrous of all were my three interceptions, two of which were turned into Iowa touchdowns.

In addition to the two touchdowns they got from interceptions, Iowa flanker Tim Dwight scored a touchdown on a punt return just seconds before the end of the half. It tears your heart out when you're already down and something like that happens. I looked up at the scoreboard, and I experienced a brief moment of panic. At the half, we were down 21-7. *Well,* I thought as I walked into the tunnel, *I got us into the situation and I'm the one who's gonna have to get us out.*

I knew it was time to reach down inside myself and decide whether I was going to lead the team up that mountain—or whether I was going to be just another Michigan quarterback with a 4-loss season. At that moment, I decided to throw out everything that happened in the first half—just put it behind me. I was going to come out and play in the second half the way I knew I could play. That decision was the turning point for me.

In the locker room, Coach Carr sat us all down and asked us a question: "Is there anyone here who doesn't think we can win?" It was a pretty somber moment. Nobody said a word. But I think that question lit a fire in the belly of that team. We were down by two touchdowns. It had taken us two quarters to lose that much ground. We had two quarters left to play. We could gain it back. Every man on that team knew we were still in the game.

Bob didn't call the Iowa game for ABC, but I would have loved to watch his on-air reaction to Brian's three interceptions. I'm sure he would have handled it a lot better than I did. I was in the stands for that game, and I was having fits! There were idiots in the stands behind me yelling, "Aw, Griese, get outta there!" I almost got into a fight with them!

All through halftime I was thinking, *Is Brian going to be able to come back? How is he going to recover from a start like this?* I should have known better.

When Brian came out for the second half, people in the stands started yelling, "Warm up Dreisbach!" I hoped Coach Carr wasn't listening. Fortunately, Coach Carr believed in Brian and stuck with him. And Brian got the job done.

—SHAY WHITNEY GRIESE

> Brian is the toughest guy I've ever coached. What he did in the Iowa game—only one in a million can regroup emotionally to do what he did. He's as tough as they get.
>
> —MICHIGAN QUARTERBACKS COACH STAN PARRISH

Brian

As we came out of the tunnel for the second half, Coach Carr took me aside. "This is why you're here, Brian," he said. "This is your time. This team is depending on you and looking to you for leadership. So have fun out there—but bring us back."

I put a lot of pressure on myself during our first drive of the second half. I knew that it would be our biggest drive, because if we scored at that point, it was only a 7-point game. So we came out swinging. We went right down the field, a 67-yard, eight-play drive. At the end of the drive, I hit Russell Shaw with a 10-yard touchdown pass. After that, I was fine.

On our next drive, with 3:11 left in the third quarter, freshman running back Anthony Thomas dashed for 58 yards to the Iowa 4-yard line. A few plays later, we had a fourth-and-inches situation at the goal line. Coach Carr told me, "Go for it." I took the snap and dived over the top, and the game was tied at 21.

Iowa instantly replied. Tim Dwight returned our kickoff to the Michigan 26, setting up a 38-yard field goal seconds before the end of the third quarter. Again we trailed, 24-21.

We came back to seal the game with a 77-yard, clock-consuming drive—maybe the biggest drive of the season—and we finished with a 2-yard touchdown pass to Jerame Tuman. We had come back, beating Iowa 28-24.

The Michigan defense deserves credit for keeping us in that game. Our guys held Iowa's Tavian Banks—the leading rusher in the nation—to 99 yards on 19 carries (he had previously averaged more than 183 yards a game). Our defense also held Iowa's quarterback, Matt Sherman, to 8 of 21 for 86 yards—and they intercepted him three times. Thanks to our defense, Iowa only gained 7 first downs compared with our 21 first downs.

You've got to give those Iowa defenders credit. They were good. Part of the reason I threw so many picks in that game was that I underestimated those guys. They played all-man coverage, and I didn't give them enough credit in the first half. In the second half, I made sure I accounted for them.

That game was a learning and growing experience for me. I discovered a lot about how you recover from a setback. People always say that when you make a mistake, don't look back, just move on—but that's easier said than done. I've seen it again and again—guys make a mistake, and it messes up their confidence so badly that you don't dare let them near the ball again. When you blow it big-time, you just have to put those things behind you and start fresh. You have to say, "There's nothing I can do about my mistakes now. I just have to go on from here and try to come back."

Bob

I didn't call that game for ABC—and I'm glad I didn't. I'm not sure I could have maintained my composure when he threw those three interceptions. What was important in that game was that Brian maintained *his* composure. Once again, he suffered a setback—and then he patiently, methodically engineered a comeback.

> College football analysts have gone as far as to say Griese, not Woodson, is Michigan's biggest asset. Craig James of CBS said Griese was his selection for All-America quarterback. Gary Danielson, a former Detroit Lions quarterback now with ABC, believes Michigan could have withstood an injury this season to Woodson, but not Griese.
>
> "I think the most valuable player in the Big Ten is Brian Griese," Danielson said. "Brian is not streaky. He makes his team go. He has the rare ability, very much like his dad, to not have to throw a lot to be good. That's a great trait, and a lot of quarterbacks can't do it."
>
> —GANNETT NEWS SERVICE, SATURDAY, DECEMBER 27, 1997

Brian

We had dodged a bullet against Notre Dame, and we had dodged a howitzer against Iowa. We were 6 and 0—still undefeated.

As we moved deeper into the season, we increasingly felt the pressure of an undefeated season. But I think all of us on the team handled it well. We didn't get tense or tight. We didn't stop playing with emotion. Most of all, we didn't stop having fun. Even with the pressure, we had fun.

That's what I tried to do the whole year—just come out and have fun. Because if you're not having fun, you're not winning. A lot of people think it's the other way around—if you win, you have fun. No, the way it works is if you have fun, you give yourself a chance to win. Fun keeps you loose. That's what we did as a team that year—we flew around the field, we had fun, and we won a lot of games.

Game seven, on October 25, was against Michigan State in Spartan Stadium. Michigan versus Michigan State is a big rivalry, and we went out and beat the Spartans 23-7 in front of a hostile Spartan crowd. Our defense played big that day, hauling in six interceptions, forcing State to field three different quarterbacks in a desperate effort to get something going. With that win, we jumped to number four in the AP and Coaches' polls.

Game eight, on November 1, was against Minnesota. Our defense smothered the Golden Gophers' offense, holding Minnesota to only 12 yards passing. We won with a final score of 24-3.

On November 8 we beat Penn State in game nine. Once again, our defense dominated with 5 sacks. On offense, Anthony Thomas, Chris Howard, Jerame Tuman, and Charles Woodson each scored touchdowns, and I had a 40-yard run.

Keith Jackson and I were in the booth for the Penn State game. Keith was calling it live when Brian scrambled up the sideline for that 40-yard run. He said, "Brian Griese scrambles out of the pocket! He's going! He's going! He's still going! The last time he ran that far, his daddy was chasing him with a stick!" The final score was 34-8. After the game, ESPN's Kirk Herbstreit declared, "Michigan football is back!" And he was right.

Brian

For game ten, on November 15, we went to Badger country and played Wisconsin in a snowstorm. The Badgers fought hard, hoping for an upset, but we won that game, 26-16. One of the memorable moments of that game was when Woodson and I reversed roles—*he* completed a 28-yard pass to *me*.

Ohio State, your couch is ready.

Psychoanalysis may be the Buckeyes' ticket now. They have played their football season. Now they face the boogie man.

Michigan is out there waiting. Like Jack the Ripper. No wonder the Buckeyes displayed slight neuroses Saturday, most of them refusing to utter the word. Michigan Who?

—GANNETT NEWS SERVICE, MONDAY, NOVEMBER 24, 1997

Brian

Our final game of the regular season—game eleven of our undefeated season—was the Michigan-Ohio State grudge rematch in Michigan Stadium. We knew the Buckeyes would be gunning for us after what we had done to them the previous year. David Boston, Ohio State's talented but overly talkative wideout, predicted the Buckeyes would beat us by two touchdowns, maybe three.

But on game day, Boston dropped the first two passes thrown his way. When he finally caught one for a touchdown, just barely beating Michigan cornerback Charles Woodson, he drew an unsportsmanlike conduct flag for taunting Woodson and wagging the ball in his face. Woodson, with true Michigan class, ignored Boston like he wasn't even there. I couldn't figure out what Boston thought he was celebrating. While he was taunting Woodson, the Buckeyes were down by two touchdowns.

Ohio State quarterback Stanley Jackson threw only two interceptions all season—and he threw *both* of them in that game. One of those interceptions came on a second and goal from the Michigan 7. Jackson took a three-step drop, then tried to force the ball into the middle of the end zone—but Charles Woodson was right there to intercept it, almost as if he'd been in the Buckeye huddle. "Stanley Jackson threw me a great pass," Woodson said with a wink when the game was over.

Jackson's second interception was snatched by Andre Weathers, who returned it 43 yards for a touchdown, giving us a 20-to-zip lead. The only play in the game that could top Weathers's touchdown-on-turnover was Charles Woodson's touchdown on a 78-yard punt return.

Ohio State used a two-quarterback system, and they brought Joe Germaine in to close the game. Trailing 20-14 with just over a minute and a half remaining, Germaine had the ball at his own 16. He had one last chance to redeem Ohio State's season with a touchdown drive. But he couldn't pull it off. The Buckeyes' last four snaps of the game produced a sack, an incompletion, a pass for 7 yards, and a fourth-down, last-gasp pass attempt that never reached the receiver.

We won. Michigan was going to the Rose Bowl.

Charles Woodson had all but sewn up his Heisman.

And we had clawed our way almost to the top of the mountain. We could see the summit—but we weren't there yet. Not yet. We had an appointment in Pasadena.

When the game was over, I went into the locker room with my teammates. We celebrated and sang "The Victors," but that wasn't enough. I wanted to go back out to the field. The fans were still out there in the stands, celebrating and cheering, and I thought it would be fitting if we celebrated the victory together. So we went back out into the stadium. Though the wintry Michigan sky threatened rain, 106,982 voices cheered from the stands.

At that moment, it really hit me that I had just played my last game in that stadium. I had spent five years of my life at the University of Michigan, and there was a big part of me that didn't want to leave. So I went around the stadium, shaking hands with the fans and savoring the moment.

Keith Jackson and I were sitting outside in the elements in our topcoats, scarves, and Scots-knit tam-o'-shanter hats. We were bantering back and forth on-camera, and even though the game was over, the crowd behind us was still cheering as loudly as if the game were still going on. It was quite a commotion. Then Keith said, "It was an incredible moment for both their lives—the father and the son. A moment, Bob, that you'll never forget, and one the son will never forget."

"I think back to about a year ago," I said. "Brian was frustrated, not getting to play, because he really thought he could help the team if he got a chance to play. He was wondering whether to go back to Michigan, and I said, 'Brian, I think you can help the team. I think you should go. But it's your decision.' And when he decided to go back, he was playing the best football of his career. He played well all year long."

They went to a shot of Brian, and the network had a linkup so we could interview him on-camera. Keith said, "You want to see a face that is full of 'Whoopee!'—well, there it is!" And Keith was right. Brian's face was lit up like a Christmas tree. He had a Michigan cap on his head, and he was holding the earpiece to his ear. Keith said, "Not a bad day! Not a bad season, huh?"

"Not bad at all!" yelled Brian, grinning from ear to ear. "I mean, I've been waiting a long time for this! This team has been waiting a long time for this! And I'm just happy for every senior on this team, because this is the way we wanted to go out!"

I called out, "Hey, Brian!"

"Hey, what's up, Pops?"

"Listen," I said, "this is the twenty-fifth anniversary of our undefeated team, the '72 Dolphins. And now you're going undefeated, too! What's going on here? Are you happy that you went back to Michigan? Tell us what you're feeling right now."

"Unbelievable!" he said. "Everything we talked about when I was deciding whether to come back—I mean, the most important thing to me was coming back to Michigan and having fun playing football. And I'm sure glad I did, because if I'd just stayed home with you, I'd have been a pain in the butt, driving you crazy! But I feel a lot better now that I'm up here!"

"I tell you," said Keith, closing out the interview, "this has been a great day in the life of the father and the son." And there was an even greater day ahead, out in sunny Pasadena.

The 1997 season was a magical year for Brian: an undefeated season; selected All Big Ten Conference; the National Football Foundation and Hall of Fame Scholar-Athlete Award; Big Ten Player of the Week in the Colorado game; ESPN Player of the Week in the Indiana game; ABC Sports/Chevrolet Player of the Game in the Penn State game; the NCAA Today's Top VIII Award; and many other top awards. And coming up: a trip to the Rose Bowl.

Brian completed 193 of 307 passes (62.9 percent) for 2,293 yards, 17 touchdowns, and 6 interceptions. He broke the school's previous record (189 of 296) set by Todd Collins in 1993. And only Collins and Jim Harbaugh have thrown for more yards in a season for Michigan—and Brian accomplished this with the fourth lowest interception percentage in Michigan history (1.95 percent).

Unfortunately, Brian's stellar performance in Michigan also caused a few million bucks' worth of havoc down in his home state of Florida. I'm on the Orange Bowl committee, and we were planning to have a big national championship game in Miami. The previous couple of years, we'd seen national championship games played in the Fiesta Bowl and the Sugar Bowl, and finally it looked like we were going to have a title game in the Orange Bowl.

But in the closing weeks of the college season, a number of things happened that threw a wrench in the championship equation. First, Steve Spurrier's Florida Gators upset then-number two Florida State. Then Brian and the Wolverines beat Ohio State, capping an undefeated season, and ending up number one in both the Associated Press and the ESPN–USA Today polls. As a result, the Rose Bowl became the national championship game, and the Orange Bowl ended up being an entertaining, but not very meaningful, consolation game featuring number two Nebraska and number three Tennessee. Overnight, the Orange Bowl's value to sponsors and advertisers dropped by an estimated $3 million.

Before he went on to the Rose Bowl, Brian came home to Florida for Christmas. He and I went out on the golf course to knock some balls around, and just after we finished the last hole, we heard a buzzing sound. I pointed skyward and said, "Hey, Brian! Look at that!"

Flying over the golf course was a plane pulling a banner behind it. The banner read: CONGRATS TO BRIAN GRIESE—YOU OWE US $3 MILLION! —O.B.C.

Brian's jaw dropped. "O.B.C.?" he asked.

"The Orange Bowl Committee," I explained.

Brian groaned. "This is *your* doing!"

"Don't look at me!" I innocently protested. "Go ask Ron Cordes. This is the kind of stunt he would pull."

"Well, you had to be in on it. Otherwise, how would he know I'd be on the golf course today? I know you had a hand in this!"

I just laughed. "I'm not saying I did," I said, "and I'm not saying I didn't."

Ron Cordes had done this kind of thing before. In fact, he had even hired a plane for a flyover at Brian's graduation from Michigan. The graduation was held at Michigan Stadium, and Ron found a tow plane operator in Ann Arbor who agreed to do the job. The message on the banner was to read CONGRATS BRIAN GRIESE NO. 14, ALL MY LOVE, JULIE. Brian had dated two different Julies in high school—and the name of his girlfriend at Michigan was Laura, not Julie. Ron figured Brian would have a lot of explaining to do when that plane flew over the graduation exercises. As it turned out, the plane was grounded because of bad weather. At dinner after the graduation, I told Brian what Ron had planned to do. When I told him what the message would have been, Brian literally turned pale.

Host Lisa McRee: You don't have to be a football aficionado. In fact, you can be sports-challenged and still love this story, a storybook ending like you rarely see at this year's Rose Bowl—Michigan quarterback Brian Griese leading his team to victory over Washington State, then being named Most Valuable Player. That's not bad for someone who almost decided not to play this year . . . Bob, as a father in the booth, what did you feel that moment?

Bob Griese: Well, I'd been in the booth for five Michigan games during the season, and this was Brian's last game in college. I was doing fine there until the end, when they named him the MVP . . . When I saw him up on that stand, getting the MVP, there were

---

a lot of emotions that went through my mind, a lot of flashbacks. And it was a great moment for Brian and his team . . .

Lisa McRee: Brian, it's been said that your greatest strengths are in leader-ship and the sheer will to win. What is it that inspires you to be a leader to your team?

Brian Griese: So many things. I enjoy playing the game and playing with my teammates. I don't play for national championships, but for the fans and for the sheer love of the game. That's what's driven me, and I'm just sad that my career at Michigan is over.

–ABC's *GOOD MORNING AMERICA*, MONDAY, JANUARY 5, 1998

Brian

It was a miracle year—and we topped it all off with a 21-16 New Year's Day victory over the Washington State Cougars in the Rose Bowl. We won the big game and the national championship.

And after all the shouting and celebrating, after we did the inter-views with ESPN and *Good Morning America*, after things quieted down and I had a chance to reflect, I just sat in amazement and thought about the fact that I had come so close to giving it all up. I came so close to never knowing what it felt like to play a season undefeated, to win a championship, to hold a Rose Bowl trophy in my hands. I'll always be thankful that I listened to my brother Jeff and returned to Michigan for that final year.

I went through such a gamut of emotions after the Rose Bowl. But of all the thoughts and feelings that swirled around inside me, the one thing I focused on more than anything else was my mother. I knew she was there in spirit, sharing the moment with me. Before she died, she was afraid she was going to miss moments like that, and that's why she fought so long and hard against the cancer. She wanted to be with us, so that she wouldn't miss a thing.

Well, she *didn't* miss a thing. She saw it all and heard it all and felt it all. She had the best seat in the stadium.

I was happy for my dad, too. I was glad that he was in the ABC booth calling the biggest game of my college career. The thing I liked most about being named MVP of the game was not what it said about me as a quarterback, but what it did for my dad—it focused the national spotlight on him. My father has always had a reputation for being cool, cerebral, and even unemotional. So I was glad that millions of people got to see the Bob Griese I know—Bob Griese the proud father, the tough Dolphins quarterback who cries on camera when his son holds up the Rose Bowl trophy, the father whose example has taught three sons what it means to be a man, to be strong, to demonstrate courage, and yes, to show emotion. I wanted that moment to be a tribute to the man who is MVP in my life, and who set aside his own life to be both father and mother to me when his wife, my mother, passed away.

1 2

AN UNDEFEATED LIFE

One of the Broncos' most talked-about selections of the 1998 draft was quarterback Brian Griese. Son of Pro Football Hall of Famer Bob Griese, Brian has been in the spotlight for most of his life, and has performed well in that situation. Griese is a very smooth player who has an aggressive approach to the game every time he steps on the field, one of the qualities that helped him lead the Michigan Wolverines to their first national championship in 49 years as a senior in 1997.

—WWW.DENVERBRONCOS.COM

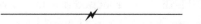

Griese is more of a quarterback for the '90s than he is a chip off the old block. His dad retired when Brian was 5 years old. It's Elway and the current generation of quarterbacks who've taught him about playing the game.

—*DENVER POST,* WEDNESDAY, APRIL 22, 1998

> **Brian**

The weeks after the Rose Bowl victory were really crazy. People were pulling at me from every direction, and it was hard to find any time to just get away and relax. I played in the Hula Bowl, did a lot of media interviews, went to autograph signings, card shows, and awards banquets—something was going on all the time. I managed to spend some time with my family in Coral Gables before going to the NFL combine in Indianapolis in early February.

The combine is kind of a meat market for pro football teams. They subject you to physicals and workouts; they probe you and poke you. It's no fun, but you endure it because it's one of the hoops you jump through on your way to the NFL draft. You also get to meet with coaches and trainers from around the league. After the combine, I returned to Ann Arbor and went through some workouts for scouts from a number of teams, including the Lions, the Steelers, the Bengals, the Jaguars, and the Falcons.

I wasn't considered a superhot prospect for the NFL. The quarterbacks everyone was scrambling to draft were Peyton Manning from Tennessee and Ryan Leaf from Washington State. I knew that at best I was going to be picked in the third round. I wanted a shot at the NFL—but if it didn't happen, I would survive. I had my degree, and I was prepared to go back and get my master's and eventually get into the field of international development. A lot of guys who are good, but just a cut under NFL level, will go play pro football in Europe—but that wasn't for me. If I didn't make the NFL, I was going to hang up my pads and head for the real world.

In April, as the NFL draft approached, my father could see I was getting anxious, and he tried to downplay it. "Look," he said, "we're not going to have any draft day party or anything. This is gonna be a normal Saturday, just like any other Saturday around here. I'm just gonna do my Saturday chores—you know, mow the lawn, wash the windows, weed the flower bed—"

"Oh, right, Dad," I said. "And while you're at it, don't forget to change all the lightbulbs, clean the oven, sweep the garage floor, straighten the attic, yadda, yadda, yadda. Sure, Dad." Like he really does all that every Saturday!

Bob

I was just saying I've got things to do on Saturday and maybe Brian ought to keep himself busy, too. I told him, "Look, you'll go crazy just sitting around and watching the draft on TV—and you'll drive the rest of us crazy. So why don't you take your girlfriend out to lunch, or go to the beach and have a nice relaxing day?"

Brian

That sounded like a good idea. So my girlfriend and I went out to lunch, along with my brother Jeff and some other friends. After lunch, we went out to the beach for a while, then came back home and hung out around the pool. We kept the TV on and tuned it to ESPN so we could listen with one ear—

Bob

He was a nervous wreck. After the first couple of rounds, it was clear that all the teams he had talked to had already drafted their players, and Brian hadn't been picked. The first day of the draft was almost over. There were only about four or five picks left in the third round, and that would be it for Saturday's draft.

I kept saying, "Why don't you turn off the TV? Why don't you just count on getting picked in tomorrow's rounds and stop worrying about it? That way, you won't be disappointed. If you get picked today, the phone will start ringing and you'll find out soon enough."

Brian

The ultimate pessimist—that's my dad.

Bob

That's not pessimism. That's realism. I told Brian, "Hey, it's not the end of the world if you don't get drafted. Remember, at this point last year, you didn't have the wildest notion of being drafted by the NFL."

Shay and I were in the kitchen, throwing some food together to feed all these kids. Most of them were out by the pool, but Brian had come inside and had gone into the den and was kind of circling around in front of the TV like a tiger pacing his cage. All of a sudden, Brian's name was called on TV. The Denver Broncos—the reigning Super Bowl champs—had taken Brian in the third round. Though he was the 91st pick overall, the sports commentators quickly began referring to Brian as the "heir apparent" to John Elway.

Brian

I was stunned when I heard my name on TV. It was what I wanted, it was what I'd been hoping for—but when it happened, I was not really prepared to believe it. The Broncos had really not shown that much interest in me before the draft. It sort of came out of the blue.

As soon as my name was called, everybody started screaming and yelling and running into the house from the pool. And then the phone call came from the Broncos, congratulating me on being selected. I could hardly believe I was going from a national championship university team to a world championship NFL team.

I had been pulling for John Elway and the Broncos in Super Bowl XXXII because of what Elway had been through. He had paid his dues—fifteen seasons in the NFL, four trips to the Super Bowl, but no ring until that game. He deserved it. I really respect a guy who perseveres over the long haul and finishes as a champion. I was really hoping John would return for a sixteenth season, and fortunately for me, he did. I'm on a veteran team where everyone aboard knows what it takes to get to the Super Bowl.

Then, in January 1999, I was there when Elway led the Broncos to a second consecutive world championship in Super Bowl XXXIII—and without even having to get my uniform scuffed, I got a Super Bowl ring! It's made me hungry for the chance to go out and earn one myself.

Bob

Time will tell. Meanwhile, I'm glad for Brian's sake that John returned for another season. That gave Brian the chance to study him—see how he prepares, how he handles pressure situations, and how he demonstrates leadership in moving his team toward a championship. When I was in my thirties, my attitude was, *If I had known ten years ago what I know now!* When my body was in peak shape, my mind wasn't fully prepared for the job—and by the time I was mentally at my peak, my body was kind of beat-up and getting ready for retirement. I know that John Elway is getting to that point where he's pretty well done it all and he's got nothing to prove—but I'm glad he stayed a while longer. The more Brian can learn from him, the better quarterback he'll be in the long run.

He just carries a persona with him that says "I'm a leader." I know it was rumored that his arm was not very strong, but that is totally false. It's stronger than anybody thought, and this kid has probably come along further in the first two months than anybody I've ever had.

—DENVER BRONCOS OFFENSIVE COORDINATOR GARY KUBIAK

We're not only impressed with Brian's playing ability, his mechanics and football awareness and elusiveness, but also how he handles himself off the field.

—DENVER BRONCOS HEAD COACH MIKE SHANAHAN

Bob

The 1998 preseason proved that Brian has the makings of a good quarterback. In late August of that year, I was on the sidelines at Denver's Mile High Stadium for the last game of the preseason, a rematch of the Super Bowl XXXII teams, Green Bay and Denver. The preseason, of course, is the shakedown cruise, when every player is battling to prove his worth, make the cut, and remain on the roster. It was a Monday night game on ABC, and one of the graphics they put up on the screen when Brian was on the field, late in that game, showed that Brian had the highest pass rating among all NFL quarterbacks in the 1998 preseason (a pass rating is arrived at by computing together a QB's stats for pass attempts, completions, passing yards, touchdowns, and interceptions):

1998 Preseason Highest Pass Ratings	
Brian Griese, Denver	138.9
Randall Cunningham, Minnesota	130.5
Steve Young, San Francisco	124.9
Koy Detmer, Philadelphia	123.5
Chris Chandler, Atlanta	112.7
Vinny Testaverde, N.Y. Jets	108.3

I looked at that graphic and thought, *Man, that's pretty distinguished company! The kid's off to a great start—even if it is only the preseason.* Top it off with the fact that Brian's coach in Denver is Mike Shanahan—a brilliant, offense-minded coach who is single-minded about winning championships. Mike just signed a seven-year contract with Denver before Brian got there, and that means a lot of stability for Brian over his first few years in Denver. You can't ask for a better opportunity than that.

Brian

I've been given a great opportunity, and I intend to make the most of it. Shortly after I was drafted, I went back to my old school, Christopher Columbus High, and I gave a talk to the kids there. I wanted each of those kids to dream big dreams and make the most of their opportunities. When people fail to achieve, I think it's usually not so much because they didn't have opportunities, but because they didn't recognize their opportunities—and they shortchanged themselves in the process.

I urged the students to work hard at their studies, so that they could better themselves. And I urged them to get involved in their community, so they could improve the world around them.

"Driving here," I said, "I stopped at a stoplight, and I saw a man with a cardboard sign, asking for money. Seeing him literally begging in the street, I realized how fortunate I am. Who knows how that guy ended up in the street with a cardboard sign and his hand out? Maybe he didn't have the opportunities I've had—the opportunities you have right now. But then again, maybe he just didn't make the most of the opportunities God gave him. There are people in this world who would give anything to be where you are right now, getting a good education, getting a shot at a bright future. Don't waste your opportunities. Seize them. Use them. Make the world a better place."

One of the things I've learned from my dad is that football is a metaphor for life. I don't know that he ever told me that in so many words—I think I learned it from living with him and watching him. I figured out that just about every lesson you learn in football can be applied to the way you live your life, and every principle that's important in life can be applied to playing football.

My dad had an undefeated season with the Dolphins, and I had an undefeated season at Michigan. But one thing I've figured out from living with Bob Griese and watching him and learning from him is how to live an undefeated life. Because in life—just as in football—we all take big hits, we all get sacked, we all get intercepted, we all fumble. All of us have times when we look up at the scoreboard and see that we're down by two or three touchdowns—and we begin to lose hope. Sometimes we get run over, and we get our heads kicked in, and they have to carry us off the field. But none of those things has to defeat us.

It takes a lot of confidence to play football. But it also takes a lot of confidence just to get up in the morning and live an effective, meaningful life. Where does confidence come from? Well, to a degree, it comes with experience. After you've done something a few times, you've got it down, and you feel confident about it.

But what about the challenges you've never tackled before? Where do you get the confidence to try something new, something hard and a little scary? Well, in part, I think that kind of confidence comes from preparing yourself the right way. You study, you practice, you drill, and you do everything you can to be as ready as you can possibly be to take on a new challenge.

But the last part of it, and for me the most important part of being confident, comes in simply not taking things too seriously. When I go out and play football, I know I can play this game. I never think, *What if I make a mistake? What if I don't perform to my peak today?* I don't take myself too seriously, and I don't take the game too seriously. I think of it this way: *It's just a game. I'm going to go out and have fun.*

That kind of thinking takes a lot of the pressure off, because there's a lot of pressure at the quarterback position. You've got to be serious about winning, and your teammates have to know you're serious. But at the same time, you have to have a bit of nonchalance in order to be calm, cool, and levelheaded in situations where most people would lose their composure.

Bob

That's really true. You've gotta be serious—but focused. If you get *too* serious about the game, then you tense up; you forget to have fun. When you get uptight, you're afraid to take risks. You can't play football all worried and tense—and you can't live your life that way, either. You have to stay loose.

I don't think anybody ever became really successful at anything without confidence. If you really want to win at anything, you have to give up the luxury of always worrying that someone's gonna knock your head off. You really have to say, "I don't care if someone's gonna knock my head off— I'm gonna play my game."

I'm not saying you take stupid chances or that you don't care what happens to you. But winning has to be more important to you than a little pain or injury. If you don't want to get hurt, don't play the game. As a quarterback, if you worry too much about getting hurt, you're gonna be underthrowing, you're gonna be distracted, or you're gonna be looking at the guy who's rushing you instead of targeting your receiver. You've got to have people in your life you can depend on, you have to have a solid offensive line, and you've got to have confidence in those guys to keep the opponent out of your backfield.

When you get sacked—and this is true in both football and everyday life—you've got to pick yourself up and say to yourself: *All right, I just got my clock cleaned. Whose fault was it? Well, I guess it was my fault. What could I have done better? What should I do next time? Well, I have a few options. I might tell my linemen to make sure they account for that guy. I might call a play that will keep him out of the backfield. I might be ready to check off to a different play and not let him come in. There are a lot of things I can do to handle the situation better.*

If I decide to leave the play on, then I've got to have confidence in that play. I've got to trust my teammates and play my game, take my seven-step setup, look downfield, and throw. If I get creamed, I get creamed. It's gonna happen some. It's part of the game. You just hope it won't happen too often. But you can't play this game and win unless you're poised in the pocket. That's certainly true of football. And when you think about it, you can see that it's true of anything you do in life.

Brian

I remember after I threw those three interceptions in the Iowa game, and I came back out to the sidelines after halftime, there were fans yelling and booing and telling Coach Carr to pull me out of the game. I just shut it out. I couldn't let that kind of thing get to me, or I never would have gotten back into my rhythm in the second half.

When you're down, when you've had a setback, you just have to accept whatever's happened and go on from there. People are fickle—they love you when you're doing well and hate you when you're not. That's human nature and there's nothing you can do about it. The only thing you can control is the way you play the game—and the way you live your life. Beyond that, why worry about it?

> Football is a by-product of everything else. It's their job and they love it. But it's love that holds them together. That's their glue.
>
> —SHAY WHITNEY GRIESE

Bob

It's been really interesting working on this book and listening to Brian talk. I've been hearing things I've never heard him say before. Ever since Brian was a kid, there have been lessons, ideas, and principles I have tried to get across to him—but until now, I wasn't sure how many of them went in. Sometimes when we'd be out on the golf course, for example, I'd try to tell Brian where to hit the ball and how to putt, and he'd say, "No, I don't think so. I'm hitting it over here."

Now, years later, we are talking over our lives and memories and the way we approach life and football, and I hear Brian sounding a lot like I did three, four, five years ago. I used to say these same things to him that he's saying today, and he'd be looking away with that expression that says, "I don't need to hear this." And now I'm thinking, *Hey, it sank in, didn't it?* Either it sank in, or Brian went out and learned it on his own. Or maybe a little of both.

Maybe it's a matter of going out and testing the things he heard at home and finding out, *Hey, maybe the old man isn't so dumb after all!* I told all three of my sons many times: "The older you guys get, the smarter I'll become."

Brian

I listened to a lot of things he told me—but I didn't want him to know that. Of course, there were also things I had to learn for myself. Every person, at a certain age, has to find his own way and figure out what's best for him. Maybe what worked for Bob Griese won't work for Brian Griese. I've got to figure out what works best for me.

As it happened, it turned out that a lot of what I discovered was exactly what my dad had been telling me. He gave me a lot of good advice and the benefit of his experience, but I still had to go out and try things out—just so that I'd know what my own strengths are. No two people are alike, not even father and son. And no two quarterbacks are alike, not even father and son quarterbacks.

Even though he and I are often compared, I don't think I learned that much about football from my dad. I learned a lot more from him about character and confidence, about handling a crisis and pressure, about the right attitude for recovering from a setback. He taught me these lessons by the way he lived his life more than by the things he told me. And maybe those were the most important lessons he could ever teach me.

Bob

One thing I've seen very clearly as we've been working on this book is that there is a lot of Judi in these three young men, Scott, Jeff, and Brian—and I'm even seeing a lot of Judi in her beautiful granddaughters, Reneé Judith and Claire Marie. Judi was the most compassionate, caring person I've ever known—she was always putting others ahead of herself, always involved in making life better for other people. When I see all the things that Brian has been involved in—the hospital visits he did all five years at Michigan and all the other projects and programs and individual acts he has been involved in to help other people—I can see that Brian takes a part of Judi along with him wherever he goes. I know she's been happy to see all that Brian has done for people and all the lives that have been made better because of him.

When we started talking about this book, I thought that *Undefeated* would be such a good title for it, because of my undefeated season with the Dolphins and Brian's undefeated season at Michigan. Having reached the end of the book—not the end of the story, of course, but the end of the book—I can see that the title *Undefeated* means so much more.

I think of Judi—undefeated by cancer, undefeated by death. Sure, the cancer could take her away from us, but it could never quench her spirit or change who she was. It could never make her bitter or angry or self-centered. It could never destroy her love for us, and it could never erase her memory from our minds. In the end, it couldn't rob her of the births of her grandchildren. It couldn't even rob her of the weddings, graduations, and ball games of her kids—she was there at every one. Even during the time that ABC wouldn't let me cover one of Brian's games, Judi was there. The network could keep me away, but death couldn't keep Judi away. She was undefeated.

Brian

It's true. I feel my mother with me all the time—not just when I'm in church or when I'm playing football. She's with me when I'm about to go to sleep at night or when I'm eating my breakfast in the morning. She continues to be a big influence in my life, helping me to be calm in pressure situations, showing me how to care about people who are less fortunate than I am, and putting my whole life in perspective. She reminds me that the most important thing is family, and helps me not to take things too seriously. Death couldn't defeat her—she's still with me, helping me grow and mature and face the challenges of life. She used to tell me that God has a purpose for my life, and she's still with me, making sure I don't forget it.

Bob

Looking back, I realize that our family was undefeated—even when we lost Judi. As much as we needed her and miss her, Scott, Jeff, Brian, and I came through it. It was the hardest thing any of us has gone through, but we came through it undefeated, and even stronger. We stuck together and survived it. We're a family. We're Christians. We know that God is good, and that we're going to see Judi again.

Brian

You talk about someone who's undefeated, and I think of Jayne Uber, paralyzed from the neck down, but undefeated. And I think of Emily, a girl who died of cancer at Mott Children's Hospital. And there were so many others I met at the hospital over my years at Michigan. I mean, those kids were tough, they fought hard against their diseases and injuries, they were competitors, and they never surrendered. Even when Emily died, she never surrendered to her cancer. Those kids were champions; they were undefeated.

I really believe that's the way God meant us to live our lives. Life doesn't always go the way we plan. We kick in a window during a thoughtless moment, or we fall off a horse, or we get cancer. Life is full of turnovers and penalties, you know?

But that's not the end of the game—unless we let it be. That's not the final score—unless we surrender.

And maybe that's the note on which to close this book:

If you've had a setback or a fumble, stay cool, okay? Stay poised in the pocket. Just be patient and battle your way back into the game. People are pulling for you—and you're gonna be okay.

Bob

Hey, listen to this kid—he makes a lot of sense. After all, I taught him everything he knows . . .

AFTERWORD

Brian Griese has really impressed everybody this whole year. He picked up the offense, and he throws the ball real well. He's a lot better athlete than people say he is. Brian's going to be around for a long time.

—JOHN ELWAY

Bob

Well, Brian had the first word in this book—so I get the last word.

He spent his first season in the NFL being mentored by a football legend, John Elway. That was the year the Denver Broncos played thirteen in a row without a loss. They almost went undefeated—but then, near the end of the '98 season, they dropped two in a row and finished 14-2. Mind you, I want the Dolphins' undefeated season to stand forever—but I was really pulling for the Broncos that year. If another NFL team ever matches what we did, I'd want it to be a team Brian is playing on.

His first season in the pros, Brian built a good relationship with the two veteran quarterbacks on the team, John Elway and Bubby Brister. He trained hard, studied the complex Denver offense, and picked it up. Watching from the sidelines of Super Bowl XXXIII, Brian collected a Super Bowl ring the easy way—without getting his uniform mussed. The game was played at Pro Player Stadium in Miami, just ten miles from where he grew up, so Super Bowl week was like homecoming for Brian.

John Elway announced his retirement in April of '99; then, in late

August, coach Mike Shanahan surprised a lot of people by giving Brian the starting job. Brian had directed game-winning, come-from-behind, fourth-quarter drives in each of his first three exhibition games. With a .667 completion rate, six TD passes and only one interception, his preseason pass rating was a strong 106.5.

"Brian Griese has played so well throughout camp and preseason games," said Shanahan, "that I think he deserves the opportunity. He understands the full package, which is very unusual for a second-year guy. It's everything he does—how he handles himself; how he handles the offense, the running game, the passing game; how he handles himself in the huddle; the way he understands defenses and protection schemes; how he handles himself versus a blitz. He has really fared well."

But the '99 season proved to be a tough one. The Broncos dropped their first four games in a row, beginning with the home opener against Miami, when the glare of the spotlight couldn't have been hotter. It was a Monday night game on ABC with a special halftime ceremony to retire John Elway's No. 7 jersey. I was at Mile High Stadium that night, sitting in the owner's box with Shay and Broncos' owner Pat Bowlen, watching my old team beat up on my own son down on the field. Talk about mixed feelings!

After that 0-4 start, Shanahan decided to bench Brian and start Bubby Brister in game five against the Oakland Raiders. But when Brian arrived at the Coliseum, he learned that Brister would be out of the game due to a practice injury. That day, Brian led the Broncos to a 16-13 victory—their first for the regular season.

The following Sunday, Brian completed 19 of 30 for 363 yards and two touchdowns, one interception, to beat the Packers 31-10 at Mile High Stadium. By this time, Brian had gotten into a rhythm with wide receiver Ed McCaffrey—six of Brian's first seven career TD passes were to Eddie. Just two weeks after nearly being benched, Brian was named AFC Offensive Player of the Week for his 363-yard showing against Green Bay.

By season's end, Brian had started 13 of 16 games, and the Broncos had finished with a 6-10 record. That may sound a little lackluster for a team that had just won back-to-back Super Bowls—until you realize that: they played one of the toughest schedules in NFL history (every team they played that season finished with a winning record); most of the games they lost were extremely close (three points or less); and some of their biggest guns were sidelined by injuries—running back Terrell Davis (the NFL's 1998 season MVP), tight end Shannon Sharpe, and linebacker John Mobley, to name a few.

Speaking as a football analyst more than as a father (and yes, I think I can be objective about this), I'd say Brian had a great season. He was thrust into the spotlight and he handled the pressure well. He doesn't play in anyone's shadow—not Bob Griese's, not John Elway's. He plays his own game. He's an accurate thrower and moves well in the pocket. He doesn't bowl you over with his physical skills, but I didn't either when I was playing. With a little seasoning, a quarterback with Brian's skills and temperament can take a team to the Super Bowl.

Brian finished the season in elite company. Only eight quarterbacks have ever thrown 3,000 yards in their rookie starting season since the NFL-AFL merger in 1970—and Brian (at 3,032 yards) is one of them. So he accomplished a lot as a rookie starter, and I'm proud of that. But even more than his stats, I'm proud of the *character* he displayed. Throughout the season, he showed poise and toughness under fire. He played through the pain of a bad throwing shoulder, which he injured in the season opener against Miami, then reinjured in a 23-20 loss to Minnesota. At the end of the season, he had surgery on the shoulder, and came through it just fine.

Fact is, he came through *everything* just fine. He didn't have as much fun quarterbacking the Broncos as he had leading the Wolverines to an undefeated season—but the fun will be there again one day. Speaking as a football analyst—and okay, speaking as Brian's dad—there's no doubt in my mind that he's going to have a great career and a lot of fun.

Will he collect another Super Bowl ring? Or an undefeated season like his old man? All I can say is . . .

Stay tuned!

Notes

CHAPTER 3: A PUNCH IN THE FACE

1. Roland Lazenby, *The 100 Greatest Quarterbacks* (New York: Crescent Books, 1988), 38.
2. Nigel Cawthorne, ed., *World of Pro Football* (Secaucus, NJ: Chartwell, 1988), 110.
3. Don Shula, *The Winning Edge* (New York: Dutton, 1973), 138–139.
4. Ibid., 151–152.
5. Cawthorne, *World of Pro Football*, 109.
6. Shula, *The Winning Edge*, 156.
7. Cawthorne, *World of Pro Football*, 109–110.
8. Shula, *The Winning Edge*, 163.
9. Lazenby, *The 100 Greatest Quarterbacks*, 38.
10. John Facenda, narrator, "Super Bowl VI—Dallas Cowboys, World Champions," *NFL Films Super Bowl Memories*.
11. Cawthorne, *World of Pro Football*, 110.

CHAPTER 4: PERFECTION!

1. CNN/*Sports Illustrated*, "Super Bowl Coverage." <http://cgi.cnsi.com>.
2. Shula, *The Winning Edge*, 212–213.
3. Paul Zimmerman, "The Road to Glory," CNN/*Sports Illustrated*. <http://cgi.cnsi.com>.
4. Shula, *The Winning Edge*, 224.
5. Bob Glauber, "Unbeaten, Untied, Unsung." *Newsday*, 9 November 1997.
6. Zimmerman, "The Road to Glory."

7. Paul Zimmerman, "Miami Dolphins vs. Washington Redskins, Super Bowl VIII," *Sports Illustrated*, 2 January 1989.
8. John Facenda, narrator, "World Champion Dolphins 17–0," *NFL Films Super Bowl Memories*.
9. Tex Maule, "Unbeaten Season," *Sports Illustrated*, 15 November 1989.

CHAPTER 5: ATTACK OF THE PURPLE PEOPLE

1. Paul Zimmerman, "Miami Dolphins vs. Minnesota Vikings—Super Bowl VIII," *Sports Illustrated*, 2 January 1989.
2. Steve Sabol, narrator, "Super Bowl VIII: Miami Dolphins vs. Minnesota Vikings," *NFL Films Super Bowl Memories*.
3. John Facenda, narrator, "Super Bowl VIII: Miami Dolphins vs. Minnesota Vikings," *NFL Films Super Bowl Memories*.
4. John Madden, *One Knee Equals Two Feet* (New York: Villard Books, 1986), 35–36.
5. Facenda, "Super Bowl VIII: Miami Dolphins vs. Minnesota Vikings."

About the Authors

Bob Griese

For nearly two decades, Pro Football Hall of Famer Bob Griese has been one of network television's most respected football analysts, first for NBC's NFL coverage and currently for ABC's college game-of-the-week and bowl game coverage. His frank commentary, insider's analysis, and genial chemistry with twelve-year broadcast partner Keith Jackson have made him one of the most respected names in sports coverage.

Bob Griese's poised leadership and unerring ball control during his brilliant fourteen-year career with the Miami Dolphins (1967-1980) earned him the title "The Thinking Man's Quarterback." He helped lead the Dolphins to three straight Super Bowls, including two consecutive titles (Super Bowls VII and VIII). The victory in Super Bowl VII capped a perfect 17-0 season—the only undefeated record in NFL history.

Under Miami head coach Don Shula, Griese earned a .698 winning percentage (91-39-1) and became the fourteenth quarterback in history to join the NFL's exclusive 25,000-yard club. He appeared in six Pro Bowls, two American Football League All-Star Games, and was All-Pro in 1971 and 1977. For the first 34 years of the franchise, Griese's jersey, number 12, was the only jersey ever retired by the Dolphins.

Before playing in Miami, Griese was a two-time All-American at Purdue, voted All-Time Quarterback for Purdue's first hundred years, named to the inaugural class of the Boilermaker Athletic Hall of Fame, and is a member of the National Football Foundation's College Hall of Fame.

Bob Griese has three sons—Scott, Jeff, and Brian. He lives in Coral Gables, Florida, with his wife, Shay Whitney Griese.

BRIAN GRIESE

In 1997, Brian Griese quarterbacked the University of Michigan Wolverines to their first national championship in fifty years, capping an undefeated season with a thrilling Rose Bowl victory on New Year's Day 1998. At the end of that game, he was named Rose Bowl MVP.

Other honors and awards Griese amassed during his years in Michigan maize and blue: the NCAA Top Eight Award; the Arthur D. Robinson Award for top Michigan student athlete; three-time Academic All-Big Ten selection (1995, 1996, 1997); and National Football Foundation and College Hall of Fame Scholar-Athlete 1997.

During his undefeated season at Michigan, Brian completed 193 of 307 passes (62.9 percent) for 2,293 yards, 17 touchdowns, and only six interceptions, breaking the previous record set by Todd Collins in 1993. His interception percentage (1.95 percent) is the fourth lowest in Michigan record books. His record as a starter for Michigan is 17-5 (.773).

At Michigan, Brian shone off the field as well as on. He volunteered weekly time to visit sick children at Mott Children's Hospital; he helped found S.H.A.R.E. (Student-Athletes Helping to Achieve Reading Excellence), a reading program for elementary-age children; he served as a facilitator in the university's Leadershape summer program; and he served with the Student-Athlete Community Service Committee.

After graduating, he was drafted by the world champion Denver Broncos, where he had a chance to understudy the legendary John Elway. He was on the sidelines at Super Bowl XXXIII in January 1999, when the Broncos collected their second consecutive Super Bowl crown.

At the beginning of the 1999 season, Brian Griese was named starting quarterback of the Denver Broncos. He started in 13 out of 16 games and became one of only eight NFL quarterbacks since 1970 to throw more than 3,000 yards as a rookie starting quarterback.

JIM DENNEY

Freelance writer Jim Denney has written more than forty books with a number of different authors, including Super Bowl champion Reggie White, *Star Trek* actress Grace Lee Whitney, supermodel Kim Alexis, and Orlando Magic executive Pat Williams. He lives in California with his wife and two children.

.